Poke The Bear

(Time To Awaken Out of Sleep)

Angel Domingue

Jerusalem which is above is free, which is the mother of us all
- Galatians 4:26

Table of Contents

Preface

When I think of all the great things we have learned from the Word of God, I think of His promises, His love, grace, and mercy for His people. I think of His son Jesus Christ Our Lord and Savior who died for us. God displayed the greatest gift and demonstration of true love when He laid down his life for people who did not even deserve it.

When I look back to being a babe in Christ and how the people around me were making changes to turn away from sin and to turn to God, living the way God has called them to live, I remember I wanted that as well. I would go to church events to hear about Jesus and learn how to live for God. I would seek God. I wanted out of the misery I was in.

I know many people would like to experience God's presence. They would like to hear from Him and know that it is God they are hearing. Many people will go to church. They will read the Bible. They will even make some life changes. But they then find themselves feeling empty and stagnate so they go back into their old behaviors: like addictions, bad relationships, depression, and walking after the works of the flesh. All so they can fill the empty inner void. They start to feel like the church is no longer for them.

One of the biggest problems is we get so caught up in going to church rather than knowing that we are the church. We begin to go through the routines and emotions of guilt and then God becomes a job and not Our Father. I have written this book to provide some answers about what went wrong in our walk with the Lord and what prevents us from growing spiritually.

"Special Thanks"

I thank all my friends and family who I love. I am so grateful to have you in my life. I thank Danielle Procope Of Mertina Writing Services for taking on this huge project you are amazing!

I want to give a very special thank you to my Mom who has always shown me love by supporting me and spending time with me. Mom you have taught me so much I thank you for sharing your blessings, knowledge, and wisdom with me making my life much easier. I am so blessed to have you as my Mother I love you very much! Thank you Mom.

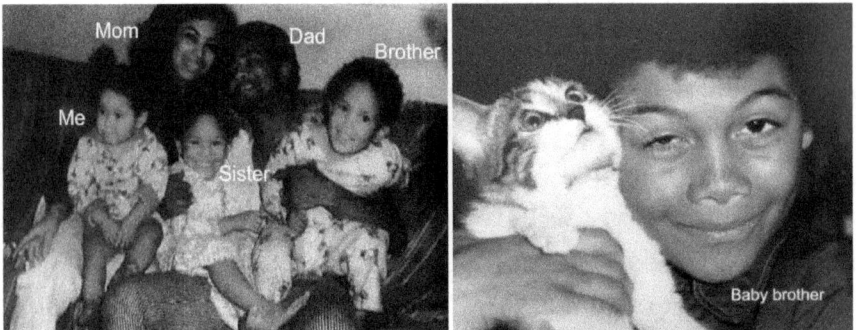

Flashback of my beautiful family

~I dedicate this book too~

This entire book is dedicated to Our Father The Great I Am That I Am, the God of Abraham, the God of Isaac, and the God of Jacob, I thank you Father for providing for me and protecting me from my enemies and most of all for giving us your only begotten Son, Our Lord and Savior we call Jesus Christ I love you.

Introduction

God said the truth shall set us free. However, many of us as believers may know the truth, but we don't want to make people feel bad or uncomfortable by having to correct their behavior. We don't speak up when we see another in the wrong or speak to a sister or a brother in the Lord who may be living a sinful lifestyle even though they may have asked you for help or your opinion.

Sometimes we do not want to speak about what is true in fear of poking the bear, so to speak. We do not want to ruffle any feathers or make anyone angry because maybe their beliefs are different and they don't feel they need to change despite them hating the condition that they are in.

They may want out of their life, but yet they continue in that dangerous cycle. Think for a minute about all the years you lived knowing your true feelings, images, traditions, and beliefs were geared around lies. Do you really want to go home to glory with a pocket full of lies or do you want to be free?

I decided to pull up my big girl panties a long time ago and say that others can believe what they want to believe, but in my house, I will serve the Lord. I love God's laws, statutes, and commandments because they keep me safe and give life to my soul. And even though I am in my sinful nature I want to walk in the spirit.

I want to rest on the Sabbath day like my Father did. I want to go back and tie up loose ends. I want to look at the pagan holidays for what they truly are and admit I was living in Babylon, and I still am today.

I had to rethink my life and say, Lord my God, I am sorry for my sins and evil desires and the evil desires of my forefathers and my parents. I know one day I will stand before God in fear and tremble knowing that I wanted to live by His word.

I find that out of all the information given in the world, the word of God is the only way of getting the true history of who you are, why you are in the condition that you are in, and how to get out of it.

To get more Information about this book " **Poke The Bear**" write or Email:

Angels On Board Prison Ministry
P.O. BOX 247121
Sacramento, CA 95824

(Time To Awaken Out of Sleep)

angelonline@att.net
(www.pokethebear.org)
(www.aturninmybelly.com)
(www.angeldomingue.com)

The Truth about Being Born of Water and the Spirit

What is God actually doing and giving the believer when they get baptized and do you have to get baptized? Did Jesus need to be baptized?

Let's go deeper in scripture and see what God's word is truly saying. This subject has caused division and arguments among many believers, but let's clear this up once and for all. It's time to get the true facts. The answer is yes, we all must be baptized and yes, Jesus had to be baptized. The reason why Jesus had to be baptized was to fulfill all righteousness.

Let's read the Biblical passage:

"Then Jesus came from Galilee to the Jordan to John, to be baptized by him. ¹⁴ John would have prevented him, saying,
"I need to be baptized by you, and do you come to me?" ¹⁵ But Jesus answered him, "<u>Let it be so now;</u> for thus <u>it is fitting for us to fulfill all righteousness."</u> Then he consented. ¹⁶ And when Jesus was baptized, he went up immediately from the water, and behold, the heavens were opened and he saw the Spirit of God descending like a dove, and alighting on him; ¹⁷ and lo, a voice from heaven, saying, "This is my beloved Son, with whom I am well pleased."
   - **Matthew 3:13-17 (RSV)**

So we see in God's word that everyone has to do what God requires. This passage says that being baptized is pleasing to God.

But let's not stop there, let's read the key to what happens when a person believes in Jesus Christ as their Lord and Savior and gets baptized.

Let's read the Biblical passage:

"And he said to them, "Go into all the world and preach the gospel to the whole creation. ¹⁶ *He who believes and is baptized will be saved, but he who does not believe will be condemned.* ¹⁷ *And these signs will accompany those who believe: in my name they will cast out demons; they will speak in new tongues;* ¹⁸ *they will pick up serpents, and if they drink any deadly thing, it will not hurt them; they will lay their hands on the sick, and they will recover."*
  - **Mark 16:15-18 (RSV)**

What is God actually doing when a person is baptized?

God is releasing something here, but what is it? Jesus commanded His disciples to go out into all the world and preach the gospel to all of creation. Then He said: *"He who believes and is baptized will be saved, but he who does not believe will be condemned and these signs will accompany those who believe in my name."*

Signs that will accompany those who believe in Jesus's name:

1) They will cast out demons.
2) They will speak in new tongues.
3) They will pick up serpents.
4) If they drink any deadly thing, it will not hurt them.
5) They will lay their hands on the sick and the sick will recover.

This reveals that God will provide the believer with prophetic powers that will only come by believing in Him and being baptized.

Let's read in this next text what is even greater about being baptized.

Peter tells the crowd on the day of Pentecost:

"Then Peter said to them, "Repent, and let everyone of you be baptized in the name of Jesus Christ for the remission of sins; and you shall receive the gift of the Holy Spirit."
- Acts 2:38 (NKJV)

Read John's words:

"I baptize you with water, but someone is coming soon who is greater than I am—so much greater that I'm not even worthy to be his slave and untie the straps of his sandals. <u>He will baptize you with the Holy Spirit and with fire."</u>
- Luke 3:16 (NLT)

Did you read that? We are to repent and be baptized in Jesus's name for the remission of sins and you will receive the gift of the Holy Spirit.

John says we will be baptized with the Holy Spirit and with fire. Baptism remits our sins and gives us the power of the Holy Spirit with Fire. The fire represents the presence and power of God. We can read this in **(Ezekiel 1:27).**

The power of God will help us to not become a slave to sin by giving us power from the Holy Spirit. God can start cutting away our sinful nature so we then become less interested and not as easily tempted in partaking in evil desires. This only happens when we turn away from our old life and truly repent by turning over our life to God, allowing Him to now lead.

We do this by reading His word and continuing to follow God's commands with our actions. Getting baptized is very important because this is what God requires.

God releases the gift of the Holy Spirit with the power to get results against sin, so if we only do what we want and not what God requires there can be no new man or new woman. We will just be the same old empty shell, only focused on ourselves. When we get baptized, God will pour out His spirit onto the believer. It is a spiritual circumcision, the cutting away of our sinful nature.

Let's read the Biblical passage:

"When you came to Christ, you were "circumcised," but not by a physical procedure. Christ performed a spiritual circumcision—the cutting away of your sinful nature. 12 For you were buried with Christ when you were baptized. And with Him, you were raised to new life because you trusted the mighty power of God, who raised Christ from the dead."

- **Colossians 2:11**

This verse tells us that there will be a change in us because God will cut away our sinful nature. We need to be trusting and have faith in Jesus Christ and what He did for us by dying on the cross for our sins. Then God can spiritually cut away the old man or woman because we trust in the power of God who raised Jesus from the dead. There will be a change in us. A believer in Jesus Christ will always become new.

Let's read the Biblical passage:

"This means that anyone who belongs to Christ <u>has become a new</u> <u>person. The old life is gone; a new life has begun!</u> [18] *And all of this is a gift from God, who brought us back to himself through Christ. And God has given us this task of reconciling people to him.* [19] *For God was in Christ, reconciling the world to himself, no longer counting people's sins against them."*

- **2 Corinthians 5:17-21 (NLT)**

When you are baptized and repent you will also receive the following:

1) Forgiveness of your sins.
2) The gift of the Holy Spirit with fire.
3) The cutting away of your sinful nature.

What about people who have been baptized in the Spirit with evidence of speaking in tongues, but were not baptized in water? Do they need to be water baptized?

The answer is yes.

Let's clear this up with a very important text. This is when the Holy Spirit falls on the Gentiles. Peter was sharing the same message with the Gentiles telling them that "whoever believes in Him will receive remission of sins" **(Acts 10: 43).**

Before Peter finished speaking, the people who heard the Word of God and received what Peter was saying were impacted. These were people who had not been baptized but Peter commanded them to be baptized <u>with water</u> in the name of the Lord.

13

Let's read this important text:

"While Peter was still speaking these words, <u>the Holy Spirit fell upon all those who heard the word.</u> ⁴⁵ And those of the circumcision who believed were astonished, as many as came with Peter because the gift of the Holy Spirit had been poured out on the Gentiles also. ⁴⁶ For they heard them speak with tongues and magnify God. Then Peter answered, ⁴⁷ <u>"Can anyone forbid water, that these should not be baptized who have received the Holy Spirit just as we have?"</u> ⁴⁸ <u>And he commanded them to be baptized in the name of the Lord</u>. Then they asked him to stay a few days."
- **Acts 10:44-47 (NKJV)**

This verse is evidence that we need to be baptized in water *and* Spirit because the two go together once we receive the truth of Jesus Christ and repent. We should always have a water baptism with no exceptions! This is what Jesus was telling Nicodemus.

⁵ Jesus answered, "I assure you, no one can enter the Kingdom of God without being born of water and the Spirit. ⁶ Humans can reproduce only human life, but the Holy Spirit gives birth to spiritual life. ⁷ So don't be surprised when I say, 'You must be born again."
- **John 3:5-7 (NKJV)**

We also read in scripture that when a person was only baptized in water without signs of the Holy Spirit, they would send Peter and John to lay their hands on them and they would receive the Holy Spirit.

Let's read the Biblical passage:

"Now when the apostles who were at Jerusalem heard that Samaria had received the word of God, they sent Peter and John to them, [15] *who, when they had come down, prayed for them that they might receive the Holy Spirit.* [16] *For as yet He had fallen upon none of them. They had only been baptized in the name of the Lord Jesus.* [17] *Then they laid hands on them, and they received the Holy Spirit."*

- **Acts 8:14-17 (NKJV)**

So why is it that people repent and are water baptized but no change happens? They are baptized as an adulterer and come back as an adulterer. Why is there no change?

We are going to go over some important scriptures that will give us an understanding about this topic so that we can be free from our struggles with sin.

We must understand that water baptism is symbolic of death to our old self. We rise as a new man or woman when we confess our sins with a heartfelt conviction that we are sinners and understand we have not followed what God commands and need a Savior.

Now this next scripture will explain what the water baptism will do once we confess.

Let's read the Biblical passage:

"For Christ also died for sins once for all, the righteous for the unrighteous, that He might bring us to God, being put to death in the flesh, but made alive in the spirit; [19] in which He went and preached to the spirits in prison, [20] who formerly did not obey, when God's patience waited in the days of Noah, during the building of the ark, in which a few, that is, eight persons, were saved through water. [21] Baptism, which corresponds to this, now saves you, not as a removal of dirt from the body, but as an appeal to God for a clear conscience, through the resurrection of Jesus Christ, [22] who has gone into heaven and is at the right hand of God, with angels, authorities, and powers subject to Him." **1 Peter 3:18 (RSV)**

When we are water baptized, it symbolizes becoming in union with Christ **(Galatians 3:26-27)**, the remission of our sins **(Acts 2:38)**, identification with Christ in His death to sin and resurrection to new life **(Romans 6:3-5)**, and becoming a member of the body of Christ **(1 Corinthians 12:13).**

The blessings of baptism are received by faith **(Romans 6:8-11)**. Now when we repent and are water baptized in Jesus's name we are appealing to God. We can come to Him with a clear conscience because we understand that we are sinners because of the commands we have broken. We will be truly convicted and eager for God to save us by knowing that Jesus died for our sins once and for all. We will be truly convicted of our lawless living.

Now if we are baptized in Jesus's name without any understanding and just go through the motions feeling that we're good people then the old person will stay. We have to know God's Law, which is the Word of God.

16

Let's read the Biblical passage:

"Well then, am I suggesting that the law of God is sinful? Of course not! In fact, it was the law that showed me my sin.
I would never have known that coveting is wrong if the law had not said, 'You must not covet.'"
- **Romans 7:7 (NLT)**

So we read in the text that it is the Word of God that convicts us and the Word of God that teaches us how to live Holy and pleasing to God. When we receive the Word of God as truth, then we are cleansed by the Word, not the water. The water baptism is admitting and confessing that we are lawbreakers and we repent meaning that we turn away from our sin and back to God.

Let's read the Biblical passage:

"He that covereth his sins shall not prosper: but whoso confesseth and forsaketh them shall have mercy."
- **Proverbs 28:13 (NLT)**

The text clearly says that if a person wants to cover their sin, make excuses, and does not see a need to really make any changes and turn back to God, that person will not prosper.

This is why we will not see a change after the water baptism if sins are being covered.

Let's read the Biblical passage:

"You are already clean because of the word which I have spoken to you. ⁴ Abide in Me, and I in you. As the branch cannot bear the fruit of itself, unless it abides in the vine, neither can you, unless you abide in Me."
- **John 15:3 (NKJV)**

When we hear the Word of God and abide in Him, God will start to cleanse us. We must believe and in our actions live our lives knowing that Jesus and Jesus alone will be the total object of our faith in all things.

Let's dig deeper in Biblical truths.

Let's read the Biblical passage:

"Husbands, love your wives, just as Christ also loved the church and gave Himself for her, ²⁶ that He might sanctify and cleanse her with the washing of water by the word, ²⁷ that He might present her to Himself a glorious church, not having spot or wrinkle or any such thing, but that she should be holy and without blemish." ²⁸
- **Ephesians 5:26 (NKJV)**

When people are baptized with no desire to change or turn back to God that person cannot have a relationship with God because of covered sin. They are unable to understand the importance of continuing in God's word so the old person will stay even after the water baptism.

The word of God is what washes us. Receiving God's word is truth and if we stay in His word we will be convicted to make that change so we can be right with God.

18

The change of heart and the confession of our sins is what will fill us with the spirit of God and cause that old person within us to die as the spirit quickens the new person to come forth.

Just going through the motions of baptism without a full understanding that we are sinners who need a Savior is all lip service because the heart is far from God. There is a difference when the Holy Spirit comes upon you and when the Holy Spirit dwells within you.

Let's read a good Biblical example of having the Holy Spirit come upon you without the indwelling of the Holy Spirit.

Let's read the Biblical passage:

"If I speak in the tongues of men and of angels, but have not love, I am a noisy gong or a clanging cymbal. ² And if I have prophetic powers, and understand all mysteries and all knowledge, and if I have all faith, so as to remove mountains, but have not love, I am nothing."
- **1 Corinthians 13:1-2 (RSV)**

This is a perfect scripture that confirms that we can have prophetic powers that come upon us by the Holy Spirit, but we need the indwelling of the Holy Spirit that gives the fruit of the Spirit. This produces love.

"But the fruit of the Spirit is love, joy, peace, patience, kindness, goodness, faithfulness."
- **Galatians 5:22 (RSV)**

So we have to make sure that we understand what being born again means and how to successfully turn back to God so we can become a child of God and not the child of the devil.

God says repent, be baptized, read the Holy Bible and follow His commands without reservation. This is the love of God. To repent of something does not mean merely to be sorry or remorseful but to stop practicing sin and turn away from it completely this is true repentance to change. Being baptized is so important. Even in Moses's day they were baptized.

Let's read the Biblical passage:

"Moreover, brethren, I do not want you to be unaware that <u>all our fathers were under the cloud,</u> <u>all passed through the sea,</u> ² <u>all were baptized into Moses in the cloud and in the sea,</u> ³ all ate the same spiritual food, ⁴ and all drank the same spiritual drink. For they drank of that spiritual Rock that followed them, and that Rock was Christ."
- **1 Corinthians 10 NKJV**

Wow, this is huge! Even the Israelites had to be baptized during the time of Moses because he was the lawgiver just like John was the baptizer in his time. The commandments were given to the Israelites. They were baptized by the Law of Moses. We all need to confess our sins and be water baptized. We must immerse ourselves in the Word so that the old man will die and the new man will come forth.

No more excuses! Let's get in the Word of God and cleanse ourselves and be baptized with The Holy Spirit with Fire. The fire is the presence and power of God and you will see a huge change when you put God's word in action.

Let's remember what it says in Ephesians 4:5,
"One Lord, one faith, one baptism."

One Lord: Jesus Christ.
One faith: Faith in what Jesus did on the cross.
One Baptism: Our Salvation is in Christ Jesus. We are baptized in the name of Jesus Christ. The Father, The Son, and The Holy Spirit.

We must all be born again of water and the Spirit. Amen!

"And now why do you wait? Rise and be baptized, and wash away your sins, calling on his name."
- **Acts 22:16 (RSV)**

The Mysteries of the Holy Spirit

Let's get right into the mysteries of the Holy Spirit, also known as "The Spirit of Truth." The Holy Spirit is God. The Holy Spirit is equated with The Father and The Son. This is why we are baptized in the name of the Father and of the Son and of the Holy Spirit. They are all one. The Holy Spirit is The Spirit of God.

"Go therefore and make disciples of all nations, baptizing them in the name of the Father and of the Son and of the Holy Spirit."
-   Mathew 28:19 (RSV)

I am Holy Spirit, filled with the evidence of speaking in the Spirit. This is also known as speaking in tongues. I want to share not only the knowledge of what the Holy Spirit can do, but also share what I have experienced as I am led by the Spirit of God.

First of all, some may ask, well do I have the Holy Spirit living in me and how do I get the Holy Spirit? Here is Jesus our Lord and Savior answering this question.

Let's read the Biblical passage:

"If you love me, you will keep my commandments. And I will pray to the Father, and He will give you another Counselor, to be with you forever, even the Spirit of truth, whom the world cannot receive, because it neither sees Him, nor knows Him; you know Him, for He dwells with you, and will be with you."

-   John 14:15-17 (RSV)

When we make the decision to repent of our sins and choose Jesus Christ as our Lord and Savior, turning our lives back to God's original plan, this is the true love of God, the keeping and following of His commands.

We only really do what we actually believe, so if someone says they love God, but they do not follow His commands, then we know they do not really love God. So if God says to get baptized and you are baptized, you have now followed His command in action. This is an act of love.

Being obedient to God by faith is always the key. You can easily tell if you are truly a follower of Jesus Christ by asking one simple question: do you listen and do what God has asked you to do in your actions? This is what being obedient to God means, doing what he asks even if you do not totally understand.

Jesus said: "If you love me, you will keep my commandments and I will pray to the Father, and He will give you another Counselor, to be with you forever, even the Spirit of truth which is the Holy Spirit" **(John 14:16).**

When we decide that we do not want to be like the world, living by the works of the flesh, and instead we want to be like Our Father and no longer follow the world, then God will give us His spirit to live in us so we will know how to live like Him. I believe in God by faith and since I have trusted in Him, I have experienced things that were written in the Bible before I even knew about it.

God is amazing and if you trust and believe you will experience the Holy Spirit and see things come to pass that will leave you in total awe.

The Holy Spirit is a person and it is not hard to believe this. Just think: we are spirits. Our bodies are just a house for our spirit. So just like us the Holy Spirit has a voice, mind, will, emotions, and He has a nature.

I will prove it. Let's read what the Holy Spirit does and read the Biblical text.

The Holy Spirit and What He Can Do

The Holy Spirit is referred to as a Him by Jesus:

"Even the Spirit of truth; whom the world cannot receive, because it seeth him not, neither knoweth him, but ye know him; for he dwelleth with you, and shall be in you."

- **John 14:17**

The Holy Spirit speaks: *"As they ministered to the Lord, and fasted, the Holy Ghost said, Separate me Barnabas and Saul for the work whereunto I have called them"* (**Acts 13:2**).

The Holy Spirit interprets Scripture: *"But the natural man receiveth not the things of the Spirit of God, for they are foolishness unto him, neither can he know them, because they are spiritually discerned"* (**1 Corinthians 2:14**).

The Holy Spirit guides us into all truth: *"Howbeit when He, the Spirit of truth, is come, He will guide you into all truth for He shall not speak of Himself; but whatsoever He shall hear, that shall He speak: and He will show you things to come"* (**John 16:13**).

The Holy Spirit indwells in the believer: *"And because ye are sons, God hath sent forth the Spirit of his Son into your hearts, crying, Abba, Father"* (**Galatians 4:6**).

The Holy Spirit grieves: *"And grieve not the Holy Spirit of God, whereby ye are sealed unto the day of redemption"* (**Ephesians 4:30**).

The Holy Spirit creates: *"The spirit of God hath made me, and the breath of the Almighty hath given me life"* (**Job 33:4**).

The Holy Spirit molds character and produces fruit: *"But the fruit of the Spirit is love, joy, peace, long-suffering, gentleness, goodness, faith, 23 Meekness, temperance: against such, there is no law"* **(Galatians 5:22–23).**

The Holy Spirit intercedes when we are weak: *"Likewise the Spirit also helpeth our infirmities: for we know not what we should pray for as we ought: but the Spirit itself maketh intercession for us with groanings which cannot be uttered"* **(Romans 8:26).**

The Holy Spirit teaches and reminds: *"But the Comforter, which is the Holy Ghost, whom the Father will send in my name, He shall teach you all things, and bring all things to your remembrance, whatsoever I have said unto you"* **(John 14:26).**

The Holy Spirit gives power: *"And, behold, I send the promise of my Father upon you but tarry ye in the city of Jerusalem, until ye be endued with power from on high"* **(Luke 24:49).**

The Holy Spirit seals the believer: *"In whom ye also trusted, after that ye heard the word of truth, the gospel of your salvation in whom also after that ye believed, ye were sealed with that Holy Spirit of promise, 14 Which is the earnest of our inheritance until the redemption of the purchased possession, unto the praise of His glory"* **(Ephesians 1:13–14).**

The Holy Spirit gives knowledge and wisdom: *"For to one is given by the Spirit the word of wisdom; to another the word of knowledge by the same Spirit"* **(1 Corinthians 12:8).**

The Holy Spirit can raise the dead: *"But if the Spirit of Him that raised up Jesus from the dead dwell in you, He that raised up Christ from the dead shall also quicken your mortal bodies by His Spirit that dwelleth in you"* **(Romans 8:11).**

The Holy Spirit Baptizes: *"For by one Spirit are we all baptized into one body, whether we be Jews or Gentiles, whether we be bond or free; and have been all made to drink into one Spirit"* **(1 Corinthians 12:13).**

The Holy Spirit calls and commissions: *"Take heed therefore unto yourselves, and to all the flock, over which the Holy Ghost hath made you overseers, to feed the church of God, which he hath purchased with his own blood"* **(Acts 20:28).**

The Holy Spirit reveals to you who Jesus is: *"But when the Comforter comes, whom I will send unto you from the Father, even the Spirit of truth, which proceedeth from the Father, He shall testify of me"* **(John 15:26).**

The Holy Spirit tells you that you are a child of God: *"But ye are not in the flesh, but in the Spirit, if so be that the Spirit of God dwells in you. Now if any man has not the Spirit of Christ, he is none of His"* **(Romans 8:9).**

This is just a brief overview of what the Holy Spirit can do. There is so much more. I remember attending a retreat and the minister was laying hands on people so that they would receive the Holy Spirit.

I was sitting there watching and I began to grow frustrated because I discerned some errors in the process. God spoke to my heart and He said that the reason why many do not receive the Holy Spirit of Fire and the evidence of speaking in tongues is because they do not know why they need it and they do not know its value. God said everyone should be taught about the Holy Spirit so they can understand the full value of its role and speak in the Spirit also known as tongues.

Without the Holy Spirit, we cannot do anything for the Kingdom of God. Listen to what I am saying! The Holy Spirit has everything we need to be successful on earth until Jesus Christ our Lord and Savior returns. The spirit of God, the Holy Spirit, gives us life and without the Holy Spirit, we are walking in darkness.

The Father, the Son, and the Holy Spirit are one and this is important for you to know. The Father is God, the Son is God, and the Holy Spirit is God. God is omniscient which means that God is all-knowing, all-wise, and all-seeing.

Because the Father, the Son, and the Holy Spirit are one they are in perfect harmony and in perfect unity. The personalities of the Father, Son, and Holy Spirit have their missions that are always in the will of God, no arguing or debate. They always look and go in accordance with God's perfect will.

A great example of this is what Jesus said in Luke 22:42:

"Father if you are willing, please take this cup of suffering away from me. Yet I want Your will to be done, not mine."

There is no way you can be a Christian without the Holy Spirit. The Holy Spirit gives you the power to be a witness to the truth of God who gave his only begotten Son, Jesus Christ.

Let's read the passage:

"But you will receive power when the Holy Spirit comes upon you and you will be my witnesses, telling people about Me everywhere — in Jerusalem, throughout Judea, in Samaria, and to the ends of the earth" **(Acts 1:8 NLT).**

Listen carefully! The biggest mystery of the Holy Spirit is this: if you say anything about the Father or the son Jesus Christ, you can be forgiven. But if you say any blasphemous utterances against the Holy Spirit you will not be forgiven.

I have heard people make fun of those of us who do speak in the Spirit with utterances. They say it is gibberish and made up. We have to be careful: just because you may not have experienced it does not mean it's not from God.

Let's read this important passage:

"Anyone who isn't with me opposes me, and anyone who isn't working with me is actually working against me. ³¹ "So I tell you, every sin and blasphemy can be forgiven — except blasphemy against the Holy Spirit, which will never be forgiven. ³² Anyone who speaks against the Son of Man can be forgiven, but anyone who speaks against the Holy Spirit will never be forgiven, either in this world or in the world to come."

- **Matthew 12:30-32 (NLT)**

When God released the gift of the Holy Spirit to me, I was at home praying on my knees. I was saying the 'Our Father' prayer when I actually felt the release.

If you can imagine someone turning a knob to open a door, I felt that mechanical turn in my belly and the release of the power of God brought an ongoing flowing of this unknown language out of my mouth as I prayed.

See, you have to open your mouth in faith and pray and when God decides He will release the gift so you can speak in the Spirit language called tongues. So if you have been wanting this gift, do not give up! Come thirsty to God and ready to receive and it will come. Everyone receives spiritual gifts at different times so never quit or stop asking God. Just continue to seek and learn as much as you can about the Spirit of God and gain understanding. The more you know the greater your desire will be to speak in tongues.

I thank God who gave me patience and the desire to want the gift to speak to Him in the Spirit. I knew I needed this gift. People would lay hands on me and pray for me to receive this gift but I never received it until I became thirsty for God and understood that I needed this precious gift.

I always felt special when it came to God. I believe He wanted to give me the gift of speaking in tongues when I was alone. I was in awe. I was so happy to speak directly to God. I became a great witness for the Kingdom of God because of the Holy Spirit that dwells in me.

I trust God and I do not care about what people think or say. I am a child of the highest God who hears me. I know at the end of the day that God is the only one who is built to last. Everything else is temporal. It is only our God the Father of Abraham, Isaac, and Jacob who gives life. I will share some mysteries of the Holy Spirit that I have learned.

I remember being really mad and upset when I heard about another sister in the Lord who was being mistreated. I was mad because this sister would give her last and did not deserve the abuse she was given. As I was driving I was thinking of all the things I would tell her abuser and the Holy Spirit reminded me of the scripture Ephesians 4:26 that says:

"Be ye angry, and sin not. Let not the sun go down upon your wrath."

I then became aware of my evil thoughts and convictions because my thoughts were far off from being Godly. While still angry but now concerned, I quickly prayed in tongues non-stop as I continued to drive.

I tell you the truth when I say that my blood pressure decreased and the love that was absent in my anger poured back into my heart. I was back to feeling peace within ten minutes of praying in tongues. I was in awe! The feeling was indescribable. Praying in the Spirit not only took away the anger and anxiety, but the conviction.

I was so happy that I called my friend and told her that God will deal with the situation. My thoughts were wrong and I knew if I prayed in the Spirit that I would be delivered from my evil thoughts. God changed my heart and brought me peace. He took away my anger. He is amazing!

The Holy Spirit will also help you when you feel scared and worried in any and all situations. Just ask Him to help you and He will show you a way out. If you are being judged or you need to speak and you do not know how to say the things that are in your heart, ask the Holy Spirit to help. He would love to help you because that is what He is here for. He lives in us to make life much easier for the believer. So when you ask Him for help that is faith in action. You are asking God to help you even though you cannot see Him.

The situation may be impossible for man but you going to God in faith is knowing *nothing* is impossible for God. We just need to always remember what activates the move of God and that is our obedience to Him: when we repent and turn away from a sinful life and look to follow Him and respond to what He tells us to do. The Holy Spirit will then guide us to what is right and what is wrong.

God convicts the world of its sinful living. The Holy Spirit gives life to our bodies and dwells in us. The Holy Spirit indwells in the believer and bears witness that you are a child of God. The Holy Spirit will always remind us of God's promises. The Holy Spirit provides many spiritual gifts. He teaches, reminds, and gives courage, inspiration, wisdom, motivation, interpretation, and the power that we need to do what God has called us to do.

No one, not even the educational system, having letters behind your name, or carrying some type of degree can ever give you the power that the Holy Spirit gives.

The Holy Spirit is very helpful in life choices, like when I wanted to buy a sister in the Lord a gift. I said okay Holy Spirit, help me and the Holy Spirit would remind me of something she wanted or enjoyed.

I love the Holy Spirit, He is my friend, my comforter, and my everything. He always has your best interest at heart without any motives other than his love for His people.

Speaking of love, another mystery of the Holy Spirit is if you have the gift to speak in the Spirit you must also have a love for people and concern for their welfare. Love for all is God's will regardless of their race, religion, or condition. We must have love and respect regardless of our differences because God calls us to love one another by honoring our parents and loving our brothers, sisters and neighbors.

We must have love, respect, and charity. Without these things, regardless of if you have the gift of speaking in the Holy Spirit or any other gift, without love it is empty and just words without any power. Love must always be present. Love covers all. Love is the greatest.

Another mystery of the Holy Spirit is that He can depart just as fast as He dwells in the believer. This can happen for many reasons, especially when God has chosen you for a special assignment and you become continuously disobedient because of pride and being too self-willed.

We see this in Saul and David. David was a man after God's heart. He wanted to obey God, and he was not a people pleaser. However, Saul was a man after his own heart, and he wanted to please and glorify himself. He was impatient and self-willed. When God asked him to do something, Saul would only go halfway. This caused him to be outside of the will of God. Since the Holy Spirit only agrees with God's will, the Holy Spirit departed.

Let's read the Biblical passage:

"Now the Spirit of the LORD departed from Saul, and an evil spirit from the LORD TROUBLED him" (1 Samuel 16:14 RSV).

When you continue to go against God and you know what He asked you to do, this is sanely going against God, not once or twice, but continuously doing the opposite of what God has asked you to do.

God will not continue in the foolishness. He is Holy and even though He chooses us, if you do not want to be obedient and live in a Godly way you do have free will. God will leave you to your free will which opens the door to tormenting spirits that come from a Godless lifestyle of disobedience.

Holy Spirit, doctrinal examples:

The doctrine stated: God is one beside Him there is no other. Divine unity compounds three distinct persons. They are different, but the same. The three cooperate with one mind and purpose. God Creates, Jesus Redeems, and the Holy Spirit sanctifies. The father testifies of the son **(Mathew 3:17),** the son testifies of the father **(John 5:19),** and the son testifies to the Holy Spirit **(John 14:26).** They have an eternal fellowship.

The Holy Spirit testifies to the Son **(John 15:26)** so we can see they are one. God cannot explain what our mind can't comprehend. Trinity is shown in the Bible even though the word Trinity is not seen.

How can you see the Trinity without the word Trinity? Read what Jesus says and you will see the three also known as the Trinity.

Jesus speaks and we can see the Trinity in operation. Let's read:

The Father loves and sends the Son. I came from my Father and I return to my Father. The Father and I will send you a Counselor and the Counselor will teach you about me. My Father will reveal me through the Counselor and the Counselor will speak only about me. We will abide in you.

God loves and sends the Son, the Son goes back to the Father and the Father and Son send the Holy Spirit. The Holy Spirit intercedes with the Father.

Don't let people lie about the Father, the Son, and the Holy Spirit. They are one and work together. When Jesus was baptized the Holy Spirit was there as a dove. Why, does God say you must be baptized in the name of the Father, the Son, and the Holy Spirit? Because they are all one.

"If any man is thirsty"

"Jesus stood and cried, saying, If any man thirst, let him come unto me, and drink. He that believeth on me, as the scripture hath said, out of his belly shall flow rivers of living water. But this spake He of the Spirit, which they that believe on Him should receive: for the Holy Ghost was not yet given; because that Jesus was not yet glorified" (**John 7:37-39 KJV**).

This passage mentions the Father, the Son, and the Holy Spirit.

"The grace of the Lord Jesus Christ, and the love of God, and the communion of the Holy Ghost be with you all. Amen.

- 2 Corinthians 13:14

I'd like to add one last thing about what the Holy Spirit will do.

He will fight any and all demonic attacks. Recently, I had a demonic attack in a dream and I remember how the attack came so quickly. I remember seeing the demons coming towards me and at the same time I lifted my hands. I told myself to not stop speaking in the Spirit and to concentrate and to keep speaking in my prayer language regardless of being bombarded by these demons yelling and coming at me in this dream.

I just kept raising my hands and praying in the Spirit. Not long after, the demons had to flee! All praises to God, I woke up free from any fear.

This is important information to know. Your prayer language is a 911 call into the Kingdom of God.

NOTEPAD

Date: _____

_____

_____

_____

_____

_____

_____

_____

_____

_____

_____

_____

_____

_____

_____

_____

_____

_____

_____

_____

NOTEPAD

Date: _____

_____

_____

_____

_____

_____

_____

_____

_____

_____

_____

_____

_____

_____

_____

_____

_____

_____

The Truth about Generational Curses

As believers, when we speak about generational curses we have to remember what Jesus did on the cross. He has redeemed us from all curses.

Let's read the Biblical passage:

"Christ has redeemed us from the curse of the law, having become a curse for us."
- **Galatians 3:13 (NKJV)**

The first thing I want to say is that when we are obedient to God, His word is so powerful that a person who was once broken can be put back in their original state. This is just how God intended from the beginning.

God is perfectly fair, holding each person responsible for their own choices. So why do we see the same curses from the past continue to visit the next generations? They are suffering from the same family experiences, even though they are Christians.

Let's first read the Bible verses that reference generational curses.

"You shall not bow down to them or serve them; for I the LORD your God am a jealous God, visiting the iniquity of the fathers upon the children to the third and the fourth generation of those who hate me."
- **Exodus 20:5 (RSV)**

When we read the text, it is clearly talking to those who "hate him" and if you're a Christian you love God, however, we must remember that regardless of whether or not a person is a believer, their parents, as well as their grandparents, can have a huge influence on them.

If a person had parents who did not believe in God or said they believed in God, but did not have a personal relationship with Him, we know their actions will show a lifestyle that is sinful despite what they say. Either way, they lived a rebellious life opposite to what God commands.

The effects of sin are naturally passed down from one generation to the next because children are likely to practice the same sinful lifestyle as their parents. This is also called learned behavior. Just like many people have learned to be racist, a person practicing sin is the one who opens the door to a domino effect.

God clearly tells us about generational curses being passed down children through the practice of sin.

Let's read the Biblical Passage:

"Having eyes full of adultery, and that cannot cease from sin; beguiling unstable souls: a heart they have exercised with covetous practices; cursed children." **2 Peter 2:14 (KJV)**

The text in Second Peter clearly lets us know that practicing sin will only lessen a person's self-control. If you continuously practice sin you are the host for generational curses that will harm your children or other people who you have influenced.

Practiced sin will always follow the next generation in the same way you were influenced. A practiced sin will always turn into iniquity.

Let's look at what iniquity means:

1. The absence of moral or spiritual values.
2. Morally objectionable behavior.
3. An unjust act.

"Iniquity" means "guilt worthy of punishment." Iniquity is seen as the worst of sin.

Anyone who does not live a Godly lifestyle will suffer due to their iniquities and trespasses. When temptation comes they find themselves powerless to do the right thing. They will bend in the direction of sin which means they are breaking God's commands. They fall into trespassing.

Trespassing means going against a person. An example of this is when someone trespasses on someone else's property. It is any violation of law, civil or moral; it may relate to a person, a community, or the state, or offenses against God.

So when a person continues to sin and trespass continuously against God it becomes a habit. This then turns into an iniquity. When you live a sinful life, absent of moral or spiritual values, this will keep blessings out and curses in.

Let's look up what the word 'curse' means:

1. The cause of evil, misfortune, or trouble.
2. An evil that has been invoked upon a person.
3. Evil or misfortune that comes as if in response to imprecation or as retribution.

'Imprecation' means to repeat and 'retribution' means the natural consequence of sin. Generational curses enter into a family through influences. What we see over and over in families are the consequences of people who have been practicing sin or have been influenced by association.

Here is a perfect example: the children of alcoholic parents frequently suffer neglect and abuse as a direct consequence of their parents' sinful behavior. Behavior studies show that these children will most likely also abuse alcohol.

The consequences of the parents' alcoholism are passed on through the generations. In this sense, the Bible says that children are punished for the sins of their fathers "to the third and fourth generation." So God is saying that we curse ourselves and our family with our sinful acts because it most likely will continue into the next generations.

This is not only in the Old Testament or the imagination, we see families suffer from repeated negative circumstances. For example, not only a father will go to jail, but also his son and when his son has a son and reaches his teen years he is now in prison as well. It becomes a family affair. You can find several suicide victims in the same family. Shall we bring up divorce? Almost everybody in my family is divorced. Can anyone keep a marriage?

Let's be honest. We see these generational curses and influences and it can cause the next generation "to bend" in the same way. God warns us to not walk in our fleshly desires.

The Works of the Flesh and their Definitions

Let's read the Biblical passage:

"But I say, walk by the Spirit, and do not gratify the desires of the flesh. For the desires of the flesh are against the Spirit, and the desires of the Spirit are against the flesh; for these are opposed to each other, to prevent you from doing what you would. But if you are led by the Spirit you are not under the law. Now the works of the flesh are plain fornication, impurity, licentiousness, idolatry, sorcery, enmity, strife, jealousy, anger, selfishness, dissension, party spirit, envy, drunkenness, carousing, and the like. <u>I warn you, as I warned you before, that those who do such things shall not inherit the kingdom of God</u>." - **Galatians 5: 16-21 (RSV)**

Adultery—If you are married and have sex with someone other than your spouse, or if you are not married and have sex with a married person.

"Let marriage be held in honor among all, and let the marriage bed be undefiled; for God will judge the immoral and adulterous."
- **Hebrews 13:4 (Leviticus 20:10) (RSV)**

Idolatry – The worship of an idol or a physical object as a representation of a god. Idols are a matter of the heart, anything that you put in front of God. It could be your husband, money, or false religion. Anything can easily be made into an idol when it blocks you from having a relationship with God and causes you to put your time and trust elsewhere. It is not just bowing down to objects.

44

"Put to death, therefore, what is earthly in you: fornication, impurity, passion, evil desire, and covetousness, which is idolatry."
- **Colossians 3:5 (RSV)**

Witchcraft – The practice of magic, especially black magic; the use of spells and the invocation of spirits. The use of supernatural power not from God; for if the power is not from God, it is of the Devil.

"But the fearful, and unbelieving, and the abominable, and murderers, and whoremongers, and sorcerers, and idolaters, and all liars, shall have their part in the lake which burneth with fire and brimstone: which is the second death."
- **Revelations 21:8 (Deut 18:10)(RSV)**

Hatred – Intense hostility and aversion usually deriving from fear, anger, or sense of injury. Hatred of the flesh is sin and not what the Spirit wants you to express to others.

"Hatred stirs up strife, but love covers all offenses."
-Proverbs 10:12 (Titus 3:3) (RSV)

Emulations – ("zeal," "earnestness," and "enthusiasm") where it is classed among "the works of the flesh" and signifies the stirring up of jealousy or envy of others, because of what we are, or have, or profess. To Imitate. Paul wishes that the Jews would "emulate" him **(Romans 11:14)**

"Do not be conformed to this world, but be transformed by the renewal of your mind, that you may prove what is the will of God, what is good and acceptable and perfect."
- **Romans 12:2 (RSV)**

Wrath – Wrath, when used by man, is the exhibition of an enraged sinful nature and is therefore always inexcusable.

"Let all bitterness and wrath and anger and clamor and slander be put away from you, with all malice."
- **Ephesians 4:31(RSV)**

Murder – The crime of unlawfully killing a person especially with aforethought malice. Killing another outside legal justification and condemnation.

"Anyone who hates his brother is a murderer, and you know that no murderer has eternal life abiding in him."
- **1 John 3:15 (Numbers 35:16)(RSV)**

Drunkenness – Given to habitual and excessive use of alcohol. Excess of the intoxicating substance causes you to lose total control of your body.

"Woe to those who rise early in the morning to run after their drinks, who stay up late at night till they are inflamed with wine."
- **Isaiah 5:11 (Ephesians 5:18)(NIV)**

Fornication – Is generally consensual sexual intercourse between two people who are not married to each other.

"Flee fornication. Every sin that a man doeth is without the body; but he that committeth fornication sinneth against his own body."
- **1 Corinthians 6:18 (KJV)**

Homosexual – Sexual behavior between members of the same sex or gender.

"If a man also lies with mankind, as he lieth with a woman, both of them have committed an abomination: they shall surely be put to death; their blood shall be upon them."
- **Leviticus 20:13 (KJV)**

"Those who indulge in sexual sin, or who worship idols, or commit adultery, or are male prostitutes, or practice homosexuality, or are thieves, or greedy people, or drunkards, or are abusive, or cheat people—none of these will inherit the Kingdom of God."
- **1 Corinthians 6:9–10 (NLT)**

Impurity – Something that is impure or makes something else impure. Following after the flesh.

"When you follow the desires of your sinful nature, the results are very clear: sexual immorality, impurity, lustful pleasures."
- **Galatians 5:19 (NLT)**

Licentiousness – Lacking moral restraint, especially in sexual conduct or vices. The lusts of the flesh, which lead to acts of uncleanness.

"For admission has been secretly gained by some who long ago were designated for this condemnation, ungodly persons who pervert the grace of our God into licentiousness and deny our only Master and Lord, Jesus Christ." - **Jude 1:4 (RSV) (Also read Ephesians 4:19)**

Sorcery – The belief in magical spells that harness occult forces or evil spirits to produce unnatural effects in the world.

"And when they say to you, "Consult the mediums and the wizards who chirp and mutter," should not a people consult their God? Should they consult the dead on behalf of the living?"
- **Isaiah 8:19 (RSV)**

Enmity – A state of deep-seated ill-will or hatred. The quality of being an enemy.

"You adulterers! Don't you realize that friendship with the world makes you an enemy of God? I say it again: If you want to be a friend of the world, you make yourself an enemy of God."
- **James 4:4 (NLT)**

Strife – Lack of agreement or harmony. Contention over carnal issues or even after the truth.

"A hot-tempered man stirs up strife, but he who is slow to anger quiets contention."
- **Proverbs 15:18 (RSV) (1 Timothy 6:3-5)**

Jealousy/Envy – A feeling of jealous envy, especially of a rival. A feeling of grudging admiration and desire to have something that is possessed by another. Coveting possession or power of another. This is a manifestation of pride.

"But if you are bitterly jealous and there is selfish ambition in your heart, don't cover up the truth with boasting and lying. For jealousy and selfishness are not God's kind of wisdom. Such things are earthly, unspiritual, and demonic."
James 3:14-15 (Also read Galatians 5:26 & 1 Corinthians 3:3)

Anger – A strong emotion; a feeling that is oriented toward some real or supposed grievance.

"Be angry but do not sin; do not let the sun go down on your anger."
- **Ephesians 4:26 (RSV)**

Unforgiving – Unwilling or unable to forgive or show mercy.

"But if you do not forgive men their trespasses, neither will your Father forgive your trespasses."
- **Matthew 6:15 (RSV)**

Selfishness – Stinginess resulting from a concern for your own welfare and a disregard of others.

"For men will be lovers of self, lovers of money, proud, arrogant, abusive, disobedient to their parents, ungrateful, unholy."
- **2 Timothy 3:2 (RSV)**

Dissension – Disagreement among those expected to cooperate. Causing division against established authority.

"Therefore, some of the Pharisees were saying, "This man is not from God because He does not keep the Sabbath." But others were saying, "How can a man who is a sinner perform such signs?" And there was a division among them."
- **John 9:16 (RSV) (Rom 16:17-18)**

Heresies – Teaching things against the truth of the Word of God.

"But false prophets also arose among the people, just as there will be false teachers among you, who will secretly bring in destructive heresies, even denying the Master who bought them, bringing upon themselves swift destruction."
- **2 Peter 2:1 (RSV)**

Party-spirit – It is partying, where the flesh is indulged, celebrated and encouraged to be out of control. Such partying usually includes many sins previously explained in this list.

Now the works of the flesh are plain fornication, impurity, licentiousness, idolatry, sorcery, enmity, strife, jealousy, anger, selfishness, dissension, party spirit, envy, drunkenness, carousing, and the like. I warn you, as I warned you before, that those who do such things shall not inherit the kingdom of God.
- **Galatians 5: 16-21 (RSV)**

Carousing – Means indulging in one's appetites excessively. Bad or immoral behavior that involves sexual sin, drugs, alcohol, etc.

"For you have spent enough time in the past doing what pagans choose to do living in debauchery, lust, drunkenness, orgies, carousing and detestable idolatry."
- **1 Peter 4:3 (NIV)**

Such As: Any expression of the flesh is condemned. The flesh being in control is by itself a sin. **(Galatians 5:16-17)**

So now we have an understanding of what works of the flesh mean. When we read this Biblical text, it is telling us that the only way to stay away from practicing sin is to continue to walk in the Fruit of the Spirit: which are love, joy, peace, patience, kindness, goodness, faithfulness, gentleness, and self-control against such there is no law. (**Galatians 5: 16-22 RSV**)

When we make a decision to continue to walk by the flesh, this is when we are open to receive a curse.

Let's read the important Biblical key texts:

"Because the carnal mind is <u>enmity against God</u>, for it is not subject to the law of God, neither indeed can be. So then they that are in the flesh <u>cannot please God."</u>

- **Romans 8:7-8**

Let's look up what the word 'enmity' means:

1. Hatred.
2. A feeling or condition of hostility; hatred; ill will.
3. The quality of being an enemy. The opposite of friendship.

Let's read the Biblical passage:

"I the LORD your God am a jealous God, visiting the iniquity of the fathers upon the children to the third and the fourth generation <u>of those who hate me."</u>

- **Exodus 20:5 (RSV)**

This gives us a clear understanding that when we are practicing sin, we are saying we hate God and become an enemy to God.

My question to you is if you are walking in the flesh, and it is not pleasing to God, how do you expect to receive God's blessings? We have to know the word of God because the word of God will always reveal why we are in the condition that we are in. It will also tell us how to get out.

One of the biggest reasons why many of us will see the same kind of curses visiting the family is because there are familiar spirits who reside with you and your family. These spirits are invited in through practicing sins such as adultery, fornication, idolatry, witchcraft, hatred, emulations, wrath, strife, murders, and drunkenness.

Familiar spirits embed themselves into our very personality and behavior so that their appetites and desires become our appetites and desires, much like drugs. This is why God says we must be led by the spirit of God. Being outside of that will lead us to being a slave to sin and in bondage, which leads to death.

Another way familiar spirits can enter into our lives is by opening the door to the occult which includes Ouija boards, tarot cards, astrology, and contacting the dead. Putting your faith in these types of devices will only lead to demonic attacks.

I remember a friend of mine told me she was using the Ouija board as an object of faith, asking it questions about other people and her life. One day she was playing with the Ouija board and the Ouija Board told her it would kill her. She became frightened and began to stay away from playing with the Ouija board and one day she was leaving the house and an evil spirit came from behind and started to choke her. Totally freaked out, she ran out of her home. She started having demonic attacks and feared for her life. She finally had to move out of that home and turned her life over to Jesus and she never partakes in the occult any longer. This is true repentance, turning to God and no longer practicing sin.

Even though you are a Christian and love God the enemy will always try to attack you using all types of temptation. It is up to us as believers to let the enemy know we are not his playground. We do this by being obedient to the word of God and keeping his commands regardless of what we want or think is best. God knows that we are not perfect, but putting our faith in the finished work of Christ is the key to our strength.

God will always fight our battles. Our faith and trust in our Lord Jesus Christ will bring us the blessings.

Let's read the Biblical passage:

"But blessed are those who trust in the Lord and have made the Lord their hope and confidence."

- Jeremiah 17:7 (NLT)

We can also get generational curses through the words that we speak. Look at what happened when Pilate handed Jesus over to be crucified. He did not want Jesus's blood to be on his hands so he told the crowd that it will be on theirs.

Let's read a Biblical text about generational curses:

"So when Pilate saw that he was gaining nothing, but rather that a riot was beginning, he took water and washed his hands before the crowd, saying, "I am innocent of this man's blood; see to it yourselves. "And all the people answered, "His blood be on us and on our children!" Then he released for them Barab'bas and having scourged Jesus, delivered him to be crucified."

- **Matthew 27:24-26 (RSV)**

Who knows what was said or done by our ancestors that may be affecting us today. Words can be spoken into existence. We must be careful about what we say and how we think about ourselves because it may change who we become over a period of time. Our words are powerful and can cause curses in our lives.

God tells us what we as believers and unbelievers need to do to close the door to these generational curses.

Let's read the Biblical passage:

"Put all your rebellion behind you, and find yourselves a new heart and a new spirit. For why should you die, O people of Israel?"

- **Ezekiel 18:31**

The key word is "Israel." This is referring to those who are in a covenant with God, which are us as believers. In this text in Ezekiel, God says to put your rebellion behind you and find yourselves a new heart a new spirit. This refers to being born again.

Let's read the Biblical passage:

"Therefore, if any man be in Christ, he is a new creature: old things are passed away; behold, all things become new."

- 2 Corinthians 5:17-21 (KJV)

If you are born again and all things become new this means your heart should be new too. So as born again believers we can see the wrong not only in ourselves but also in what was taught to us by our parents and ancestors.

Our ancestors may have been involved in hate crimes like racism, killing, lynching, rape, kidnapping, torture, enslaving, molesting, and idol worshipping. The curses of iniquity can come upon nations, lands, and families. Think of all the bloodshed that took place on the land where we live. I never forget the Biblical text when Cain killed his brother Abel.

Let's read:

"And the LORD said, "What have you done? The voice of your brother's blood is crying to me from the ground."

- Genesis 4:10 (RSV)

And even though we are not guilty or responsible for what our ancestors or parents have done, we know that it is wrong. If we say, well, we were not there and we did not do it, we have to remember that if we have a new heart in Christ we would feel horrible that our forefathers participated in living an evil lifestyle and were an enemy to our God, and also had a big influence on our disobedient behavior toward God.

So if we turn to God and say 'I love you God, but I have no remorse for what we or my ancestors have done' what would make us any different? The only thing that can make us different is our heart and having compassion and sorrow for people that we as well as our forefathers have wronged and affected. We should not have a carnal mindset and say things like oh that was a long time ago so "get over it." We must examine ourselves and be sensitive to the Holy Spirit and look at what things we may have inherited through tradition, lifestyle, and learned behaviors.

We know we all have inherited the worst sin of all which is un-forgiveness. We have seen so many of our family members fight amongst one another and have watched our families break up and divide through un-forgiveness.

Let's read the text in Mark about un-forgiveness:

"And whenever you stand praying, forgive, if you have anything against anyone; so that your Father also who is in heaven may forgive you your trespasses."

- **Mark 11:25 (RSV)**

Unforgiveness causes stress and chronic anxiety.

Un-forgiveness is classified in medical books as a disease. According to Dr. Steven Standiford, chief of surgery at the Cancer Treatment Centers of America, refusing to forgive makes people sick and can cause chronic anxiety and stress. Un-forgiveness can also cause a loss of appetite, anorexia, obesity, increased or excessive smoking or drinking of alcohol, anxiety, anger, depression, exhaustion, paranoia, and the feeling of being out of control.

Stress is linked to the six leading causes of death: heart disease, cancer, lung ailments, accidents, cirrhosis of the liver, and suicide. Un-forgiveness is a gateway to self-inflicted physical pain. Nine times out of ten, the ones who have hurt us have moved on, yet we are still living in the past.

Forgiving someone is not saying that what they have done to you was okay. It is saying that you are not going to be angry about it anymore, and that you much rather be free from the consequences of holding un-forgiveness in your heart.

When you make a decision to finally forgive all of the people who wronged you then you will realize what a burden your anger and hatred was and all the pain and sickness it caused. You will suddenly feel the heavy weight begin to melt right off your shoulders because love conquers all.

"But I say unto you, Love your enemies, bless them that curse you, do good to them that hate you, and pray for them which despitefully use you, and persecute you."
- **Matthew 5:44 (KJV)**

We have to forgive and if the person that we want to forgive is deceased, unavailable, or unsafe to speak to we must repent and ask God for forgiveness and guidance. Not forgiving someone can be a reason for why our prayers are unanswered. God says to forgive if you have anything against anyone so that your Father also who is in heaven may forgive you your trespasses.

We can start over right now God gave us the free gift to receive Jesus Christ as our Lord and Savior who died for all our sins and curses. All we need to do is repent and turn back to God and receive this free gift. This is why God says: "My people are destroyed for lack of knowledge" **(Hosea 4:6 RSV).**

When I think about generational curses I think about the curse I was under because of my actions and all the trouble I had in my life. It started when my marriage ended. I really wanted to be married and I tried to be the best wife I could, however, I did not have a solid foundation of what a healthy marriage looked like.

I was raised by my mother who had four of us babies to look after. I remember back then that the biggest worry my mom had was losing us kids. It is very difficult and hard to be a single mom with one income, as a lot of you who are single parents know. My mom always worried about not having enough money to provide so she worked all the time so I was told come straight home. I was never allowed to spend the night over at friends' houses and had to be in by dark.

I laugh writing this to myself because I remember the Kool-Aid commercial when the mom had the gallon of Kool-Aid and was pouring it out to all the kids. Well, my mom was not the Kool-Aid mom. It was all about coming straight home from school, locking the doors, and not answering the phone or the door. When my mom called she used a signal by letting the phone ring twice, hanging up, and then calling again. After that, we would pick it up right away.

So we were these little kids watching over one another. My sister was 3 years older than me and I had a brother who was two years older and a brother who was younger than I. We were all a few years apart. My mom did not bring men to the house. She did not have casual sleepovers with men. She was always cautious over us and was very strict. We all went to catechism which means we were all raised to believe in the Catholic faith.

My mom did the best she could with having all of us and only herself to manage the household. So being raised in a household without a father gave me no understanding of marriage. Not even what it would look like. So when I got married, I did not go in with unity. I went in with 'lock the doors and don't let anyone in.'

I loved my husband, he was my first love, but I came in with trust issues so I loved him but did not trust him. In the back of my mind, I would think he would cheat because all men cheat. Why did I think that? Because my mom told me so. Even though I was in love with my husband, I always remembered what my mom told me and I would think to myself would he really have an affair. I could not see myself with any other man so how could he see himself with other women when we were both in love?

I loved my husband, but not long after the marriage my husband cheated and committed adultery. He was having an affair with a secretary from his job. I moved out and made a decision to never trust a man and so the ones who had an interest in me, I would purposely hurt them and break their heart sort to speak because I was hurting. This is how the curse came in and the damage began to spread throughout my life.

When I started to date my intentions were not to find love and settle down. I was what they would call a 'player,' a person who would keep several relationships and make one believe I was totally faithful to them. I wish I knew then what I know now. I was playing myself because I had opened the door to a curse, but how?

Let's read the Biblical passage:

"For, as it is written, "The two shall become one flesh." [17] But he who is united to the Lord becomes one spirit with him. [18] Shun immorality. Every other sin which a man commits is outside the body, but the immoral man sins against his own body. [19] Do you not know that your body is a temple of the Holy Spirit within you, which you have from God? You are not your own; [20] you were bought with a price. So glorify God in your body."
- **1 Corinthians 6:13-19 (RSV)**

I was in sexual sin at its worst. I was one body sleeping with many so all of the curses on the person I was sleeping with became joined with me. This is also known as soul ties.

God says, "Let marriage be held in honor among all, and let the marriage bed be undefiled, for God will judge the sexually immoral and adulterous." God says we must honor marriage. I chose not to. I defiled my body and brought curses into my life.

These are the curses I remember having when I continued in sexual sin. I could never consistently keep a job and I was always in poverty no matter how hard I worked. I was always short. There was never enough money. I stayed broke and everything I wanted to do would never work out.

It just seemed like everything I touched always became a problem or some type of struggle. It seems easy for others but when I would try to do something to better my state it crumbled every time.

I even *felt* cursed. I remember saying to myself: why do I always have to struggle? I had a lying tongue. I would lie for no reason. I was tormented. At bedtime I would have repeated dreams of me running away from something. I would always be running, and wake up in fear. I never rested. I would have panic attacks because I worried all the time and that caused high anxiety. I remember living in hotels and sleeping on couches. I never had a place of my own. I was always taken advantage of and never had a true friend. I had even gotten really severe uncontrollable adult acne even after I had it during puberty. No matter how many acne creams I used my face got worse. I went to the doctor and he said it was internal and even when I took pills it did not get better. My weight climbed up to 257 pounds, and this caused insecurities and depression.

I contracted STD's and of course because of my lifestyle I don't know who gave it to me and who I passed it on to. I would always be reminded of my past. I was tormented with the thoughts of the past that would play back everything I hated in my life. It would play back like a tape that plays over and over again. That would make me angry and full of envy and rage that caused me to stay away from my entire family for nearly five years. I was sick because of the curse I brought upon myself that came from practicing sin.

See when we defile our bodies, we can bring sickness to ourselves. Our own thoughts will cause fear, anger, hate and all the behaviors caused by refusing to walk in the Spirit.

Having anger, pride, fear, and hate can also be a generational curse. I was living a life that was leading me to death and it showed from the inside out through sickness in my body and the outcome of my life. I know for a fact that before I turned away from living a sinful life I was bound to generational curses by sleeping around. The curses of the people I slept with became mine just like the scripture said:

"Know ye not that your bodies are the members of Christ? Shall I then take the members of Christ, and make them the members of a harlot? God forbid. What? Know ye not that he which is joined to a harlot is one body? For two, saith he, shall be one flesh.[17] *But he that is joined unto the Lord is one spirit."*

- **1 Corinthians 6:15-17**

We are influenced by generational curses. They can also be hereditary when it comes to heart problems, diabetes, cancer, and many other types of sicknesses that run in the genes. We know that when it comes to cancer 10% is hereditary and the 90% can be caused by smoking, poor diet, sunlight, chemicals, being overweight and many other reasons.

There are many sicknesses and mental illnesses that can be hereditary through generations. This is why when we go to the doctor they want to know your family history and they ask many questions about your parents, as if they are the patient.

If you are still not convinced that generational curses exist, let me show you proof: fetal alcohol spectrum disorders. They are a group of conditions that can occur in a person whose mother drank alcohol during pregnancy. Problems may include an abnormal appearance, short height, low body weight, small head, poor coordination, low intelligence, behavior problems, and problems with hearing or seeing.

Those affected more commonly have trouble in school and law enforcement, are frequently jailed, are involved in the high-risk sexual activity, and have trouble with alcohol or other drugs **(Source: Wikipedia)**

We can see how our lifestyle choices can affect others physically. However, Our Father in heaven is never sick and has no illnesses and He gave His only begotten son Jesus who took all of our sicknesses away. We do not have to suffer what our families have suffered. So we need to examine our lifestyle and see what curses we have chosen because God gave us a choice of free will.

All praise to the Most High who is merciful and loves us. When we repent and admit that our lifestyle is wrong and we turn back to God leaving the old un-Godly lifestyle we can be free from sicknesses and curses.

So how do we detach from familiar spirits and close the door to these generational curses and influences?

The only cure for generational curses has always been true repentance and turning back to God by being obedient to His commands. It has to be active and not just lip service. When Israel turned from idols to serve the living God, the "curse" was broken and God saved them. **(Judges 3:9, 15; 1 Samuel 12:10-11)**

"Yes, God promised to visit Israel's sin upon the third and fourth generations. Now in the next verse, He promised that He would show love to a thousand generations of those who love Him and keep His commandments."

-   Exodus 20:6 (RSV)

In other words, God's grace lasts a thousand times longer than His wrath. Amen!

A perfect example of confessing and repenting of generational sin is found in Nehemiah.

Let's read the Biblical passage:

"I pray, LORD God of heaven, O great and awesome God, You who keep Your covenant and mercy with those who love You and observe Your commandments, please let Your ear be attentive and Your eyes open, that You may hear the prayer of Your servant which I pray before You now, day and night, for the children of Israel Your servants, and confess the sins of the children of Israel which we have sinned against You. Both my father's house and I have sinned."

- **Nehemiah 1:5-6 (NKJV)**

I love this prayer. It gives all of us hope. It also confirms that God is merciful. Nehemiah did not just confess his own sins, but we see that he confessed the sins of not only the children of Israel but his parents' and relatives' sins. So it is only God who fights our battle using His strength. We must call unto Him.

So we must confess our sins and also apologize for our forefathers' sins admitting that it was wrong. We must then make a decision to turn completely away from the sins of death and choose life by choosing Jesus as our Lord and Savior.

We have to let these evil spirits know who we are in Christ and that the word of God cuts like a knife into the spirit killing all their attempts to deceive us and keep us in bondage.

Let's read this important Biblical text:

"The word of God is quick, and powerful, and sharper than any two-edged sword, piercing even to the dividing asunder of soul and spirit, and of the joints and marrow, and is a discerner of the thoughts and intents of the heart."

- **Hebrews 4:12 (KJV)**

Being 'asunder' means to divide and pull apart into pieces. This means you will no longer be bound because how can you be bound to something that has been pulled apart from you and is now into pieces? Let's get free now and have God pull you apart from the iniquities.

"Submit yourselves therefore to God. Resist the devil and he will flee from you."
- **James 4:7 (RSV)**

The easiest way to begin recognizing a family curse is to take the time to self-examine your life. This list of behaviors and conditions will help you identify any generational curses or influences.

Circle all of the behaviors and any conditions that you or your family have struggled with. There is a blank notepad after the list to take down notes.

Identifying Generational Curses

Circle any behaviors or conditions that you can identify with:

- ❖ Controlling
- ❖ Cursing
- ❖ Swearing
- ❖ Gossip
- ❖ Mental Illnesses
- ❖ Physical Diseases
- ❖ Cancer
- ❖ Heart disease
- ❖ Lung disease
- ❖ Kidney stones
- ❖ Stomach problems
- ❖ Migraines
- ❖ Adultery
- ❖ Divorce
- ❖ Legalism
- ❖ Selfish
- ❖ Greed
- ❖ Possessiveness
- ❖ Laziness
- ❖ Gambling
- ❖ Stinginess
- ❖ Hoarding
- ❖ Stealing
- ❖ Poverty
- ❖ Indebtedness

- Faithlessness
- Unbelieving In God
- Critical of others
- Self-righteous
- Judgmentalism
- Revenge
- Murder
- Expecting failure
- Demonic Amulets
- Pride
- Bondage
- Slavery
- Loneliness
- Hopelessness
- Anxiety
- No ambition
- Lying
- Slander
- Racing thoughts
- Swearing
- Fornication
- Pornography
- Masturbation
- Homosexuality
- Incest
- Sexual abuse
- Music that glorifies satanic, sexual and rebellious

Behaviors.

- ❖ Rape
- ❖ Lust
- ❖ Victim mentality
- ❖ Illegal drugs
- ❖ Depression
- ❖ Self Hatred
- ❖ Bestiality
- ❖ Alcohol
- ❖ Tobacco
- ❖ Caffeine
- ❖ Overeating
- ❖ Rebellion
- ❖ Bulimia
- ❖ Anorexia
- ❖ Hypnotism
- ❖ Arrogance
- ❖ Bitterness
- ❖ Hatred
- ❖ Rage
- ❖ Violence
- ❖ Aggressiveness
- ❖ Unforgiveness
- ❖ Disobedient
- ❖ Lawlessness
- ❖ Panic attacks
- ❖ Occult Involvement
- ❖ Witchcraft

- ❖ Satanism
- ❖ Psychics
- ❖ Palm reading
- ❖ Fortune telling
- ❖ Ouija board
- ❖ Horoscope
- ❖ Atheist
- ❖ False Religions
- ❖ Voodoo
- ❖ Spiritual Blindness
- ❖ Pendulum
- ❖ Fears of all kinds
- ❖ Foul mouth
- ❖ Delusions
- ❖ Suicidal
- ❖ Jealousy
- ❖ Isolation
- ❖ Lack Of Faith
- ❖ Cutting self
- ❖ Others:
- ❖
- ❖
- ❖
- ❖

NOTEPAD

Date: _____

_____

_____

_____

_____

_____

_____

_____

_____

_____

_____

_____

_____

_____

_____

_____

_____

_____

_____

NOTEPAD

Date: _____

_____

_____

_____

_____

_____

_____

_____

_____

_____

_____

_____

_____

_____

_____

_____

_____

_____

_____

_____

The first thing you want to do is get a scriptural base for release. Here are some scriptures that confirm that we are not guilty for our forefathers' sins and we have been free from the curses through Jesus Christ once we become born again believers.

Please read: Ephesians 1:7, Colossians 1: 12-14, 1 John 3:8, Luke 10:19

"Christ has redeemed us from the curse of the law, having become a curse for us."

Galatians 3:13 (NKJV)

1) Confess your faith in Christ.

2) Forgive all who have harmed you.

3) Commit to being obedient to God's commands.

4) Renounce occult activity from yourself and ancestors.

5) Confess your sins and what you know about your ancestors.

6) Commit to getting rid of any occult objects from home.

7) Then release all in Jesus's name.

"Behold, I give unto you power to tread on serpents and scorpions, and over all the power of the enemy: and nothing shall by any means hurt you."

Luke 10:19 (KJV)

A Prayer for Releasing Generational Curses

Prayer of Release

Lord Jesus Christ, I believe that you are the son of God and the only way to God. I believe that you died on the cross for my sins and rose again from the dead. You were cursed with every curse that was due to me that I might be redeemed and entered into blessings.

Lord, I confess any sins committed by me or by my ancestors. I ask for your forgiveness. I also forgive every other person who has ever harmed me or wronged me. I have forgiven them as I would have You, God, forgive me.

I also forgive myself. I renounce all contact with the occult in all forms. I commit myself to getting rid of all occult objects and now Lord, I am receiving your forgiveness by faith with the authority I have as a child of God.In the name of Jesus, I now release myself and those under my authority from any curse over our lives. I declare it by faith in the name of Jesus, I thank you, Lord, for an answer to my prayer.

Thank you, Jesus!

Do not let anyone tell you that you will suffer someone else's curse when you have put your faith into the finished works of Christ who died and rose again for all our sins.

Once we have repented, became born again, stopped practicing sin and made Jesus the total object of our faith no one can say, regardless of our condition, that we have a generational curse.

God is a miracle worker and He is merciful and just.

Let's read the Biblical passage:

"As for his father, he will die for his own iniquity, because he practiced fraud, robbed his brother, and did what was wrong among his people. ¹⁹ But you may ask, 'Why doesn't the son suffer punishment for the father's iniquity?' <u>Since the son has done what is just and right, carefully observing all My statutes, he will certainly live.</u> ²⁰ The person who sins is the one who will die. A son won't suffer punishment for the father's iniquity, and a father won't suffer punishment for the son's iniquity."

- **Ezekiel 18:17-20**

"So if the Son makes you free, you will be free indeed."

- **John 8:36 (RSV)**

The Biblical Hebrew Israelites - Some are African-Americans, Native- Americans, Hispanics, and many other races

This year I have been reading and listening to many authors, teachers, and people's opinions about where they think the Hebrew Israelites are today. I will explain why many African Americans believe that they are the Hebrew Israelites. I will show biblically how they fit the prophecies today and how they got scattered across the four corners of the earth.

When I started my own research the Holy Spirit reminded me of when I was a lot younger and in my early twenties. I remember standing in my mom's living room, reading the book of Deuteronomy, and feeling like it was describing my life. I remember not wanting to read that book any longer. I felt convicted, but I did not understand why.

Now here it is over 20 years later and it makes total sense. I started studying and reading and listening and I also have to agree and believe that the so-called African Americans, Native Americans, Hispanics and many other races can easily be a part of the twelve tribes of Israel. I believe this because God had borne witness with my spirit twenty years ago, but I just did not understand. I will share the thoughts many have as well as what I have learned in my own studies and research.

We know that the twelve tribes of Israel went into slavery. According to the Bible it was because the twelve tribes of Israel broke God's laws, statutes, and commands. They now have been scattered throughout the four corners of the earth. This is why many believe some of the blacks, Negro, and the so-called African American are Hebrew Israelites and are a part of the twelve tribes of Israel along with many other races.

Hebrew Israelites come in a variety of skin colors. They can be from the darkest black color to the lightest. So when it comes to being a Hebrew-Israelite it can't be about color because a Hebrew Israelite can come in many shades. Look at the Puerto Ricans, Dominicans, and Cubans some have blonde hair and blue eyes. It's not about color. It is about nationality.

Many believe your nationality is determined by your father according to Numbers 1:45. Others believe it goes by the nationality of your mother. However, we know that the Hebrew Israelites are through out the world.

I will prove it biblically and historically with concrete evidence that the Hebrew Israelites are in America, throughout North, Central, and South America, the west coast of Africa, South Africa, Ethiopia, India and the islands in the Caribbean and many believe they are the true descendants of the Ancient Hebrew Israelites mentioned in the Bible who were scattered throughout the four corners of the earth in places like Haiti, Cuba, Bahamas, Mexico, Portugal, Spain, West Indies, Colombia, Argentina, Brazil, Uruguay, Guatemala, Panama, Puerto Rico, Latin America, the United Kingdom, India,Cape Verde, and other places.

Well, how were they scattered? They were scattered during the Trans-Atlantic Slave Trade. The majority of the people who were enslaved were picked up in Ghana and along the west coast of Africa. These slaves were then scattered all throughout the world.

Now how did this happen that the Hebrew Israelites from the days of Moses, who lived in Israel, are now being scattered all throughout the four corners of the earth? How did the transition happen.

In the beginning God chose the Hebrew Israelites to be a special people unto God **(Deuteronomy 7:6-8)**

God said, because he loved them He would keep the oath which he had sworn unto their father, Abraham. When Abraham went home to Glory the promise was passed down to his son Isaac and then Isaac's son Jacob. Jacob's twelve sons became the twelve tribes of Israel. God's promise continues on through the twelve tribes of Israel to their descendants throughout the world.

God promised Abraham he would be exceedingly fruitful and that He would make nations through him and kings shall come from him and all nations of the earth will be blessed. Then God said He will establish this covenant between himself and Abraham and all of Abraham's descendants throughout generations. It would be an everlasting covenant for Him to be Abraham's God and a God to all of Abraham's descendants.

This proves God chooses us (John 15:16). The key word is 'everlasting.' God told Abraham that he would make him a great nation. God will bless him and make Abraham's name great, and he shall be a blessing and God will bless those who bless him and curse those who curse Abraham. In Abraham's name all the families of the earth shall be blessed
- Genesis 12:1-3

"God told Abraham that He will bless thee, and in multiplying He will multiply thy seed as the stars of the heaven, and as the sand which is upon the sea-shore; and thy seed shall possess the gates of his enemies; And in thy seed shall all the nations of the earth be blessed; because Abraham obeyed God's voice."

- Genesis 22:17-18

One of the most important covenants God made was with the Israelites. These are Abraham's descendants through his son Isaac and grandson Jacob, renamed Israel.

The apostle Paul speaks about the Israelites, he said:

"Who are Israelites; to whom pertaineth the adoption, and the glory, and the covenants, and the giving of the law, and the service of God, and the promises; ⁵ Whose are the fathers, and of whom as concerning the flesh Christ came, who is over all, God blessed forever. Amen."

- Romans 9:4-5 (KJV)

So the Hebrew Israelites were blessed through the promise of Abraham and God had a special love for the Israelites. Now when God brought the Hebrew Israelites out of bondage (slavery) under Pharaoh, God told the Israelites *"if you will indeed obey My voice and keep my covenant, then you shall be a special treasure to me above all people"* **(Exodus 19:5).**

"Moses said and if you obey the voice of the LORD your God, being careful to do all His commandments which I command you this day, the LORD your God will set you high above all the nations of the earth. And all these blessings shall come upon you and overtake you if you obey the voice of the LORD your God. Blessed shall you be in the city, and blessed shall you be in the field. Blessed shall be the fruit of thy body, and the fruit of thy ground, and the fruit of thy cattle, the increase of thy Kine, and the flocks of thy sheep. ⁵ Blessed shall be thy basket and thy store. Blessed shalt thou be when thou comest in, and blessed shalt thou be when thou goest out" **(Deuteronomy 28:1-6)**

God had agreed to provide all of the Hebrew Israelites' needs, all they had to do was have God as their only God, obey the voice of the LORD their God, and to be careful to do all His commandments.

"Moses also warned the Hebrew Israelites that if they did not obey the voice of the LORD their God or be careful to do all His commandments and His statutes which I command you this day, then all these curses shall come upon you and overtake you. Cursed shalt thou be in the city, and cursed shalt thou be in the field.¹⁷ Cursed shall be thy basket

and thy store.¹⁸ *Cursed shall be the fruit of thy body, and the fruit of thy land, the increase of thy kine, and the flocks of thy sheep.¹⁹ Cursed shalt thou be when thou comest in, and cursed shalt thou be when thou goest out"* **(Deuteronomy 28:15)**

"And the Hebrew Israelites said all that the Lord has spoken we will do" **(Exodus 19:8).**

The Hebrew Israelites said yes, God, we will agree with all that you spoke. So God told the Hebrew Israelites that if they obey God's voice and his covenant they will have all the blessings and if they broke the covenant they would get all the curses. Now a covenant is considered a legal document and it legally binds the parties to the covenant for as long as they shall live and blood was also sprinkled on the Hebrew Israelites after they agreed" **(Exodus 24:8)**

The Hebrew Israelites did not obey God's voice or covenant and started worshipping idols **(Exodus 32)**

"And They did not keep the covenant of God, they refused to walk in His law, and forgot His works and His wonders that He had shown them" **(Psalms 78:10-11)**

The Hebrew Israelites were a stubborn and rebellious generation, a generation that did not set its heart aright, and whose spirit was not faithful to God" **(Psalms 78:8).**

These are some of the reasons why the Hebrew Israelites fell under the curse. They broke the covenant with God, not just once, but over and over again. God never broke His promise. The Hebrew Israelites were so unfaithful to God and forgot all that God had done for them such as taking them out of hard bondage from under the hand of Pharaoh **(Exodus 1:13-14)**

The Israelites called out to God and He heard their cry **(Exodus 3:7-9)** and after everything God did for them they complained the whole time, broke agreements, worshiped idols, and had the nerve to say they wanted to go back to Egypt **(Exodus 16:3)** God told the Hebrew Israelites that if they did not follow His laws, statutes, and commands they would have many curses fall on them and one of the curses was that they would be back in bondage and enslaved.

The Hebrew Israelites refused to listen to God over and over again, even though God led them out of Egypt and slavery after 400 years of bondage. The Hebrew Israelites started worshiping other gods and the curse in Deuteronomy 68 was one of the many curses that fell on them. This verse is a prophecy that was written over 2000 years before it actually happened.

Let's read the Biblical passage:

"And the LORD shall bring thee into Egypt again <u>with ships</u>, by the way whereof I spake unto thee, Thou shalt see it no more again: and there ye shall be sold unto your enemies for bondmen and bondwomen, and no man shall buy you."
-   **Deuteronomy 28:68 (KJV)**

Bondmen - Male slaves.
Bondwomen - Female slaves.
Buy - Means to redeem. No man will save you from that condition.
Egypt - **Also** Means bondage.

Let's read the Biblical passage:

"I am the LORD thy God, which have brought thee out of the land of Egypt, out of the <u>house of bondage</u>."
-     **Exodus 20:2**

Let's also read Exodus 13:3:

"And Moses said unto the people, remember this day, in which ye came out from Egypt, out of the house of bondage; for by strength of hand the LORD brought you out from this place."

Bondage definition:

1. The state of one who is bound as a slave.
2. A state of subjection to a force, power, or influence.
3. The practice of being physically restrained, as with cords or handcuffs, as a means of attaining sexual gratification.

    So Egypt was also referred to as the house of bondage. This is also known as slavery. The Israelites spent hundreds of years being enslaved, however, God said you're going back into bondage, but this time by way of <u>ships</u> and you will no longer see your homeland.

    From the time the Hebrew Israelites broke the covenant with God, they could not get out of slavery, no matter where they went. When the Hebrew Israelites came to America, they were sold and forced into slavery again.

Let's start from the beginning: the Israelites came out of Egypt as slaves, then they came down to the land of Israel, then the Assyrians captured the Israelites and put them back into slavery (2 Kings 17:6). Then the Israelites came out of Assyria and went back to Israel, then the Babylonians came to the land of Israel and made the Israelites slaves again **(1 Chronicles 9:1)**

No matter where they went they would be enslaved, just as God told them. The Hebrew Israelites could not see their way out. Then after the Babylonians enslaved them the Israelites went back to Israel. The Persians then arrived and put the Israelites back into slavery again **(Ezra 9:9).** Then the Israelites went back to Israel and even rebuilt the temple then the Greeks took the Israelites and again made them slaves. **(1 Malachi 8:18)** Then the Israelites went back into Israel and the Romans enslaved them again.

It was so evident that the Hebrew Israelites continued in bondage (slavery) just like God said. Even Jeremiah had to ask is Israel a servant? Is he a homeborn slave? Why is he spoiled?
- **(Jeremiah 2:14)**

Now when the Romans arrived, the Hebrew Israelites knew this was prophesied by Jesus Christ our Lord and Savior. He told the Israelites that when they would see Jerusalem surrounded by armies, belonging to the Roman Empire, then they would know that desolation has come near and to let those who are in Judea flee to the mountains, and let those who are inside the city depart, and let not those who are out in the country enter it for these are the days of vengeance, to fulfill all that is written. **(Luke 21:20).**

This was a sign to the Hebrew Israelites that since they rejected God, destruction had come. They knew they needed to flee to the mountains and to the countryside. So when you look at any geographical map around Jerusalem and around the land of Israel you see Egypt and Ethiopia.

The Hebrew Israelites went down along the eastern coast and the western coast. These are the areas where they were captured and again became slaves. Jesus Christ our Lord and Savior prophesied this. He said that the Hebrew Israelites would fall by the edge of the sword and be led captive <u>among all nations</u> and Jerusalem will be trodden down by the Gentiles until the times of the Gentiles are fulfilled **(Luke 21:24).**

When the Hebrew Israelites ran for their lives from the Roman Empire they knew they would be killed if they were caught. They had to run into the land of Egypt. They hid amongst the other people. The mountains Jesus was talking about were located in Africa. The Hebrew Israelites went right into Africa fleeing from the Romans just like Joseph did when he took baby Jesus and his wife Mary. They had to flee into Egypt to get away from Herod **(Matthew 2:13)**

This Biblical prophecy came to pass in the year 65 BC and was documented and written in the book Babylon to Timbuktu.

"In the year 65 BC, the Roman armies under General Pompey captured Jerusalem. In 70 AD, General Vespasian and his son Titus put an end to the Jewish state, with a great slaughter... many outrages and atrocities were committed against the residue of the people. During the period from Pompey to Julius, it has been estimated that over 1,000,000 Jews fled into Africa, fleeing from Roman persecution and slavery. The slave markets were full of black, Jewish slaves." **(*Babylon to Timbuktu*, Page 84)**

So it was true that over one million black Hebrew Israelites fled into Africa while running away from the Romans. Some Israelites ended up being caught and sold, and forced into slavery.

The Hebrew Israelites fled to areas where Rome did not have any jurisdiction. The Israelites migrated from Israel and started living in different parts of Africa because the Romans wanted to put all the Hebrew Israelites to death. Even Biblical scholars know the history of the Hebrew Israelites migrating and living all throughout the northern and western parts of Africa.

In the 1930's, they even found some Israelites that were not captured into the slave trade and still practiced the Hebrew faithfully knowing who they were. They had a Torah written in Aramaic. This is the ancient language.

So the Hebrew Israelites migrated and got settled into a new land, then the Africans got together with the Grecians. The Africans started selling the Israelites into slavery that were dwelling on the West Coast of Africa. The women were sold into slavery for wine. We know this prophecy to be true **(Joel 3:3-8).**

Tyre and Zydan were ancient African Hamite nations. They are the children of Ham. They sold the Hebrew Israelites into slavery so the Europeans, Arabs, and the Africans were all selling, and buying the Hebrew Israelites.When the Hebrew Israelites were enslaved by the Arabs this is when some of the Hebrew Israelites converted to Islam. They were converted because they were enslaved by the Arabs and had no choice. If they did not convert they would be killed.

A lot of Israelites became crypto-Jews. They would practice Judaism in secret even though the appearance looked Muslim. But behind closed doors, they worshiped the one true God of Abraham, Isaac, and Jacob.

So the Africans turned against the Hebrew Israelites and sold them to the Europeans, Arabs, and others into slavery for guns, wine, and cheap trinkets. The Africans sold the Hebrew Israelites because they were not the same people. Even though they were both dark people the Israelites were set apart. The Hebrew Israelites were migrants to the African land.

The Africans knew the Hebrew Israelites were not their people. The Hebrew Israelites had their own customs. They were different all the way around except the color of their skin. That was how they were able to migrate and be hidden.

So Africans who were native to their own land were selling Israelites that migrated into Africa. We also know that the Igbo tribe are Hebrew Israelites, not only because they kept the customs, but because many of them were also sold out of Africa and came to America after being forced into slavery during the Trans-Atlantic Slave Trade. The Majority of people who were taken out of Africa and forced into slavery are believed to be Hebrew Israelites.

Now remember what was written in prophecy:
*"And the LORD shall bring thee into Egypt again with **ships.**"*
This is when the Trans-Atlantic Slave Trade began and when ships began to pull into the West Coast of Africa taking thousands of Hebrew Israelites and selling them abroad **(James1:1)**

When you think of all the different races that were enslaved the so-called African Americans and Native Americans, we know they went by ships with a yoke of iron upon their neck **(Deuteronomy 28: 48)** Also **Joel 3:3-8** tells us that the tribe of Judah was sold into slavery by the Africans to the Europeans and the Arabs. They traded the Israelite men and women for wine, artillery, and cheap trinkets.
The Israelites were sold into slavery all over the world.
This is all prophecy.

And it shall come to pass in that day, that the Lord shall set his hand again the second time to recover the remnant of his people, which shall be left, from Assyria, and from Egypt, and from Pathros, and from Cush, and from Elam, and from Shinar, and from Hamath, and from the islands of the sea.

12 And he shall set up an ensign for the nations, and shall assemble the outcasts of Israel, and gather together the dispersed of Judah from the four corners of the earth. **Isaiah 11:11-12 (KJV)**

Let's read what God told Moses and the Hebrew Israelites:

"But it shall come to pass, if thou wilt not hearken unto the voice of the Lord thy God, to observe to do all his commandments and his statutes which I command thee this day; that all these curses shall come upon thee, and overtake thee."
 -      **Deuteronomy 28:15**

The Hebrew Israelite Curses

The Evidence: The Curses.

Let's identify who fits these curses:

"And the LORD shall bring thee into Egypt again <u>with ships</u>, by the way whereof I spake unto thee, Thou shalt see it no more again: and there ye shall be sold unto your enemies for bondmen and bondwomen, and no man shall buy you."

- **Deuteronomy 28:68 (KJV)**

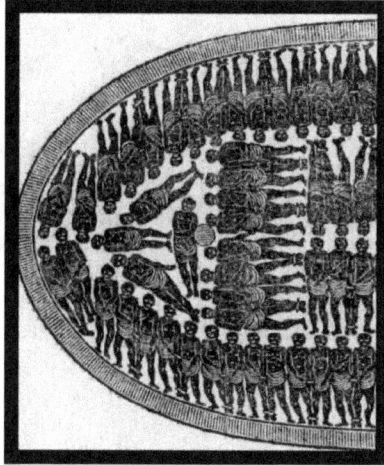

(From Wikimedia Commons)
Creative Commons Attribution 4.0 License http://creativecommons.org/licenses/by/4.0/

This is how African Americans (Israelites) were shipped as cargo aboard ships:

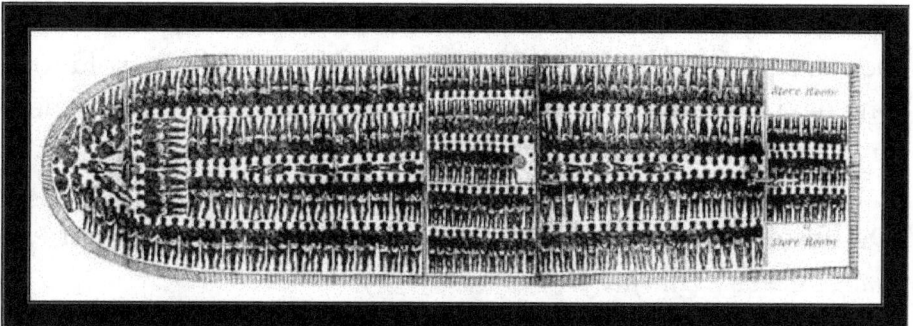

Deuteronomy 28:48: *"Therefore shalt thou serve thine enemies, which the LORD shall send against thee, in hunger, and in thirst, and in nakedness, and in want of all things: and he shall put a yoke of iron upon thy neck until he has destroyed thee."*

(The slaves, the so-called African American, had yokes of iron upon their necks as they were taken from West Africa and sold throughout America and had to depend on the slave master for food, water, clothing, and anything that they needed.)

Arab Muslim slave trade. (From Wikimedia Commons)
Creative Commons Attribution 4.0 License http://creativecommons.org/licenses/by/4.0/

Slaves tied together with yokes of iron around their necks.

Deuteronomy 28:32: *"Thy sons and thy daughters shall be given unto another people, and thine eyes shall look, and fail with longing for them all, the day long: and there shall be no might in thine hand."*

(When the Israelites were sold into slavery their children were also exported and sold into slavery and the mother had no power to get her children back. The mother would be sold to one part of the world and her child would be sold to the other and would see each other no more.)

Deuteronomy 28:16: *"Cursed shalt thou be in the city, and cursed shalt thou be in the field."*

(This Nation of people would stand out when you look at how many African Americans are being killed in their own city and the guilty party nine times out of ten will walk free. This curse is nationwide, so no matter where they would go the curse follows. The overall majority of African Americans live in low-income housing and ghettos. They are in a low state compared to other races. When slaves were brought over they worked in the cotton fields, sugar cane fields, tobacco fields, and rice plantations doing hard labor in hot weather and in distressed conditions and many died due to the conditions.)

Deuteronomy 28:37: *"And thou shalt become an astonishment, a proverb, and a byword, among all nations, whither the LORD shall lead thee."*

(When it comes to the African American people, many are astonished. They ask questions like why are the fathers not in the homes. A proverb is a saying so some people would say things like the blacks are lazy, they are not good for anything, and always on welfare. They are always playing the race card. A 'byword' is a name called outside of your own like black, African American, Negro, Sambo, Coon, Tar Baby, Nigger.. etc

Deuteronomy 28:17: *"Cursed shall be thy basket and thy store."*

(We see that so-called African Americans do not prosper like the other nations. They do not own any restaurant chains, grocery stores, banks, distribution centers. Overall, the so-called African American even goes to the Chinese to buy their hair products. I am not talking about individuals having businesses, I am talking about as a nation. If you notice the African American as a nation, it does not prosper in big businesses like all the other nations.)

Deuteronomy 28:30: *"Thou shalt betroth a wife, and another man shall lie with her: thou shalt build a house, and thou shalt not dwell therein: thou shalt plant a vineyard, and shalt not gather the grapes thereof."*

(During slavery, slave owners often took the wives of the slaves and slept with them. A lot of free labor was gained from slavery. How many countries have prospered richly off the back of the people enslaved? They benefitted greatly off of slavery, even to this day, but in comparison the so-called African American gathers nothing.)

Deuteronomy 28:61: *"Also, every sickness, and every plague, which is not written in the book of this law, them will the LORD bring upon thee, until thou be destroyed."*

(African-Americans have the highest rate of HIV and cancer in the U.S. and the highest rates of heart disease, diabetes, high blood pressure, sickle cell anemia, strokes, thyroid, lupus, and sexually transmitted diseases. Also on the slave ships, many were thrown over either because they died or because they were so sick with yellow fever, malaria, and so many other sicknesses. These diseases follow African Americans just as prophecy said they would.)

Deuteronomy 28:64: *"And the LORD shall scatter thee among all people, from the one end of the earth even unto the other; and there thou shalt serve other gods, which neither thou nor thy fathers have known, even wood and stone."*

(Now that they are in a new land they will start serving gods that they never knew. They will follow false doctrines not knowing who they truly are. They will seek after idols. We see this today, many follow after man's doctrine.)

Deuteronomy 28:41: *"Thou shalt beget sons and daughters, but thou shalt not enjoy them; for they shall go into captivity."*

(Look at how many African Americans are behind bars today. Let's look at all the black-on-black crime and killings. The parents cannot enjoy their kids due to death or incarceration.)

Deuteronomy 28:45: *"Moreover all these curses shall come upon thee, and shall pursue thee, and overtake thee, till thou be destroyed; because thou hearkened not unto the voice of the LORD thy God, to keep his commandments and his statutes which he commanded thee."*

(When the chains came off and the slaves became free through the Emancipation Proclamation they were so destroyed that even when they became free many went right back to their slave master. They did not know how to do anything else. Just like when God brought them out of Egypt under Pharaoh's bondage they wanted to go back to Egypt. The Israelites by this time had lost their identity, customs, and language. They did not remember their homeland any longer. After so many years of being enslaved in the New World, it became theirs. Remember the name African American was given to African Americans around 1986-1987. Before that they were given names like Colored, Negro, and black. There are 18 nations in the Bible. What nation are you from?)

"The ox knows its owner, and the ass its master's crib; But Israel does not know, My people do not understand." **Isaiah 1:3 (NKJV)**

The important part about this prophecy is that regardless of what people think at the end of the day God said what would happen to the Nation of Israel. We see all the curses in **Deuteronomy 28** and in **Leviticus 26** are still affecting the so-called African Americans, Native Americans, Hispanics and others so we know that there is a huge possibility that they are a part of the twelve tribes of Israel. This is the reason why no one continuously suffers like the so-called African American.

We know God told Abraham that his descendants will be strangers in a land that is not theirs and will serve, and they will afflict them for four hundred years **(Genesis 15:13).**

Prisoners being held by the Pharaoh

If you go and examine some of the different pyramids, you will see pictures of the Hebrew Israelites, the so-called Negro, on the walls and monuments as slaves. You can see evidence from the book *"Picture History Of Jewish Civilization"* Below, there is a photo from this book showing the slaves that were found painted on the walls of Ramses II. We can see clearly by color and features what the Hebrew Israelite slaves looked like back then. So we know by Biblical prophecy and documented evidence that the so-called African American Negro can possibly be a part of the twelve Tribes of Israel.

Picture History of JEWISH CIVILIZATION

The thousands of war captives who were transformed into slaves made it possible for the Egyptian kings to implement their feats of engineering. Chained captives are shown on these painted clay facing plaques from a building erected by Ramses II in honor of the king's brave warriors. From the period of the XIXth Dynasty.

Prisoner tomb of Ramses III
(CA 1187-1156 B.C.E)

We are also told Biblically what the Hebrew Israelites looked like in scripture. Let's Read:

I clothed you in embroidered cloth and gave you sandals of badger skin; I clothed you with fine linen and covered you with silk.
I adorned you with ornaments, put bracelets on your wrists, and a chain on your neck.

And I put a jewel in your nose, earrings in your ears, and a beautiful crown on your head. Thus, you were adorned with gold and silver, and your clothing was of fine linen, silk, and embroidered cloth. You ate pastry of fine flour, honey, and oil. You were exceedingly beautiful, and succeeded to royalty.

Your fame went out among the nations because of your beauty, for it was perfect through My splendor which I had bestowed on you," *says the Lord GOD. **Ezekiel 16:10-25***

What did the Ancient Israelites Look Like?

The Israelite men wore long coats and would keep their beard. They wore gold earrings **(Exodus 32:1-4)** and bonnets or caps upon their heads **(Leviticus 8:13).** They also wore fringes in the borders of their garments **(Numbers 15:37-38)** and a girdle of fine twined linen (a belt) around the waist **(Exodus 39:29)**

Pic (1) Ancient Egyptian Relief of Horemheb's tomb - 18th dynasty of Egypt 1332-1323 BCE By Saq Horemheb Under Creative Commons Attribution S-A 3.0 Pic (2) Tile inlays from the mortuary tomb of Ramses III, found in the funerary temple. - Approx. 1440 Creative Commons Attribution 4.0 License http://creativecommons.org/licenses/by/4.0/

| Ancient Israelites wearing fringes | Israelites went into captivity By the Assyrians (701 BCE) | Ancient Israelites wore caps. |

Creative Commons Attribution 4.0 License http://creativecommons.org/licenses/by/4.0/

The Hebrew Israelite women wore braided hair, earrings that were gold, or pearls **(1Timothy 2:9).** They wore dresses and would also put jewelry on their children **(Exodus 32:1-4).**

Israelite women (Wikimedia Commons)   Israelite family
Creative Commons Attribution 4.0 License http://creativecommons.org/licenses/by/4.0/

"In like manner also, that the women adorn themselves in modest apparel, with propriety and moderation, not with braided hair or gold or pearls or costly clothing, but, which is proper for women professing godliness, with good works."
-    **1 Timothy 2:9-10**

When we look at women today, it's the so-called African America's and Native Americans that are wearing the braids. We know the Hebrew Israelites migrated to Africa and were captured and forced into slavery, brought to America, and throughout North, Central, and South America, the west coast of Africa, South Africa, Ethiopia, and the islands in the Caribbean.

This is why you see so many mixed features and different shades of skin color with the Hebrew Israelites. The Hebrew Israelites, Egyptians, and others mixed the races when they encountered one another we see this biblically.

95

Not all have mixed their races, however, DNA proves today that millions have. We see the mixed races, throughout Biblical times. Exodus 12:37-39 and Leviticus 24:10-11

Hebrew Slaves Making bricks
(Wikimedia Commons circa 1350-1300 BCE)
Creative Commons Attribution 4.0 License http://creativecommons.org/licenses/by/4.0/

Hebrew Israelites were living amongst the Egyptians while they were enslaved under Pharaoh. They then migrated to Africa and throughout the four corners of the Earth.
We see the blending of the nations. Even though some of the nation's mixed during their captivity, they still are not the same people. **(Exodus 12:37-38)**

What is interesting is when you read about Noah and his three sons, Shem, Ham, and Japheth, God said each one was divided and had their own lands, language, after their families, in their nations **(Genesis 10:32)**

So we see that again they are not the same people. They represented their own culture, beliefs, language, and government. They were different all the way around.

Another interesting point is even the scholars identified that the Negro or so-called African American are different people compared to Africans.

Let's read what the scholars wrote in the Bible Dictionary:

Ham: "The youngest son of Noah, born probably about 96 years before the Flood; and one of eight persons to live through the Flood. He became the progenitor of the dark races. Not the Negroes, but the Egyptians, Ethiopians, Libyans and Canaanites" **(Zondervan Compact Bible Dictionary, page 330)**

Don't you find this interesting, "not the Negro?" The scholars even know that the so-called African American is different.

Just because a group of people has the same color skin does not make them the same people. We also learned through scripture that the Hebrew and Egyptian were not the same people. I believe that due to the migrating in each other's land they had interracial relationships and mixed to make the race we see today.

There is nothing new under the sun. We see the confusion because of the similarities in their skin color. Let's look at Moses for instance. Moses was born at a time when his people, the Israelites, were increasing in numbers and the Egyptian Pharaoh was worried that they might ally with Egypt's enemies. Moses' Hebrew mother, Jochebed, secretly hid him when the Pharaoh ordered all newborn Hebrew boys to be killed in order to reduce the population of the Israelites.

And when she could not hide Moses any longer she put him in a basket and Moses floated along the river bank. His sister stood at a distance to see where he would end up.

Now the daughter of Pharaoh came down to bathe at the river and her maidens walked beside the river. She saw the basket among the reeds and sent her maid to fetch it. When she opened it, she saw the baby crying. She took pity on him and said, "This is one of the Hebrews' children."

Now we read that it is very clear that they are two different people. Pharaoh's daughter adopted Moses and raised him and when Moses grew up, he went to his people and saw how badly they were treated. He saw an Egyptian beating a Hebrew, one of his people. He looked this way and that and seeing no one he killed the Egyptian and hid him in the sand **(Exodus 2)**.

Moses refused to be called the son of Pharaoh's daughter and rejected them **(Hebrews 11:24-27)**. Also we read that Moses killed the Egyptian not for himself, but because he was protecting his people.

Exodus 2:17-19 is a great example of misidentifying again.

Let's read the Biblical text:

"And the shepherds came and drove them away, but Moses stood up and helped them, and watered their flock. And when they came to Reuel their father, he said, How is it that ye come so soon today? And they said, An Egyptian delivered us out of the hand of the shepherds, and also drew water enough for us, and watered the flock" **(Exodus 2:17-19)**.

Now we know Moses was a Hebrew Israelite, however, they assumed he was an Egyptian. Why? Because he was the same color. He probably had on attire that an Egyptian would wear because they raised him, but he also had the same skin color as an Egyptian. If not, how could Pharaoh explain raising up their enemy in his home? Moses blended right in because they shared the same dark skin.

Think about it, when Moses told Pharaoh to let his people go it was also to be able to pray and worship the one and only true God. Remember Pharaoh had them worshipping him and his gods, so these were totally different people even in their beliefs.

"Then the LORD said unto Moses, Go in unto Pharaoh, and tell him, Thus saith the LORD God of the Hebrews, Let my people go, that they may serve me" **(Exodus 9).**

A Libyan, a Canaanite, a Syian, and a Nubian, bow to pharaoh. XVIIIth Dynasty

Let's not forget, they even thought Paul was an Egyptian as well.

Let's read the Biblical text:

"Then, as Paul was about to be led into the barracks, he said to the commander, "May I speak to you?" He replied, "Can you speak Greek? Are you not the Egyptian who some time ago stirred up a rebellion and led the four thousand assassins out into the

wilderness?" But Paul said, "I'm a Jew from Tarsus, in Cilicia, a citizen of no mean city; and I implore you, permit me to speak to the people" **(Acts 21:37-39).**

So we read over and over again about how they would misidentify the Hebrew and Egyptian. Why? Because the skin color was the same. We see time and time again that they were considered different people. Look at Joseph for instance. When his brothers came to Egypt to buy grain and they saw their brother Joseph, who was now the governor of the land of Egypt, they did not recognize him. But Joseph recognized his brothers again. They had a similar color, but Joseph was a Hebrew not an Egyptian **(Genesis 42:6).**

We have to also remember that the Egyptians did not even eat with Hebrews. It was considered detestable to Egyptians **(Genesis 43:32).** So Paul, Moses, and Joseph were all the same color as the Egyptian's black.

Remember in Exodus 4:6 we can clearly see what the color of Moses was when God was talking to Moses and told him to put his hand in his bosom.

Let's read what color Moses was:

"And the LORD said furthermore unto him, Put now thine hand into thy bosom. And he put his hand into his bosom: and when he took it out, behold, his hand was leprous as snow. And he said, Put thine hand into thy bosom again. And he put his hand into his bosom again; and plucked it out of his bosom, and, behold, it was turned again as his other flesh" **(Exodus 4:6-7).**

So what color was Moses's hand before it turned leprous and the color of snow? If you are already white, then if you turn leprous you are still going to be white. However, Moses's flesh turned back to its original color.

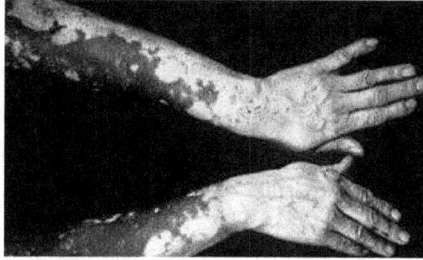

Many people believe that the Hebrew and the Egyptian are the same. However, God makes it clear they are not the same and there is a difference.

Let's read the Biblical text:

"But against any of the children of Israel shall not a dog move his tongue, against man or beast that ye may know how that <u>*the LORD doth put a difference between the Egyptians and Israel"*</u> **(Exodus 11:7).**

When we talk about Black people in Ancient times many scientist and scholars believe that Africa was the birth place of the human family and that the first members of what we now describe as the modern human race were black Africans and all human beings around the world share common roots. God is saying the Hebrew Israelites are similar but different as people.

Watch A History of the True Hebrews (Documentary):
https://www.youtube.com/watch?v=biPDp8pGqGg

Dr. Morton Proves the Negroes were Slaves in Egypt

Samuel George Morton
Attrib S-A 4.0 Creative Commons
Attribution 4.0 License http://creativecommons.org /licenses/by/4.0

Dr. George Morton was a physician and natural scientist. In Morton's major craniometry publications, Crania Aegyptiaca, or, Observations on Egyptian Ethnography, Derived from Anatomy, History, and the Monuments was published in 1844.

The anthropologist Aleš Hrdlička called Morton "the father of American physical anthropology." In this study, Morton extended his analysis of human races to ancient Egypt and by 1872 his collection numbered 1,225 of human crania or skulls.

Dr. George Morton reported in his publication that the Negro were represented in Egypt as slaves in ancient times just as in modern. This publication was written in 1844.

Let's read his actual publications:

THE NEGROES.

We have the most unequivocal evidence, historical and monumental, that slavery was among the earliest of the social institutions of Egypt, and that it was imposed on all conquered nations, white as well as black.§ So numerous was this unfortunate class of persons, that it was the boast of the Egyptian kings, recorded by Diodorus, that the vast structures of Luxor and Karnak were erected by the labour of foreigners alone. Of Negro slavery, in particular, the paintings and sculptures give abundant illustration. "Black people," says Sir G. Wilkinson, "designated as natives of the *foreign land* of Cush, are generally represented on the Egyptian monuments as captives or bearers of tribute to the Pharaohs;" and the attendant circumstances of this inhuman traffic appear to have been much the same in ancient as in modern times. It is curious, also, in a numerical point of view, to observe that Arrian, who wrote in the second century, gives three thousand as the number of Negroes annually brought down the Nile

* Voyage à Meroë, II., p. 276.   † Edinburgh Review, Vol. LX., p. 311.
‡ Idem., p. 307. The antiquity of the name Nubia, is of some importance in this discussion. Heeren and others state that it first occurs in history during the epoch of the Ptolemies; but Rosellini has now discovered that it is at least as old as the age of Meneptha I., (B. C. 1600,) on whose monuments it is found.

(Publication Crania Aegyptiaca By Dr. George Morton published in 1844)

When we talk about the Egyptians and the Hebrew Israelites being different people, many struggle because they say how is it that the Hebrew Israelites are not the same as Egyptians but they are black and have lived in Africa?

Where did Race come from? These video's should be watched by everyone:

The myth of Race, debunked in 3 minutes:
https://www.youtube.com/watch?v=VnfKgffCZ7U

A visual sociology documentary on race and ethnicity:
https://www.youtube.com/watch?v=aDz3BJDPXHA

"And thou shalt say unto Pharaoh, Thus saith the LORD, Israel is my son, even my firstborn" **(Exodus 4:22).**

"And all the firstborn in the land of Egypt shall die, from the firstborn of Pharaoh that sitteth upon his throne, even unto the firstborn of the maidservant that is behind the mill; and all the firstborn of beasts.⁶ And there shall be a great cry throughout all the land of Egypt, such as there was none like it, nor shall be like it any more.⁷ But <u>against any of the children of Israel</u> shall not a dog move his tongue, against man or beast: that ye may know how that <u>the LORD doth put a difference between the Egyptians and Israel</u>" **(Exodus 11:7)**

Other Negro delineations which can be identified with the age to which they belong, are found on the monuments of Horus, Rameses the Second, Rameses the Third, &c. in various places in Egypt and Nubia; and the first of these kings, (who dates with the nineteenth dynasty,) is represented standing on a platform which is supported by prostrate Negroes.§

For the purpose of illustration, we select a single picture from the temple (hemispeos) of Beyt-el-Wâlee, in Nubia, in which Rameses the Second is represented in the act of making war upon the Negroes; who, overcome with defeat, are flying in consternation before him. From the multitude of fugitives in this scene, (which has been vividly copied by Champollion‖ and Rosellini, and which I have compared in both,) I annex a fac-simile group of nine heads, which, while they preserve the national features in a remarkable degree, present also considerable diversity of expression.

* Rosellini, Appendix, No. 13.—Wilkinson, Ancient Egyptians, Vol. III.

† Hoskins, Travels in Ethiopia. Procession, Part First.

‡ Topography of Thebes, p. 196.

§ Champollion, Monumens de l'Egypte, Plate CX.

‖ Vide Champollion, Monumens de l'Egypte, Tom. I., Plate LXXI., LXXII.; and Rosellini, Monumenti, M. R., Tav. LXXV. A glance at these illustrations will convince any one that the slave-hunts or *ghrazzies*, as now practised by the Arabs, Tuaricks and Turks, and which are so feelingly described by Cailliaud, and by Denham and Clapperton, were in active operation, with all their atrocities, in the most flourishing periods of Pharaonic Egypt.

16

The hair on some other figures of this group is dressed in short and separate tufts, or inverted cones, precisely like those now worn by the Negroes of Madagascar, as figured in Botteller's voyage.

(Publication Crania Aegyptiaca By Dr. George Morton Page 16, 62 published in 1844)

Dr. Morton had hundreds of skulls and did an in-depth study and he found that after looking at the skulls and the cranial remains, that the Hebrew Israelites (Negroes) were not the same people as the Egyptians because the head shapes and sizes did not match. The characteristics were not the same, even though some had similar lips. The only match he did find were that the pictures of the Negroes in captivity shown on the walls of Egypt matched the Negroes he saw in modern time with the same complexions, features, expressions, and every other attribute of the race. They were depicted precisely as we are accustomed to seeing them in our daily walks said Dr. Morton.

He was amazed that the Negro was shown in servitude positions in ancient times. The same people who were slaves in Egypt are the same people God told Moses to lead out of Egypt, out of the hands of Pharaoh. These are the Hebrew Israelites, many are called the so-called African Americans.

105

Dr. Morton concluded that although "Negroes" (Hebrew Israelites) were numerous in Egypt, their social position in ancient times was the same that it has been in the United States, that of servants and slaves (**Crania Aegyptiaca, page 60-62).**

Now, when we compare Bible prophecy and American history of the enslaved blacks and their descendants today, there is a perfect match. The only conclusion a reasonable person can make is, among the blacks in America you may also find some of the Hebrew Israelites, descendants of Abraham, Isaac and Jacob, they are also the "chosen people of God."

"THEY LEFT BLACK...."

The WAR for Israel

When he was asked about peace in the middle east....The late president of Egypt, Gamal Abdel Nasser, stated.... *"The Jews will never be able to live here in peace, because they left here black but came back white. "*

Gamal Abdel Nasserwas the second President of Egypt
(Serving from 1956 until his death in 1970)

Ancient Hebrew Israelites History:
https://www.youtube.com/watch?v=blvk4LQSVyM
https://www.youtube.com/watch?v=8by5GXVp2_s
http://deuteronomy28.org/curses.html
https://www.youtube.com/watch?v=COqZS9MnTF8

Adolf Hitler also knew who the real Jews were. I have a book called *Nazis World War II.* Below, I show a picture of Adolf Hitler from a book where he shares his knowledge about the original Jews. He is watching an instructional documentary film showing the origins of the true Jews the Negro, the so-called African American.

He shares the different mixes of the genetic heritage of the original Jew. As you notice he calls the Jewish man at the bottom a bastard. This history has been known that the so-called African American may also be a part of the twelve Tribes of Israel along with many others. You can read exactly what was written in Adolf Hitler's book entitled *Nazis World War II.*

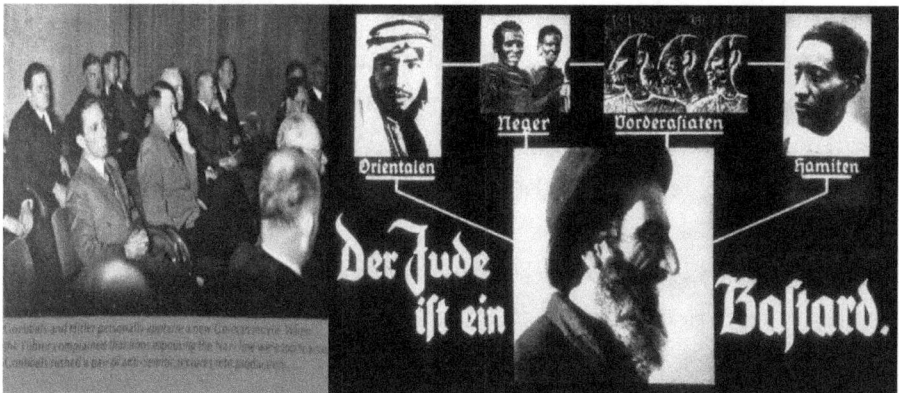

The Book Nazis World War II Page 132 Courtesy National Archives, photo no.(242-HB-9717)
(Time Life Books What Hitler said about "Jews")

"Goebbels and Hitler personally appraise a new German movie. When the Fuhrer complained that films espousing the Nazi line were too scarce, Goebbels rushed a pair of anti-Semitic pictures into production. In one segment of a Nazi 'instructional' film... the genetic heritage of the Jews is purportedly traced to Oriental, Negro, near Asian, and Hamitic peoples. Hence, the film concludes, the Jew is a bastard."

The Jewish Encyclopedia says that 96% of all Jews known today are descendants of the Khazar tribes of Russia, Eastern Europe, and Western Mongolia. These are the Ashkenazi Jews. They are the same European people who used to be known as Khazars before they started their exodus out of their homeland of Khazaria towards eastern and then western Europe. Very few are Israelites, the descendants of Abraham, Isaac and Jacob (Ref: ttps://www.youtube.com/watch?v=GpBrUfDgNCA)

"And a bastard shall dwell in Ashdod, (Israel) and I will cut off the pride of the Philistines."
- Zechariah 9:6

The Jewish people in the land of Israel today are not all real Jews. Most of them are Ashkenazi. They are Khazars (European Origin), not Hebrew Israelites. They are "Jewish," meaning their ancestors picked up the "Jewish" religion many centuries ago. So If almost 90% of JEWS we know today are NOT Semitic, wouldn't the term ANTI-SEMITIC be null and void?

Due to widespread ignorance and assumptions, after many generations, people just assumed that they were the descendants of the ancient Jews. Most of the Jews in Israel are not the descendants of Abraham, Isaac, and Jacob. God told us how we would identify the Hebrew Israelites today. We know the Jewish people in the land today have not gone into slavery by ships, nor did they have yokes of iron around their neck. God said "Judah mourneth, and the gates thereof languish" **(Jeremiah 14:2).**

The prophecy is that the true Jews would be in mourning. They would not own their own sports teams or have their own resources. The true Jew is in mourning.

The Jewish man or woman is not in mourning. They own the major media outlets, they have their own banking systems, publishing houses, and so much more. That sure does not sound like anyone is mourning to me.

The so-called African American is shot to death on camera time and time again and they are continuously in mourning, even still today. The so-called African American fits the prophecy God spoke that the Israelites would go into captivity by way of ships with yokes of iron on their neck. The Jewish people were taken by freight trains to concentration camps. Slavery was evil at its worst when it came to its treatment of black slaves.

And we all know how truly barbaric slavery was. It was so bad that people hate to talk about it today, mainly because of guilt and sorrow and the fact that many benefitted from slavery throughout generations. Even today, where it is the wealthiest is only because of free labor from hard working slaves who suffered and even died for this country and throughout the world so others can have the so-called "Good Life."

This is why I tell people we must repent for our ancestors as well as ourselves and our family. The black slaves were oppressed, raped, lynched, mocked, tortured, beaten, and their nationality was taken. Even their language, culture, and their whole state of being were taken from them. So slavery was not new but the slavery that the black people experienced was not like previous types of slavery that others experienced.

This slavery was evil at its worst. When the blacks went into slavery, it was nothing less than cruel. Just think about it when someone makes a movie about slavery, it's always about the blacks being slaves. Why not the Chinese or the Italians or

Jewish people? It is always black because nothing was worse than when the blacks were slaves. It is more realistic and truthful.

What we see going on today is all based on prophecy. The true Hebrew Israelites are not all back in the land yet because God said in the last days He will bring Israel and Judah back together. So we know the people in Israel are not all the true Biblical Israelites.

Rabbi Harry Rozenberg shared some knowledge about the many true Hebrew Israelite tribes that were still in the land of Africa. He spoke about how one of the people from the tribe wrote letters to Israel when it became a state. They told them that they were Israelites living in Africa. They reached out to Israel because Israel had just started the 'right to return' and they being Israelites also wanted the right to return to their land.

Rabbi Harry said they laughed at them and did not believe them. They later decided to go to Africa and check out their claims. A professor from Duke University went there and did DNA testing on them. They found out that these men had the 'y' chromosome designating them as a priest. It was a lineage that followed Moses's brother Aaron so if you had this type chromosome your lineage would show that you are a descendant of Aaron and carry this genetic marker. This tribe was from South Africa and called the Lemba Tribe. They carry the same DNA marker that proves they are descendants of Abraham, Isaac, and Jacob.

Rabbi Harry Rozenberg went on to talk about the slave trade and how a lot of Israelites were taken out of the western Nigerian ports and brought into America to be enslaved. He says there are people all over the world who are also Israelites because they have been scattered and dispersed through slavery. In Nigeria they have another tribe called the Ibos and there are over 40 million of them who are also Israelites. So he knows that the African American is also a part of the twelve Tribes of Israel along with other tribes like the Yoruba's of Nigeria, the Ashanti's of Ghana, the Mandingos' Temne, Krio's Fulani Tribes, the Mende of Sierra Leone, the Ewe tribe of Nigeria & Togo, the Wolof tribe of Senegal, the Bamileke tribe, the Ga, Fanti, Sefwi tribes of Ghana and so many more.

Rabbi Harry Rozenberg is an Ashkenazi Jew who admits that some of the greatest sages in the transmissions of the Torah were written by Jewish converts from Rome. He said he would not rule out any African American that believes they are the real Jew, a Hebrew Israelite, because he knows they went into slavery and prophecy is being fulfilled.

"I know thy works, and tribulation, and poverty,
(But thou art rich) and I know the blasphemy of them which say they
are Jews, and are not, but are the synagogue of Satan."
                    - Revelations 2:9

Some people may think that the identities of these people no longer serve any purpose. The truth is that after Christ's return, God has many more plans for the Israelites who have descended from the twelve tribes of Israel.

It's time to know who you truly are and repent and get out of these curses that we put upon ourselves because of being a stiff-neck people and disobeying God's law, statues, and commandments. If you're still breathing it is not too late to repent and turn back to God.

God Will Restore Israel

"And the people shall take them, and bring them to their place: and the house of Israel shall possess them in the land of the LORD for servants and handmaids: and they shall take them captives, whose captives they were; and they shall rule over their oppressors."
- **Isaiah 14:2** (Also read **Revelation 7**)

God is a just God. We have to repent and follow God's way and not man's. We will all be judged and it's not about white privilege or playing the race card or the grace card nor who is an illegal alien. God is at the borders of us all. In these last days we must wake up from sleep and examine ourselves. Our thoughts should be to one another, our motives, and the intent.

Let's tie up all the loose ends and turn to God in good conscience because we now know the truth and have true repentance.

"He that leadeth into captivity shall go into captivity, he that killeth with the sword must be killed with the sword. <u>Here is the patience and the faith of the saints.</u>"
- **Revelations 13:10**

The only way to keep God's commandments is to put your faith in the finished works of Christ Jesus and the Holy Spirit will do the work in you. Anything outside of faith in the only true God and you will find yourself with the curses and not the blessings. Many have already woken up out of sleep and have returned to seek the Lord their God.

"Afterward shall the children of Israel return, and seek the LORD their God, and David their king; and shall fear the LORD and his goodness in the latter days."

- **Hosea 3:5**

"Yet the number of the children of Israel shall be as the sand of the sea, which cannot be measured nor numbered; and it shall come to pass, that in the place where it was said unto them, Ye are not my people, there it shall be said unto them, <u>Ye are the sons of the living God</u>."

- **Hosea 1:10 - Romans 9:24-28**

Amen to this!!!

This is the last captivity, so the ones who do not choose to trust in God and instead continue to fulfill the desires of their flesh will face death.

"But the fearful, and unbelieving, and the abominable, and murderers, and whoremongers, and sorcerers, and idolaters, <u>and all liars shall</u> have their part in the lake which burneth with fire and brimstone: which is the second death."

- **Revelation 21:8**

"For it is the day of the LORD's vengeance,
The year of recompense for the cause of Zion."

- **Isaiah 34:8**

"He who kidnaps a man, whether he sells him or he is found in his possession, shall surely be put to death."

- **Exodus 21:16**

113

The Gate Of No Return

The Gate Of No Return (Benin, West Africa)
(Resource: https://www.youtube.com/watch?v=TXB7W_-ebE8)

The Gate of no return is found in the South of Benin, near to the Atlantic Ocean. The road of no return is a departure point where thousands and thousands of African slaves were marched in shackles to await slave ships that would take them away. Once they walked through this gate, they would never see their home again.

Once the Africans were captured, they were brought to the chiefs and the kings. Then they would be sold into slavery and in return, the chiefs and kings would get cannons and weapons. In Africa, there are four gates used for the huge population of slaves that went out to be transported all over the world.

Slaves would walk side by side with a huge log on their shoulders to keep them all walking together. If the slaves would cry, they would burn their mouth with a hot iron to keep them quiet. From here many slaves were traded by the Portuguese, French and English. The road of no return is just one of the four gates in Africa used as a departure point for slaves.

The last ship that picked up slaves was in 1846. Benin was involved in the slave trade for over 200 years and the last trade took place in the mid 19th century.

The Gate Of No Return   Harriet Tubman circa 1885
Other names: Minty, Moses
Artist: H. Seymour square,
1848 - 18 Dec 1905

When I think of Harriet Tubman my heart smiles. Who would not want to have a friend like Harriet. God gave her a ministry and that was to set the captives free Amen to that! She was born into slavery in Maryland in 1820, and successfully escaped in 1849. She led hundreds of enslaved people to freedom along the route of the Underground Railroad. Her occupation was a Civil War Nurse, Suffragist, Civil Rights activist. Harriet Tubman may become the face of the new $20 bill, relegating President Andrew Jackson to the reverse side of the currency.

I freed a thousand slaves, I could have freed a thousand more if only they knew they were slaves. ~Harriet Tubman~

115

Being Grafted In

When you look at the root of a tree from top to bottom you will notice that some of the tree branches start to grow wild. These wild shoots represent the children of Israel who have gone wild and forgotten about the most high God and do not keep His commandments. They will be destroyed if they do not repent.

Let's read the Biblical scripture:

"The LORD of hosts, who planted you, has pronounced evil against you, because of the evil which the house of Israel and the house of Judah have done, provoking me to anger by burning incense to Ba'al."
- **Jeremiah 11:17**

Paul is talking to the house of Israel who angered God through worshiping idols. They worshipped the gentile gods, Baal and Beelzebub, and many other Satanic gods. God had broken Israel off from His blessings because they had become fruitless. The branches had been broken off.

This is when God grafts in the Gentiles.

"But if some of the branches were broken off, and you, a wild olive shoot, were grafted in their place to share the richness of the olive tree."
- **Romans 11:17**

So God is saying okay Israel, because of your disobedience I have broken your branches off. However, now you Gentiles are a wild olive tree who I will put in the place of the Israelites to share the richness. To share means not all of Israel is broken off.

However, God is letting the Gentiles partake in sharing the richness of the olive tree as well. The Gentiles are not any better. This is why God refers to the Gentiles as a wild olive tree. They are not fruitful either.

God is telling everyone, Jew and Gentile, to produce good fruit or they will be cut off. The Gentiles being grafted into the branches that were cut off gives them the opportunity to share in the same promises given to the Israelites: the descendants of Abraham, Isaac, and Jacob. This is what the richness of the olive tree means. There will be Gentiles who will produce amazing fruit for the most high God and serve God in the way that is pleasing to Him. These Gentiles will exclude paganism and become partakers in the richness of the olive tree.

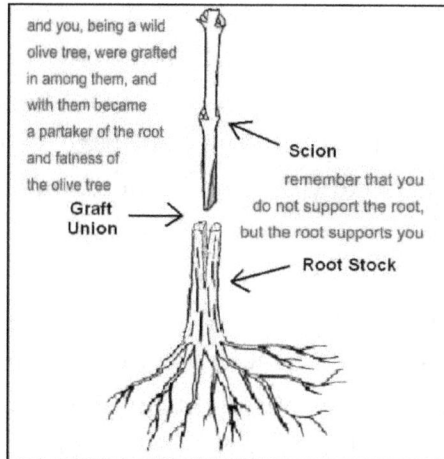

and you, being a wild olive tree, were grafted in among them, and with them became a partaker of the root and fatness of the olive tree

Graft Union ⟶

Scion

remember that you do not support the root, but the root supports you

Root Stock

This will not be easy for all Gentiles. Let's read why:

"For if you have been cut from what is by nature a wild olive tree, and grafted, contrary to nature, into a cultivated olive tree, how much more will these natural branches be grafted back into their own olive tree." - **Romans 11:24**

God is saying that Gentiles are wild by nature. This means paganism is a norm for Gentiles because Israel was chosen of God to Himself and the Gentiles were able to worship other gods such as the moon, stars, and horoscopes. This was natural for Gentiles.

Remember the Israelites were set apart and the Gentiles were not. The Gentiles were serving many false gods because this was natural for them. So we see the Israelites have broken God's commandments and become like the Gentiles. God is saying the Gentiles are a wild branch by nature and the Israelites are a wild branch by disobedience and unbelief.

This is why if you look at Christianity today there are many false doctrines. God is cutting branches off from both the Gentiles, and the Israelites. These false doctrines are being cut off. God will not allow any fruit to remain fruitless with lies and deceit. Look at how quick people want to say we do not have to keep any commandments and that we're not under the law. They continue to abuse God's grace. This is natural for the Gentiles.

This is what being contrary to nature means. Gentiles are wild by nature. This is not to put anyone down, but to get an understanding of why we all struggle. God will prune us and keep us if we trust in Him by keeping his commands. This will produce good fruit.

God said, *"Jew nor Greek, there is neither slave nor free, there is neither male nor female; for you are all one in Christ Jesus"* (Galatians 3:28).

So we all have to be grafted into Christ Jesus and this can be painful because to be grafted in God needs to cut the branches. You can be grafted in by cutting away friends who are a bad influence, social circles, Paganism, traditions, idols, and bad relationships. Anything and everything that gets in the way of producing Godly fruit has to be cut off. No more self-serving behavior. Be ready to be grafted into a good olive tree, serving only one God and what He commands.

So now when Paul says how much more these natural branches will be grafted back into their own olive tree he is talking about the Israelites. If the Gentiles who are wild by nature can be grafted in then so can the Israelites who were the natural branches to begin with.

Even though it will only be a remnant that will be saved anyone can be saved if he so chooses. God is giving all an opportunity to be grafted in, wild by nature or not. Some churches teach that Israel was cut off for good, however, that is a false doctrine. God said Israel can be grafted in again as well.

"And even the others (Israel) if they do not persist in their underlined unbelief, will be grafted in, for God has the power to graft them in again."
        -   **Romans 11:23**

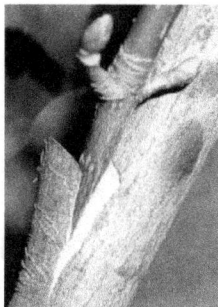

Picture of being grafted in

119

"So I ask, have they stumbled so as to fall? (Meaning Israel) By no means! But through their trespass salvation has come to the Gentiles, so as to make Israel jealous."

- **Romans 11:11**

God will now break off branches and graft in the Gentiles, which God calls the wild Olive tree. God is saying to all who received Him, who believed in His name. He gave the power to become children of God. Amen to this!

"Every branch of mine that bears no fruit, he takes away, and every branch that does bear fruit he prunes, that it may bear more fruit."

- **John 15:2**

God is not interested in any branches that are wild and do not bear good fruit. When you have a tree with wild branches, they will tend to grow wild all around the bottom of the tree. If you allow it to continue growing wild it will then curve downwards and grow into the ground. It will then start wrapping around the tree and choking it. Now if these wild branches produce any fruit it will be of very poor quality because it should have been used to sustain the branches on the top of the tree. The wild branches robbed the nutrients that the good quality branches at the top should have gotten. Instead, these wild branches are useless and will stop the entire tree from producing Godly fruit.

So God cuts them off before that happens. God says these branches have to be pruned and cut off. This is the reprobate Israelites being cut off from the vine. The tree trunk represents Christ and we are the branches that have to produce Godly good fruit. The only way to do this is to be attached to Christ and not cut off from Him.

120

"I am the vine, ye are the branches: He that abideth in me, and I in him, the same bringeth forth much fruit: for without me ye can do nothing."

- **John 15:5**

So all the branches that produce good fruit are attached to the main vine which is Jesus Christ our Lord and Savior. And they will produce good fruit and will abide in Him and not be cut off. This is what grafting in means.

Now God says to be humble and do not boast about being grafted over the branches. He said,

"if you do boast, remember it is not you that support the root, but the root that supports you. <u>You will say, "Branches were broken off so that I might be grafted in." That is true.</u> They were broken off because of their unbelief, but you stand fast only through faith. So do not become proud, but stand in awe. <u>For if God did not spare the natural branches, neither will he spare you.</u> Note then the kindness and the severity of God severity toward those who have fallen, but God's kindness to you, provided you continue in his kindness; otherwise you too will be cut off." (**Romans 11:18-25**)

Being grafting in is a part of being born again. You must cut where the original fruitless branch was and graft in another branch that is fruitful. The grafting in will be all nations to become as one, but first, you have to strip away all the world's fleshly desires that stop people from producing good fruit.

Read Romans 3 entirely this explains why we need
Jesus Christ as our personal Lord and saviour.The gift of the
sinless Christ, who freely offered himself as a substitute
sacrifice for sin on behalf of all who, through faith, are willing
to receive the redemption provided this is pleasing to God. It
was only Jesus Christ who kept the law perfect.

Other Scriptures To Read:
Baptism of Holy Spirit: Acts 2:38, Acts 19:1-6
It Is Finished: John 19:30
Fruits of the Spirit: Galatians 5:22-23 & Colossians 3:12-15
They Are One In Us: John 17:21
Seek Things Above: Colossians 3:1
You Are Born Of God Now Through Jesus/Yeshua: 1 John 3:9
You Are The Temple Of God: 1 Corinthians 3:16-17,
You Are God Building: 1 Corinthians 3:9
Temple Of God: 1 Corinthians 6:19-20
You Are a Royal Priest: 1 Peter 2:9,
You Are Kings and Priests: Revelations 1:6,
You Are Joint Heirs With Christ: Roman 8:17-18

The Ten Commandments: God's Moral Law

1) I am the Lord your God. You shall have no other gods before me: No one can serve two masters; for either he will hate the one and love the other, or else he will be loyal to the one and despise the other. You cannot serve God and mammon. **(Matthew 6:24) (Matthew 4:10)**

2) You shall not make for yourself an idol: We are his offspring. And since this is true, we shouldn't think of God as an idol designed by craftsmen from gold or silver or stone. **(Acts 17:29:31) (1 John 5:21)**

3) Do not take the name of the Lord in vain: Let as many servants as are under the yoke count their own masters worthy of all honor, that the name of God and his doctrine be not blasphemed. **(1 Timothy 6:1)**

4) Remember the Sabbath and keep it holy: And he said unto them, The Sabbath was made for man, and not man for the Sabbath. **(Mark 2:23-27)** (Hebrews 4:4-11)

5) Honor your father and mother: Children, obey your parents because you belong to the Lord, for this is the right thing to do. "Honor your father and mother." This is the first commandment with a promise. If you honor your father and mother, "things will go well for you, and you will have a long life on the earth." **(Matthew 11:28) (Matthew 19:19)**

6) You shall not murder: Anyone who hates another brother or sister is really a murderer at heart. And you know that murderers don't have eternal life within them. **(1 John 4) (Romans 13:9)**

7) You shall not commit adultery: Let marriage be held in honor among all, and let the marriage bed be undefiled, for God will judge the immoral and adulterous.
(Hebrew 13:4) (Leviticus 20:10) (Matthew 19:18)

8) You shall not steal: Let him who stole steal no longer, but rather let him labor, working with his hands what is good, that he may have something to give him who has a need.
(Ephesians 4:28) (Romans 13:9)

9) You shall not bear false witness against your neighbor:
Therefore, putting away lying, "Let each one of you speak truth with his neighbor," for we are members of one another.
(Ephesians 4:25) (Romans 13:9)

10) You shall not covet your neighbor's wife. You shall not covet anything that belongs to your neighbor:
But fornication, and all uncleanness, or covetousness, let it not be once named among you, as becometh saints. Neither filthiness, nor foolish talking, nor jesting, which are not convenient: but rather giving of thanks. For this ye know, that no whoremonger, nor unclean person, nor covetous man, who is an idolater, hath any inheritance in the kingdom of Christ and of God. **(Ephesians 5: 3-7) (Romans 7:7)**

If you follow the two commandments below in (Matthew 22:36-40) then these Ten Commandments will be followed automatically.

"Thou shalt love the Lord thy God with all thy heart, and with all thy soul, and with all thy mind. This is the first and great commandment. And the second is like unto it, Thou shalt love thy neighbor as thyself. On these two commandments hang all the law and the prophets." **(Matthew 22:36-40)**

124

Ten Commandments (Exodus 20 KJV)

And God spake all these words, saying, I am the LORD thy God, which have brought thee out of the land of Egypt, out of the house of bondage. Thou shalt have no other gods before me. Thou shalt not make unto thee any graven image, or any likeness of anything that is in heaven above, or that is in the earth beneath, or that is in the water under the earth. Thou shalt not bow down thyself to them, nor serve them: for I the Lord thy God is a jealous God, visiting the iniquity of the fathers upon the children unto the third and fourth generation of them that hate me; And shewing mercy unto thousands of them that love me, and keep my commandments. Thou shalt not take the name of the LORD thy God in vain; for the LORD WILL not hold him guiltless that taketh his name in vain. Remember the Sabbath day, to keep it holy. Six days shalt thou labor and do all thy work. But the seventh day is the Sabbath of the LORD thy God in it thou shalt not do any work, thou, nor thy son, nor thy daughter, thy manservant, nor thy maidservant, nor thy cattle, nor thy stranger that is within thy gates. For in six days the LORD made heaven and earth, the sea, and all that in them is, and rested the seventh day, therefore, the LORD blessed the Sabbath day and hallowed it. Honor thy father and thy mother: that thy days may be long upon the land which the LORD thy God giveth thee. Thou shalt not kill. Thou shalt not commit adultery. Thou shalt not steal. Thou shalt not bear false witness against thy neighbor. Thou shalt not covet thy neighbor's house, thou shalt not covet thy neighbor's wife, nor his manservant, nor his maidservant, nor his ox, nor his ass, nor any thing that is thy neighbor's.

What did Jesus Look Like According to the Bible

The Bible reveals that Jesus is black and a man of color, not only in one scripture but in several. Let's read the very important passages from the King James Bible in **Revelations 1:10-15:**

"I was in the Spirit on the Lord's day, and heard behind me a great voice, as of a trumpet, Saying, I am Alpha and Omega, the first and the last: and, What thou sees, write in a book, and send it unto the seven churches which are in Asia; unto Ephesus, and unto Smyrna, and unto Pergamos, and unto Thyatira, and unto Sardis, and unto Philadelphia, and unto Laodicea.[12] And I turned to see the voice that spake with me. And being turned, I saw seven golden candlesticks; [13] And in the midst of the seven candlesticks one like unto the Son of man, clothed with a garment down to the foot, and girt about the paps with a golden girdle. [14] His head and his hairs were white like wool, as white as snow; and his eyes were as a flame of fire; [15] And his feet like unto fine brass, as if they burned in a furnace; and his voice as the sound of many waters."

(Pic 1) Earliest known image of Jesus Christ, from the Coptic Museum in Cairo, Egypt this painting of Jesus is older than the image of the black Jesus Christ in the Church of Rome, which is from the 6th century. (Wikimedia Commons) (Pic 2) An Image Of Jesus Christ carved out of wood from the Philippines Photo by Ramon F Velasquez under the C C Attrib S-A 4.0 Creative Commons Attribution 4.0 License http://creativecommons.org/licenses/by/4.0/

In the scripture John sees the color of Jesus Christ's skin and described the color as <u>fine brass, as if they burned in a furnace</u>. John wanted to put an emphasis on Jesus's skin color being dark by saying it is as if they burned in a furnace. John also said he heard behind him a great voice, as of a trumpet. This lets us know that John the apostle was not asleep when he witnessed this. He was wide awake.

Question: Why does it matter what color Jesus is or looks like?

Answer: Jesus said: "What thou sees, write it in a book." Why would Jesus say, write this in a book? Because it mattered to Him and He wanted the reader to know. So if it does not matter to you that is one thing, however, it matters to Him.

Maybe He wanted to see how people would feel or react to seeing an image of Him in a totally different light. How would you and other people react to an image of a beautiful Black Messiah, a man of color? Can they still love Him even though He looks nothing like the image we see today?

Black Christ inside Iglesia de San Felilpe in Portobello, Panama

Definition of Revelation: Usually a secret or surprising fact that is made known. Something that is revealed by God to humans.

Christ washes the feet of the Apostles.16th century
Under the CC Attrib S-A 4.0 Public Domain
Creative Commons Attribution 4.0 License http://creativecommons.org/licenses/by/4.0/

Again, here is some more proof that Jesus is a man of color:

"And unto the angel of the church in Thyatira write; these things saith the Son of God, who hath his eyes like unto a flame of fire, and his feet are like fine brass." **(Revelations 2:18)**

This is a 150-year-old painting blessed by Pope Leo XIII and is just one of a handful of paintings based on the cloth used to dab Jesus' face before he was crucified. This is known as the Veil of Veronica, which according to legend bears his likeness. This painting was stolen. They tried to sell it to St. Joseph, the Workerville Church in Madisonville for $3,000. The church, realizing what it was, reported it to the authorities. This church is now working with officials in Rome to appraise the piece, which if determined to be authentic could make it invaluable. The linen artwork features a waxed seal stamped with the Pope's ring.

Let's read another Biblical text describing how God looks:

"Then I lifted up mine eyes, and looked, and behold a certain man clothed in linen, whose loins were girded with fine gold of Uphaz: His body also was like the beryl, and his face as the appearance of lightning, and his eyes as lamps of fire, <u>and his arms and his feet like in color to polished brass</u>, and the voice of his words like the voice of a multitude."

- **Daniel 10:5-6 (KJV)**

Please notice that Daniel has the same exact description of Christ as the Apostle John did. They both saw the color of His arms and His feet.

129

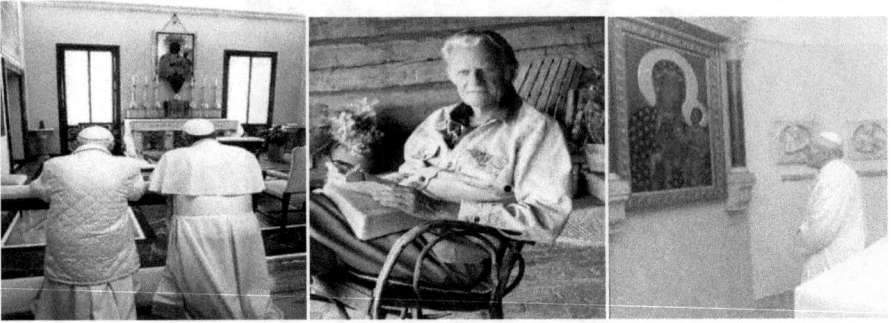

Billy Graham and the Pope both knew Jesus was a man of color.
(Billy Graham, who is Jesus http://s1.zetaboards.com/Express_Yourself/topic/4463615/1/)
Pope Francis and Pope Emeritus Benedict XVI pray together in front of the Black Madonna & baby Jesus

Reverend Billy Graham is the most respected Christian preachers in America, and maybe the world. He said that Jesus wasn't a white man. He said that Jesus had dark skin and grew up in Africa so he believes he was black along with the man who helped Jesus carry the cross that He was crucified on.

Some of us may have a personal testimony of seeing or hearing the voice of God. We have heard people's testimony, saying that they have seen Jesus and He was white. My best friend's grandmother said she has seen Jesus in a dream and He was white with blue eyes. My mom also saw Jesus and she described Him as white. I had a dream that I was at a party and I was standing behind a table. I started saying out loud "God is coming." I began to try and hide because I did not want God to see me at a party so as I started to duck and hide under the table as God began to walk into the party.

I slowly crept up and saw him walking in from a side view and he was tall with a long white coat that looked like cashmere. He had on a hat. I remember being surprised because He had an Afro and He was a man of color. As He was walking into the room, He had an entourage of people with Him but I could not see them. I just knew there were many with Him. Then the dream switched over. I am now driving down a freeway and as I am driving again, I see God to my right, hitchhiking. I once again wanted to hide from Him by quickly driving by Him, but I could not. I was too scared so I stopped the car and asked Him what is He doing out on the freeway. But as soon as my car slowed down God came in my car, sat next to me, and put His hand on my knee. He smiled and said everything is going to be alright. Then I woke up.

This dream happened around the time my dad was dying of throat cancer and I was worried. My testimony is I have seen God in a dream as a black man.

(Pic 1)"The Savior's Transfiguration", an early-15th-century icon from the Tretyakov Gallery, Attributed to: Theophanes the Greek. (Pic2) The Black Madonna & baby Jesus of Częstochowa, Poland.

"The firmament over their heads was the likeness of a throne, in appearance like a sapphire stone; on the likeness of the throne was a likeness with the appearance of a man high above it. [27] Also from the appearance of His waist and upward, I saw, as it were, the color of amber with the appearance of fire all around within it; and from the appearance of His waist and downward I saw, as it were, the appearance of fire with brightness all around. [28] Like the appearance of a rainbow in a cloud on a rainy day so was the appearance of the

brightness all around it. This was the appearance of the likeness of the glory of the LORD." **(Ezekiel 1:26-28)**

I beheld till the thrones were cast down, and the Ancient of days did sit, whose garment was white as snow, <u>and the hair of his head like the pure wool</u>: his throne was like the fiery flame, and his wheels as burning fire. **(Daniel 7:9 KJV)**

Also, we read in the scripture that His hair was white like wool. So we know by these descriptions that Jesus is a man of color and not like the images we see today.

I found a study by Samuel George Morton to be very interesting. He was a physician and natural scientist. He did a study back in 1839 about the characteristics of four races: the European, Asian, Native American, and African American. When he described the type of hair, for each group, let's read what he came up with.

Europeans: The hair, fine, long and curling, and of various colors.

Asians: Long black straight hair.

Native Americans: Long, black, lank hair.

African American: Black, wooly hair.

"It is pretty clear in scripture that Jesus was of Hebrew descent, his genealogy being attested as of the Hebrew patriarchs in the Gospel of Matthew and the Gospel of Luke. By the Middle Ages a number of documents, generally of unknown or questionable origin, had been composed and were circulating with details of the appearance of Jesus. These documents are now mostly considered forgeries. While many people have a fixed mental image of Jesus, drawn from his artistic depictions, these images often conform to ethnic-European stereotypes which are not grounded in any serious research on the historical Jesus but are based on second - or third-hand interpretations of spurious sources." **(Wikipedia Encyclopedia)**

Brass is already brown, like a doorknob. Anything burned has to get very dark from oxidation. And Christ's feet were the same color as the rest of his body: dark brass!

No where in the bible describes that, Jesus, looks like this.

This is the color of brass.

There is no scripture in the Holy Bible that describes Jesus to look like the images portraying Him today as being European looking. No matter what anybody believes about how Jesus looks I will always believe the word of God and He tells us what He looks like. The devil can tell you things and show you false Images, but the Holy Spirit will bear witness to the believer's spirit and reveal the truth.

Here is a demonstration of what burning brass looks like:
https://www.youtube.com/watch?v=WNDNRtMBDdo

133

When we see pictures of Jesus, we never see His hair like wool and skin like the color of brass.

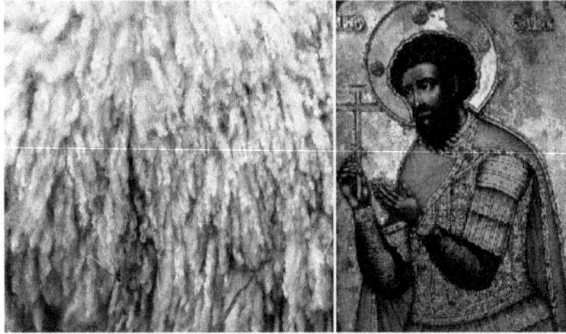

This is what wooly hair looks like. Jesus (circa 6th Century)

The Transfiguration of Jesus, during which he was glorified with "His face shining as the sun. John's vision of the Son of Man: "... and His feet were like unto burnt brass, His head and His hairs were white like wool, as white as snow." Other translations say: "burnished bronze."

"Her Nazarites were purer than snow, they were whiter than milk, they were more swarthy in body than rubies, their polishing was of sapphire: Their visage is blacker than coal." **(Lamentations 4:7-8)**

The definition for Nazarites: One who is separated from others and consecrated to God.

The definition for 'visage': The face appearance.

- Nazarene (title): A title applied to Jesus Christ
- Nazirite, in Biblical times: Someone who took a vow described in Numbers 6:1–21.

It is quite obvious that Jesus our Lord and Savior and the Israelites were people of color.

There is a book called Russian Icons by Vladimir Ivanoff. This is a book of paintings that celebrates 1000 years of Christianity. This book used to cost about $80.00 Now it costs around $500 to buy. Why? Because people have started to become wise to the fact that inside of the book you can actually see proof of how the pictures of Jesus Christ were originally painted as a man of color. In the book there is an artist who actually copies an original picture of Jesus Christ as a man of color and repaints it to look European.

Russian Icons by Vladimir Ivanoff

"Wherein the heathen had sought to paint the likeness of their Images. They brought also the priests' garments, and the first fruits, and the tithes and the Nazarites they stirred up, who had accomplished their days. Then cried they with a loud voice toward heaven, saying, What shall we do with these, and whither shall we carry them away? For thy sanctuary is trodden down and profaned, and thy priests are in heaviness and brought low."
- **Malachi 3:48-51 KJV**

"The earth is given into the hand of the wicked: he covereth the faces of the judges thereof; if not, where, and who is he?"
- **Job 9:24 KJV**

The Good Shepherd,   Twelve-year-old child Jesus in the temple
Catacombs of Rome, 3rd century   (Russian icon, 15th or 16th century)
Creative Commons Attribution 4.0 License http://creativecommons.org/licenses/by/4.0

Here is an image of Jesus from a Byzantine coin
Of the second reign of Justinian II, 705-711 c. e.
(Photo Gold-stater.com)

During the Renaissance era, the dark ages, which were from the 14th to the 17th century in Europe, went into a whitewashing stage. They destroyed and threw away original paintings of the Hebrews and drew new paintings in their image.

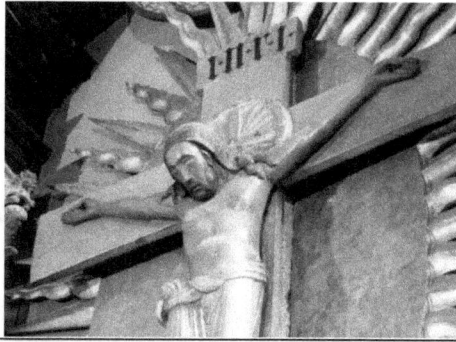

The Gero Crucifix. Cologne Cathedral, Germany. c. 970
Photo by Elke Wetzig Attrib S-A 4.0 Creative Commons
Attribution 4.0 License http://creativecommons.org /licenses/by/4.0

Healing of the Paralytic is the earliest visual depiction
of Jesus on a wall of the Syria and dated 235 A.D.
Resource: http://realhistoryww.com

This fresco of Christ Among the Apostles is in an arcosolium
of the Crypt of Ampliatus in the Catacombs of St. Domitilla in Rome.
Dated from the 2nd through 4th centuries.
Resource: http://realhistoryww.com

(More Pictures on page 259)

The Progenitor of the Dark Races

Now these are the generations of the sons of Noah, Shem, Ham, and Japheth. It's written that the sons of Ham are Cush, Mizraim, Phut, and Canaan **(Genesis 10:6)**
Ham is known as the progenitor of the dark races: Egyptians, Ethiopians, Libyans, and Canaanites. The Egyptians identified themselves as black people and saw themselves as descendants of a black man, Ham. 'Progenitor' means to originate. We find this information in the Compact Bible Dictionary by Zondervan under the name Ham which also indicates that he is Noah's son. Now when we look up Cush, it says the eldest son of Ham, who was the son of Noah. When you look up Mizraim, again, it says the son of Ham is the progenitor of the Egyptians, the people of North Africa, the Hamitic people of Canaan. Mizraim is the Hebrew and Aramaic name for the land of Egypt. We can already see the dark race started from the beginning.

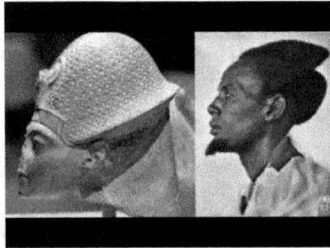

We can also read in scripture that Jacob was black if his son Simeon was black wouldn't that mean he was black?

Let's read:*"Now there were in the church at Antioch prophets and teachers, Barnabas, <u>Simeon who was called Niger,</u> Lucius of Cyrene, Manaen a lifelong friend of Herod the tetrarch, and Saul."* **(Acts 13:1)**

The nickname *Niger* means "black", and refers to a dark complexion or African descent.

Niger: Latin word meaning black, or dark. Simeon is the second son of Jacob by Leah. **(Gen 29:33)**

How about King David I believe he was also a man of color why? Let's read the biblical text:

Now he was <u>ruddy, and withal of a beautiful countenance</u>, and goodly to look to. **(1 Samuel 16:12-13)** *And when the Philistine looked about, and saw David, he disdained him, for he was but a youth, and <u>ruddy, and of a fair</u> countenance.* **(1 Samuel 17:42)**

So we see King David was Ruddy and fair, let's see what fair and ruddy mean's in the Compact Bible Dictionary by Zondervan.

Fair: Fair in this context means he was attractive, good looking, and beautiful.

Ruddy: A word used to refer to a <u>red or fair complexion, in Contrast to the dark skin Hebrews.</u> Which means either two things one King David was not dark skinned, King David was a handsome light skinned, fair complexion Hebrew Israelite not dark. Or two he was brown skinned with a beautiful countenance. (*Definitions: Compact Bible Dictionary by Zondervan*)

The Lord has commanded, saying: 'Speak to the children of Israel, that they bring you a red heifer without blemish, in which there is no defect and on which a yoke has never come.
- Num 19:1-2

Who Wrote the Bible?

The King James Version (KJV), also known as the Authorized Version (AV) or King James Bible (KJB), is an English translation of the Christian Bible for the Church of England begun in 1604 and completed in 1611. The most influential version of the most influential book in human history was the work of a committee. Earlier translations into English had been the daring and illegal work of individual reformers or hasty compilations of several translations, with a minimum of revision and with marginal notes reflecting the theological bias of the editors (the Geneva Bible 1560, the Bishop's Bible 1568) When James became King of England he was urged to sponsor a new English Bible that might be authorized for use in all Anglican churches, and be acceptable to all church parties and displace the Geneva Bible, growing in popularity as the puritans grew in political strength. James himself was a Bible student and had published a metrical version of the Psalms to be the patron of a major scholarly undertaking appealed both to his vanity and to his politics. In 1604 he appointed 54 distinguished professors and churchmen to undertake the task and had his Archbishop draw up detailed rules to guide them.

We also see this truth in scripture. Let's read:

"Knowing this first, that no prophecy of the scripture is of any private interpretation. For the prophecy came not in old time by the will of man, but holy men of God spake as they were moved by the Holy Ghost." **(2 Peter 1:20-21)**

They labored independently and together in six teams, checking one another's work, until 1611 the King James Version, at last, appeared the most majestic, beautiful and graceful book in the English language. More than one thousand editions appeared before 1800 and it is still the Bible for millions of readers, 368 years later. King James authorized the bible which means he approved that it would be translated from the Hebrew to the Greek and English. Some say he was a homosexual, which later was found out to be a lie and a rumor by Sir Anthony Weldon. King James, in fact, had a wife and eight kids. Further, an examination of King James' numerous extant writings shows him to be a true man and a father; in deep love with his wife.

For complete and detailed research on this issue, I refer you to the book King James VI of Scotland & I of England, Unjustly Accused?, by Stephen A. Coston, which goes into exhaustive detail. We know that King James was not a homosexual. Besides, what homosexual would authorize hundreds of scriptures that speak against that lifestyle in scripture such as Lev 20:13 which says if a man also lies with mankind, as he lieth with a woman, both of them have committed an abomination they shall surely be put to death their blood should be upon them? So we know that rumor was nonsense and God moved Godly men to bring out His truth.

Let's read what God said about His word:

"The Lord gave the word: great was the company of those that published it." **(Psalms 68:11)**

Amen to this!!

The Apocrypha

In the beginning, there were 80 books in the King James Bible: 39 in the Old Testament, 14 in the Apocrypha, and 27 in the New Testament. The word 'Apocrypha' means 'hidden books.' the Apocrypha is a selection of books which were published in the original 1611 King James Bible.
The Apocrypha was a part of the KJV for 274 years until being removed in 1885 A.D.

The Apocrypha and Deuterocanonicals support some of the things that the Roman Catholic Church believes and practices which many others feel are not in agreement with the Bible. Examples are praying for the dead, petitioning "saints" in Heaven for their prayers, worshipping angels, "alms-giving," and atoning for sins. Some of what the Apocrypha / Deuterocanonicals say is true and correct.

What is interesting is when you read through the book of Daniel 7-8 and when you go through the orders of the empires you read about the Babylonians, Medes, Persians, Greeks, and the Romans. Then when you get to the last book of the Old Testament you are in the book of Malachi. We know that the Persians are ruling at that time and when you turn one page over you are in the New Testament and Rome is ruling. So where is the history of the Greeks? It is in the Apocrypha, in the book of Maccabees.

Also, when you go to the book of John, and read John 10:22-23 it talks about the feast of dedication. Let's read:

"And it was at Jerusalem the feast of the dedication, and it was winter. And Jesus walked in the temple in Solomon's porch." **(John 10:22-23).**

We see Jesus celebrated this holiday. The Feast of dedication, also known as "Feast of Lights" or Hanukkah we cannot find any information about the Feast of Dedication in the 66 books of the Bible. Why? Because it was taken out and it can be found in the Apocrypha in 1 Maccabees 4:56. Also, when you read in Daniel 8:14 about the sanctuary being cleansed, that information is also in the Apocrypha, 1 Maccabees 4:41-64, 2 Maccabees 1:18, and 2 Maccabees 6:2. So many people believe in some of the validity of the Apocrypha and still read it today.

One last thing about the Apocrypha in the book of 2 Esdras you will find 70 missing verses that are not in the Bible, however the Oxford university actually published the missing verses in their Bibles and study materials. You can find the missing verses in the Oxford Revised Standard Version Bible. You can also get these verses in the book called "Cambridge Annotated Study Apocrypha" you will not find these verses in the KJV Bible they have been removed. These verses give further information in regards to Hell (The Pit of Torment) It also gives more information on what happens after the spirit leaves the body. The missing verses are 2 Esdras 7:36-105 RSV/NRSV Here is a PDF version you can read online:

(http://www.polohco.com/get/70verses.pdf)

Ancient Kemet (Egypt & Christianity)

When we think of Ancient Egypt, a lot of us think of the Pharaoh and how he was so stubborn about letting God's people go. We also think about Moses leading the Israelites out of Egypt under Pharaoh. The reason why I wanted to talk about Ancient Egypt is because God created everything and all things including the civilization of Ancient Egypt. Remember, God allowed the Egyptians to raise Moses from a baby.

Let's read the Biblical text:

"And Moses was learned in all the wisdom of the Egyptians and was mighty in words and in deeds." **(Acts 7:22)**

Akhenaton - 18th Dynasty Amama 1340 BCE   Nefertiti (ca. 1370 BC - CA. 1330 BC)
Akhenaton was married to Nefertiti
(Creative Commons Attribution 4.0 License http://creativecommons.org/licenses/by/4.0/)

Nefertiti is one of the most fascinating Egyptian rulers in history. She was a queen, but she was also a priestess some believe she may have even been a Pharaoh. She was married to Amenhotep IV (aka Akhenaten) they threw out all of the old known gods and set up, the sun as god in the form of Aten. This didn't make the couple very popular, but it did give them absolute power over their subjects.

144

God also allowed Joseph to live and rule amongst the Egyptians. Why? Because God knew how advanced and smart the Egyptians were because God gave them their spiritual gifts.

I believe without a shadow of a doubt that the Father of Abraham, Isaac, and Jacob was also the God of the Ancient Egyptians and as we see in scripture over and over again, God puts out his expectations and everyone agrees to God's commands. Just like today man breaks treaties and agreements and the Egyptians did as well. God said all right, let's see how you do on your own. Then we see the Ancient Egyptians idol worshipping and going to a desolate place. Today we see what is left the pyramids and the hieroglyphics on the walls by the Egyptian scribes.

Picture of the Great Pyramid C Commons Attribution-Share Alike 3.0 Author Alex Ibh

All Glory to God who was the only one able to bless the Egyptians with the knowledge that they had. I'm going to share some knowledge about the civilization of Ancient Egypt and some of the similarities to Christianity.

145

Pharaoh Ramses II had a sanctuary of the Holy of Holies and they also believed in a triad like we call the trinity: the Father, the Son, and the Holy Spirit. Well the Egyptians had God the father, God the Goddess, and God the son. All three were referred to as a God.

On the walls at Abu Simbel, Egypt there are hieroglyphics of the Egyptians slaying their enemies. Some say the pictures of the enemies being slain were Hittites, Israelite slaves and captives. The Egyptians created hieroglyphics by using a chisel and a small hammer that they carved into stones, marble, and granite. After they chiseled the drawings they would put a layer of plaster over it. They made paint for these drawings out of clay and dyes and they would get the colors from flowers and trees to make the different color stains.

It's amazing that on the walls, they show the purification rights or the baptism of the Pharaoh. They show him getting baptized like Christians do. Inside the temple were hieroglyphics of an ankh and a cross.

Ptolemaic Frieze "The Cross Revealed"
By Crichton E. M. Miller
Creative Commons Attribution 4.0 License http://creativecommons.org/licenses/by/4.0/

Senusret I with Ankh He was the second Pharaoh
Of the Twelfth Dynasty of Egypt

The Egyptian gods are often portrayed carrying an Ankh by its loop, or bearing one in each hand, arms crossed over their chest.

The ankh appears in hand or in the proximity of almost every deity in the Egyptian pantheon (including Pharaohs) It represents the concept of life, also called "The Key Of Life" which is the general meaning of the symbol.

Additionally, an ankh was often carried by Egyptians as an amulet, either alone, or in connection with two other hieroglyphs that mean strength and health. It also represents the male, female, and child. Ancient Egypt has a lot of mysteries, however, we know God created them just like he created us.

"Do not despise an Egyptian, because you resided as foreigners in their country." **(Deuteronomy 23:7 NIV)**

Also, the drawings in the pyramids show people in Egypt playing instruments. They show the harp, tambourine, flute, and electric guitar. The Egyptians had the musical instruments before the Europeans. They even show them using a harpoon. The Egyptians also had a calendar based on the lunar, a calendar based on the moon and the sun. Their calendar was not 12 months in a year. They had 13 months, 12 months of thirty days in each and 1 month of 5 days. They also used what was called a sundial against the shadows to tell what time of day it was. We also read this in the Bible.

Let's read the Biblical text:

"Behold, I will bring again the shadow of the degrees, which is gone down in the sundial of Ahaz, ten degrees backward. So the sun returned ten degrees, by which degrees it was gone down."
- Isaiah 38:8

The Egyptians were very advanced and skilled in engineering and were masters in architecture. They were professional craftsmen, they were highly intelligent. Egypt had many other inventions before we did, such as the toilet. They actually made a toilet with a water system using a bucket and a troth that opened to release the water to flush. This was found at the Temple of Ramses the III at the West bank at Luxor. The Statues of Ramses II are breathtaking and they are huge. The detail is beautiful and all of his statues are made out of marble and limestone.

Ramses II, also known as Ramses the Great, was the third Pharaoh
of the Nineteenth Dynasty of Egypt. He is often regarded as the greatest,
most celebrated, and most powerful Pharaoh of the Egyptian Empire.
(Wikipedia Died: 1213 BC) C Commons Attribution-Share Alike 4.0
Creative Commons Attribution 4.0 License http://creativecommons.org/licenses/by/4.0/

Many believe Egypt is the mother of the Western world and the whole world should look to Egypt If you're Jewish, Christian, Muslim, Greek, or Roman this is the beginning of where it all started. God says, "but Jerusalem above is free, which is the mother of us all" **(Galatians 4:26)**
Dr. Yosef Ben believes that the United States used Egypt to set up the symbols for the country and was based on the Masonic order which he believes was copied from Egypt in the 22 tablets taken from the country.

He said they were stolen by England and then they used the tablets for their symbols. For instance the pyramid on the United States money and the "ever seeing eye" are also on the money along with other hidden symbols that are also seen in Ancient Egypt. Also in the Supreme Court they use the scale for Justice like the Egyptians have on their walls.

Another similarity between Christians and Ancient Egypt is that Christians have the Ten Commandments and the Ancient Egyptians had what is called the Ma'at, 42 Negative Confessions. Out of the 42 negative confessions, ten of them are also found in the Ten Commandments that were given to Moses. Remember Moses was learned in all the wisdom of the Egyptians and was mighty in words and in deeds. **(Acts 7:22)**

The 42 Divine Laws of Ma'at • The 42 Negative Confessions

1. I have not committed sin.	2. I have not committed robbery with violence.
3. I have not stolen.	4. I have not slain men or women.
5. I have not stolen food.	6. I have not swindled offerings.
7. I have not stolen from God/Goddess	8. I have not told lies.
9. I have not carried away food.	10. I have not cursed.
11. I have not closed my ears to the truth.	12. I have not committed adultery.
13. I have not made anyone cry.	14. I have not felt sorrow without reason.
15. I have not assaulted anyone.	16. I am not deceitful.
17. I have not stolen anyone's land.	18. I have not been an eavesdropper.
19. I have not falsely accused anyone.	20. I have not been angry without reason.
21. I have not seduced anyone's wife.	22. I have not polluted myself.
23. I have not terrorized anyone.	24. I have not disobeyed the Law.
25. I have not been exclusively angry.	26. I have not cursed God/Goddess.
27. I have not behaved with violence.	28. I have not caused disruption of peace.
29. I have not acted hastily or without thought.	30. I have not overstepped my boundaries of concern.
31. I have not exaggerated my words when speaking.	32. I have not worked evil.
33. I have not used evil thoughts, words or deeds.	34. I have not polluted the water.
35. I have not spoken angrily or arrogantly.	36. I have not cursed anyone in thought, word or deed.
37. I have not placed myself on a pedestal.	38. I have not stolen what belongs to God/Goddess.
39. I have not stolen from or disrespected the dead.	40. I have not taken food from a child.
41. I have not acted with insolence.	42. I have not destroyed property belonging to God/Goddess.

Maat or Ma'at was the ancient Egyptian concept of truth, balance, order, harmony, law, morality, and justice. Maat was also personified as a goddess regulating the stars, seasons, and the actions of both mortals and the deities, who set the order of the universe from chaos at the moment of creation. The earliest surviving records indicating that Maat is the norm in nature and society, in this world and the next, were recorded during the Old Kingdom, the earliest substantial surviving examples were found in the Pyramid Texts of Unas
(CA. 2375 BCE and 2345 BCE)

The Book of the Dead

The Papyrus of Ani: is a papyrus manuscript with cursive hieroglyphs and color illustrations created c. 1250 BCE, in the 19th dynasty of the New Kingdom of ancient Egypt. Egyptians compiled an individualized book for certain people upon their death, called the Book of Going Forth by Day, more commonly known as the Book of the Dead, typically containing declarations to help the deceased in their afterlife.

Book of the Dead circa 1200 B.C From Papyrus of Ani, based on the weighing of the heart
Tomb of Ani - 19Th Dynasty C Commons Attribution-Share Alike 4.0
Creative Commons Attribution 4.0 License http://creativecommons.org/licenses/by/4.0/

This picture is a part of the Papyrus of Ani showing what was called the "Weighing of the Heart."

After you died, the ancient Egyptians believed your heart had to be weighed. This is why you see the picture of a scale with a heart on one side and a feather on the other. Your heart had to be lighter than a feather. To find out if your heart qualified for the trip to the afterlife, your spirit had to enter the Hall of Maat. The God Anubis would lead you into the Hall of Maat to have your heart weighed. If your heart was light, you were considered to be pure and free from sin. This meant you had passed the test and entered your afterlife led by Horus to Osiris.

BUT, if your heart was heavy because your deeds were not good, the God Ammut would suddenly appear... and eat you up!

The word hieroglyph is Greek for "Sacred writing" or "God's words." "The "Book of the Dead" is an illustrated papyrus scroll placed in the tomb as a guidebook for the deceased during his journey to the afterlife. It also contains prayers, hymns, and rituals. The actual title of the "Book of the Dead" is "The going forth by day."

The Papyrus of Ani was stolen from an Egyptian government storeroom in 1888 by Sir E. A. Wallis Budge, as described in his two-volume *By Nile and Tigris*, for the collection of the British Museum where it remains today. Before shipping the manuscript to England, Budge cuts the seventy-eight-foot scroll into thirty-seven sheets of nearly equal size, damaging the scroll's integrity at a time when technology had not yet allowed the pieces to be put back together.

In the Valley of the Kings in the 19th dynasty they found the tomb of King Tut. In his tomb, they found solid gold, alabaster and other precious minerals not intended for the eyes of the living but to accompany the young King into the afterlife. The Egyptian "Book of the Dead" was a guide for the afterlife. The Egyptians valued the afterlife, so they would put things in their coffins believing that their favorite things would accompany them in their afterlife. God teaches us not to hold on to stuff like the Egyptians did.

Golden Mask of Tutankhamen at the Egyptian Museum
Author: Carsten Frenzl (Under Creative Commons Attribution S-A 3.0)

"Do not lay up for yourselves treasures on earth, where moth and rust destroy and where thieves break in and steal But lay up for yourselves treasures in heaven, where neither moth nor rust doth corrupt, and where thieves do not break through nor steal."
- **Matthew 6:19-20**

God was right because the memory of the ancient world and its highest artistic creations were turned into decorations, adornments on a shelf, and divorced from historical context and ultimately from all meaning. Grave robbers usually sell their goods on the black market. Though some artifacts may make their way to museums or scholars, many end up in private collections. Egypt was raped of the Nile. They took the heritage out of the country and now it is everywhere.

Precious grave sites and tombs were robbed before scholars were able to examine them so the information was destroyed. God says don't bother storing up anything because

I will provide all your needs, even through the afterlife keep your faith in the finished works of Christ, not in stuff.

We can learn from the Ancient Egyptians to remind us that we need to trust in the one and only true God.

Let's read what God said in His word:

"Remember the former things of old: for I am God, and there is none else; I am God, and there is none like me." **(Isaiah 46:9)**

Ancient Egypt, shows us that God never changed. He always wanted us to follow His laws, statutes and commands and not to follow false gods and worship idols or to live in fear.

So when we look at Ancient Egypt, they have helped us by leaving us their testimonies of fearing what will happen to them after they died and wanting declarations written for them to help in their journey to the afterlife. They would spend half of a year's wage getting a papyrus created for them. At their burial they would have someone roll it up and put the declarations in their coffin to help them with their journey on to the next life.

The Egyptians would have some instructions written inside of their coffins. They called this the coffin text. The Egyptians valued the afterlife more than life itself, however, they feared the journey getting there. The 'Book of the Dead' is a Bible to the Egyptians. It is the oldest known religious text in the world. Even the 42 negative confessions was a list of sins you should not commit, such as the Ten Commandments. It is known that some of the text from the 'Book of the Dead' is similar to what is written in the Holy Bible, the Old Testament and also the Koran.

153

It has been said that the Christian imagery was influenced by Ancient Egypt, comparing the images of Osiris, Isis, and Horus to when we see images of Mary with baby Jesus sitting on her lap. They feel the idea was based on Isis's statues where she is holding Pharaoh. Ancient Egypt believed in one God they called Osiris. This has made some believe that they had copied Ancient Egypt's 'The Book Of The Dead' because they both had some things in common, however, the truth is there is only one God who never changed so of course there would be similarities until one starts believing in idol worshipping and false Gods.

We see proof that God has always wanted us to follow his laws, statutes, and commands and to have order. The Egyptians' "Book of The Dead" was basically the first text about the thought process of the first human being's thinking about the afterlife. The oldest text is the pyramid text around 2300 BC. The people that did all of the writing in Ancient Egypt were called 'scribes.' They had to attend scribal school in the temple to learn hieroglyphs. This was considered an esteemed profession because they controlled knowledge, which is power. To be a scribe took many years of training to master the writings. The Ancient Egyptians knew words were powerful and believed that words aim to create a blessed afterlife.

When Egyptians died, after wrapping the deceased they would put amulets all around the body, front and back. The Egyptians believed this would help in the journey to the afterlife. They also spent a lot of time preserving the bodies of the deceased so the soul could return to the body in the afterlife which would be perfectly preserved.

They would remove the lungs, liver, stomach, intestines and place them in ceremonial jars which would later be united with the body. This was their belief. They did not keep their brain. That was removed and disposed of.

After everything was removed they would melt resin and pour it through the nose and roll it all around the head so the crania were coated to protect it. The heart was the only organ that would stay within the body. That was the only organ they felt carried a sense of intelligence and feeling and they would need it in the afterlife. Then they would wash the body out and dry it using neutron, a baking soda kind of mixture, wait about 40 days, and then apply oil all over the body and then wrap the body with ceremonial rituals. This would be the end of the mummification and then they were ready to be buried.

They felt that after you die you go through a series of tests on your way to the afterlife. "The Book Of The Dead" provided answers and protection written in a form of a papyrus scroll. There were over 180 chapters that you could pick through that would be placed in your coffin once you were deceased. They were believed to guarantee eternal life. Having "The Book Of The Dead" was the answer.

The Ancient Egyptians believed that the heart was the most important organ to possess because they believed all your thoughts and beliefs were in the heart. Having it was a big part of getting into the afterlife, so it was very important to protect it. They did this by placing a scarab over the heart, a beetle meaning rebirth. They would also inscribe the back of it.

Heart Scarab
Date between 1070 and 736 BC

They also feared that the heart might reveal certain things that they had done while they were living that may hurt them in the afterlife. So for protection they inscribed declarations on the back of the scarab and placed it on top of the heart of the deceased.

The difference between Ancient Kemet and Christianity is that Ancient Egyptians knew that there was life after death and they valued the afterlife. They spent a lifetime preparing for the afterlife while Christians focused on the here and now.

Despite all historical efforts of Eurocentric specialists to conceal, misrepresent, degrade, downplay and plagiarize this truth, Black African scholars and specialists have successfully refuted all systematic efforts to separate this great Black African history of Black African people worldwide.

The ancient Egyptians built monuments that served as a blueprint for modern civilization. They invented law, mathematics, music, agriculture, writing, arts, science, time, calendar, and speech.

Resource: https://www.youtube.com/watch?v=9WOZ0C4gPAI

How They Built the Pyramids

One of the most sought out answers is how the Egyptians build the pyramids. Many believe that aliens may have been involved. Many believe that extraterrestrials gave the pyramid builders the knowledge to fulfill the task needed because they felt that the Egyptians did not have the capabilities or the equipment needed to align those big heavy stones with the stars.

I believe what Dr. Maat said because we know that the Egyptians were very smart, full of wisdom, and if anyone wanted to align the stones up to the stars the Egyptians would have been the ones to do it. They could have aligned whatever they wanted to and moved two-ton blocks because when you really study the Egyptians they had the ability and they had God the father of Abraham, Isaac, and Jacob, who verified that the Egyptians were full of wisdom. This is why God allowed Moses to be raised up by Pharaoh.

The Egyptians understood math and they understood physics. All they needed was math, physics, astronomical science and observation to align the pyramids. Archaeologists have found the oldest evidence of symbolic thought. Not only did they find the oldest evidence of symbolic thought, they also found the oldest evidence of mathematical thought. This is why Dr. Maat confirms the claim that the Egyptians did not need any help from the aliens to build these pyramids. These ideas were born in South Africa. They reached Central Africa first and then eventually culminated in Kemet allowing our ancestors to build great structures like the pyramids and the sphinx.

The way the Egyptians built the pyramids, worked with granular structures, and aligned things with the true north of the stars was nothing more than a system and a methodology. The Egyptians implemented what they knew and that was how they were able to maneuver granular structures and align what they needed to align. The way they moved 2 to10 ton rock was by using algebra, geometry, trigonometry, astronomical science, mechanics, material science, and physics. They needed knowledge in these areas to build ramps.

So the question is how they were able to move these heavy rocks as well. There is an article you can look up. It is in the physical review letters entitled "Sliding Friction on Wet and Dry Sand." This paper states that they did an excavation on a pyramid from 1900 B.C.E. and found the names of the pyramid builders written in red ochre. Since they found the names of these Egyptians who actually did the work we know the Egyptians did the building and not the aliens who would not have written their names on the pyramid stones in red ochre. The history of writing things in red ochre goes back to body painting. Painting yourself is known to be an African tradition. This is powerful information and you can also look up this history for yourself.

The Egyptians started investigating the effect of using water and sands. They experimented with different amounts of water on the sliding friction of a variety of sands by measuring the force necessary to pull the sled. They poured water onto the sand to decrease the friction. This allowed them to pull a sled that was weighted down by a statue or a block. So during their research, they computed the friction coefficient. Friction is resistance so they computed what was called a 'shear modulus' which measures the stiffness of a material. They found that the friction coefficient and the 'shear modulus' are inversely proportional. When you pour water onto the sand capillary bridges form. When these capillary bridges form that increases the shear modules. When the shear modulus increases that decreases the friction allowing you to pull something that is heavy.

The Egyptians formed several teams that worked together in order to move these limestone blocks. Each team wrote their names in red ochre on the pyramid blocks as a record of works written. The evidence of the Egyptians moving blocks and statues are drawn on the wall in the ancient tomb of Djehutihotep, 1900 B.C.E. On the wall is a painting of a group of 172 men. They are hauling an immersed statue using ropes attached to a sled with another man in front pouring something on the sled.

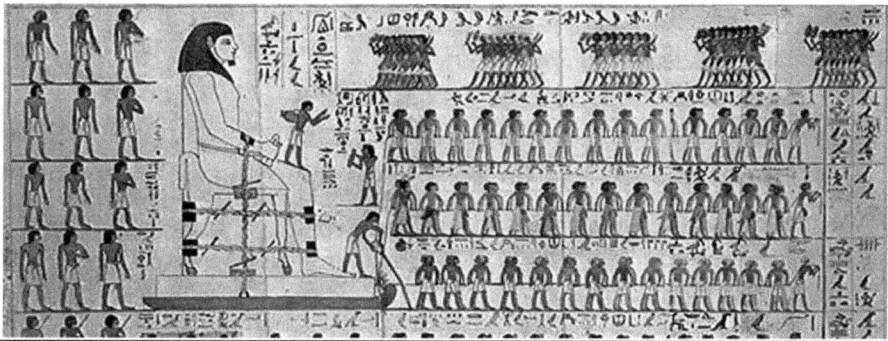

Djehutihotep 1900 B.C.E. Wikipedia,

By far, Djehutihotep is best known for the famous decoration inside of his tomb that represents the transport of a colossal statue of him that was nearly 7 meters (23 ft) high. It was transported by 172 workers using ropes and a slide, in an effort that is facilitated by pouring water in front of the slide. Unfortunately, no traces of this colossus have ever been found. The colossus' depiction itself was irremediably vandalized and destroyed in 1890.

Original transport of a colossal statue damaged. (Wikipedia)

Dr. Maat also spoke about this article called "The Coast in Color." This article describes the pinnacle point which is located in Mossel Bay at the bottom of Africa. Pinnacle point is a cave that was occupied over 164,000 years ago. In this cave they found several items. They found shellfish remains, a red pigment, and stone "bladelets." They also found 57 pieces of hematite, an iron ore that can be ground up to produce a blood-red pigment called red ochre. Red ochre came out of the South and the pyramid builders wrote their names in red ochre on the pyramid blocks. We know this tradition comes from South Africa.

There is evidence on the walls about how our ancestors built these pyramids, moved stones, and worked as a team to get the most beautiful pyramids built. Dr. Matt has done an excellent job sharing this information.

You can also watch Dr. Matt explain this in more detail at: https://www.youtube.com/watch?v=Z9zhroI9bFg

Who Can Be Saved?

"But in every nation, he that feareth him, and worketh righteousness, is accepted with him."

- ### Acts 10:35

God will save everyone and anyone who repents and believes in God and obeys His commands and puts their faith in the finished works of Jesus Christ, who was crucified for our sins.

When we walk by faith we have to remember that faith is always an action word. God wants us to understand the truth about trusting in Jesus Christ and having Jesus as our only personal Savior because He bore the judgment for our sins. He died in our place and has risen again so we can have eternal life, and be saved from our enemies, and get out of the mess that we are in.

Praise God for Jesus! We now have a direct relationship with God who has given us the gift of the Holy Spirit that comforts us. This is good news! We will all come before God on judgment day so we must be Christ-like and ready to come before Our Father.

"For God shall bring every work into judgment, with every secret thing, whether it be good, or whether it be evil."
- ### Ecclesiastes 12:14

For the Lord will have mercy on Jacob, and will yet choose Israel, and set them in their own land: and the strangers shall be joined with them, and they shall cleave to the house of Jacob. **- Isaiah 14:1**

God also says worketh righteousness. If we are true Christians, then we are followers of Christ and we will keep God's commandments.

"And it shall be our righteousness if we observe to do all these commandments before the LORD our God, as he hath commanded us."

- Deuteronomy 6:25

"And, behold, one came and said unto him, Good Master, what good thing shall I do, that I may have <u>eternal life</u>? [17] And he said unto him, Why callest thou me good? There is none good but one, that is, God: but if thou wilt enter into life, <u>keep the commandments</u>."

- Matthew 19:16-25

When we read God's word, it is very clear that we can all be saved. He said "all Nations" so that means that race, color, age or gender does not matter. God said <u>every Nation</u> can be saved and accepted by Him. Fearing God protects us from false doctrines so if anyone tells you to do the opposite of the word of God, then you know it's wrong. God is our Judge so we must do what is written and obey His word regardless.

"And many false prophets shall rise, and shall deceive many. And because <u>iniquity shall abound</u>, the love of many shall wax cold. But he that shall endure unto the end, the same shall be saved."

- Mathew 24:11-13

False teachers will start lying to you with smooth lips and say that you can't possibly keep what God commands and because you're saved by grace you do not have to follow His commands. If you trust in the finished works of Jesus Christ and allow the Holy Spirit to work in you to cut back your sinful nature and follow God's commands that's being obedient and this is what keeps you from sinning, obedience to God's word.

162

Yes, we are saved by grace, however, God says if you love me, you will keep my commands so grace is an action plan. Just like faith is an action, when we choose God there must be a change in us.

God is looking for us to continue being obedient to His word by no longer practicing sin. Don't let people deceive you with their false doctrines that you can stay practicing sin and not change, just playing the grace card.

"Thou shalt love the Lord thy God with all thy heart, and with all thy soul, and with all thy mind. This is the first and great commandment. And the second is like unto it, Thou shalt love thy neighbor as thyself. On these two commandments hang all the law and the prophets."
- **Matthew 22:36-40**

"And it shall come to pass, that ye shall divide it by lot for an inheritance unto you, and to the strangers that sojourn among you, which shall beget children among you: and they shall be unto you as born in the country among the children of Israel; they shall have inheritance with you among the tribes of Israel."

- **Ezekiel 47:22**

This is beautiful. All nations who want to be saved shall share in all the promises that God has to give. What he means by the 'stranger' are the Gentiles, everyone that is not a Jew. God will share an inheritance among all nations.

In this next verse, God reminds us to take heed to His word because we have a special covenant with Him and we must take hold of it by faith. We know faith is an action word. We must be doers of His word.

163

"Also the sons of the stranger, that join themselves to the LORD, to serve him, and to love the name of the LORD, to be his servants, every one that keepeth the Sabbath from polluting it, and taketh hold of my covenant; ⁷ Even them will I bring to my holy mountain, and make them joyful in my house of prayer: their burnt offerings and their sacrifices shall be accepted upon mine altar; <u>for mine house shall be called a house of prayer for all people</u>." **Isaiah 56:6 -7**

"This is the love of God, that we keep his commandments: and his commandments are not grievous."
- **1 John 5:3**

Yet if they shall bethink themselves in the land whither they were carried captives, and repent, and make supplication unto thee in the land of them that carried them captives, saying, We have sinned, and have done perversely, we have committed wickedness;48 And so return unto thee with all their heart, and with all their soul, in the land of their enemies, which led them away captive, and pray unto thee toward their land, which thou gavest unto their fathers, the city which thou hast chosen, and the house which I have built for thy name:49 Then hear thou their prayer and their supplication in heaven thy dwelling place, and maintain their cause,50 And forgive thy people that have sinned against thee, and all their transgressions wherein they have transgressed against thee, and give them compassion before them who carried them captive, that they may have compassion on them:51 For they be thy people, and thine inheritance, which thou broughtest forth out of Egypt, from the midst of the furnace of iron- **1 Kings 8:47-51**

And he said, It is a light thing that thou shouldest be my servant to raise up the tribes of Jacob, and to restore the preserved of Israel: I will also give thee for a light to the Gentiles, that thou mayest be my salvation unto the end of the earth.- **Isaiah 49:6**

A False Relationship with God

Some people say I am doing me and that is all I can do. But the truth is they can be Christ-like and live for God and not for self.

We hear people say this all the time: "I got to do me." But the truth is you can be born again. Get baptized in Christ and be filled with the Holy Spirit of God. Many people who have been baptized have since backslid and many are fornicating and doing other things that lead into practicing sin thinking they have a relationship with God because they had been previously baptized.

You can share the word of God with people who have this mindset and they will tell you that they do not have time to get into God because they are focusing on looking for a job right now and they will make many other excuses for why they are not trusting in God and choosing to live an empty, unfulfilling life.

God told us to work in His vineyard. He gives us a new heart and a new spirit so we can worship God in spirit and in truth. Many will say, "I pray to God every day" as they go about their daily lives continuing in fornicating and whatever else "I got to do me" requires.

We have to know that we are set apart as God's holy people and that God has chosen us.

You did not choose Me, but I chose you and appointed you that you should go and bear fruit, and that your fruit should remain, that whatever you ask the Father in My name He may give you.
- John 15:16

It is a blessing when someone corrects us in love to get us back in the right mindset of trusting in God and living by His word by being obedient to God. This is the move of the Holy Spirit, when we are shown that we are practicing sin. God will use all kinds of ways to correct His children and He uses our brothers and sisters in the Lord who love God and love their brethren. God wants to always remind us that He loves us and we are His Holy people that belong to Him.

"For you are a holy people, who belong to the Lord your God. Of all the people on earth, the Lord your God has chosen you to be his own special treasure."
- Deuteronomy 7:6

Can You Judge? What is Righteous Judgment?

When God uses our brothers and sisters in the Lord to give instructions for a sinner to "repent" some may be offended and get mad and say "you cannot judge me."

"Judge not according to the appearance, but judge righteous judgment."
- **John 7:24**

The answer is yes, a born again believer that's not practicing sin and knows and lives obedient to God's word can judge righteously. Never to condemn, but to help his fellow brethren stay encouraged in the faith and to not let him stumble.

"But he who is spiritual judges all things, yet he himself is rightly judged by no one. For who has known the mind of the LORD that he may instruct Him? But we have the mind of Christ."
- **1 Corinthians 2:15-16**

What is Righteous Judgment?

"How can you think of saying to your friend, Let me help you get rid of that speck in your eye,' when you can't see past the log in your own eye? Hypocrite! First, get rid of the log in your own eye; then you will see well enough to deal with the speck in your friend's eye."
- **Matthew 7:1-5**

If no one corrects God's chosen people they will continue breaking God's laws and continue in bondage. They will stay in captivity and be tormented by their enemies.

Remind them to be subject to rulers and authorities, to obey, to be ready for every good work, ² to speak evil of no one, to be peaceable, gentle, showing all humility to all men. ³ For we ourselves were also once foolish, disobedient, deceived, serving various lusts and pleasures, living in malice and envy, hateful and hating one another. ⁴ But when the kindness and the love of God our Savior toward man appeared, ⁵ not by works of righteousness which we have done, but according to His mercy He saved us, through the washing of regeneration and renewing of the Holy Spirit, ⁶ whom He poured out on us abundantly through Jesus Christ our Savior, ⁷ that having been justified by His grace we should become heirs according to the hope of eternal life.⁸ This is a faithful saying, and these things I want you to affirm constantly, that those who have believed in God should be careful to maintain good works. These things are good and profitable to men.

- Titus 3:1-8

Avoid Dissension: *But avoid foolish disputes, genealogies, contentions, and strivings about the law; for they are unprofitable and useless. ¹⁰ Reject a divisive man after the first and second admonition, ¹¹ knowing that such a person is warped and sinning, being self-condemned.* **- Titus 3:9-11**

The Whole Duty of Men and Women

"Let us hear the conclusion of the whole matter: Fear God, and keep his commandments: for this is the whole duty of man."
-Ecclesiastes 12:13

God Created Man in His Image

"God created man in His own image; in the image of God He created him; male and female He created them."

-   Genesis 1:27

What a blessing that God loves us so much that He made us in His image. This means God has toes, eyes, hands, a face, hair, and ears just like we do. We should see God in each one of us.

Moses Sees God

"Moses said, "I pray thee, show me thy glory." And He said, "I will make all my goodness pass before you, and will proclaim before you my name 'The LORD', and I will be gracious to whom I will be gracious, and will show mercy on whom I will show mercy. But," he said, "you cannot see my face; for man shall not see me and live." And the LORD SAID, "Behold, there is a place by me where you shall stand upon the rock; and while my glory passes by I will put you in a cleft of the rock, and I will cover you with my hand until I have passed by; then I will take away my hand, and you shall see my back, but my face shall not be seen."

-   Exodus 33:18-23

Moses makes a request to God and that's to see Him. God lets us know that when we have a relationship with Him, He will do countless things for the ones who follow His commands. He told Moses, I will be gracious to whom He chooses as well as merciful because Moses trusted God and had a personal relationship with God.

God says no one can see His face and live so we know that God has a face as well as hands. God also told Moses, I will let you see me from the back as I pass by. So God is showing us in scripture that yes, He has a body and our body is formed like Our Father in heaven.

"After this I looked, and, behold, a door was opened in heaven: and the first voice which I heard was as it were of a trumpet talking with me; which said, Come up hither, and I will show thee things which must be hereafter.

And immediately I was in the spirit: and, behold, a throne was set in heaven, and one sat on the throne.

And he that sat was to look upon like a jasper and a sardine stone: and there was a rainbow round about the throne, in sight like unto an emerald."

- **Revelations 4:1-3**

Even though we cannot see God's face, He always shows Himself and is described as a man of color. We see this in many different scriptures. Some people may say, well, I do not believe that you can see the colors in the spirit. But we just read in **Revelations 4:1-3** that there was a rainbow around about the throne.

We know that only God and Jesus will sit on the throne so God is telling us a lot in this scripture. Just think about it: when it rains we see a rainbow in the sky. This rainbow we see today can be straight from Gods throne. He did make a promise that He would not flood the earth and a rainbow was a sign of this promise.

"And I will remember My covenant which is between Me and you and every living creature of all flesh; the waters shall never again become a flood to destroy all flesh. 16 The rainbow shall be in the cloud, and I will look at it to remember the everlasting covenant between God and every living creature of all flesh that is on the earth." 17 And God said to Noah, "This is the sign of the covenant which I have established between Me and all flesh that is on the earth."

-   Genesis 9:15-18 NKJV

Why did Jesus Come and Who Rejected Him?

"The saying is sure and worthy of full acceptance, that Christ Jesus came into the world to save sinners. And I am the foremost of sinners."

- **1 Timothy 1:15**

"He that committeth sin is of the devil; for the devil sinneth from the beginning. For this purpose the Son of God was manifested, that he might destroy the works of the devil."

- **1 John 3:8**

Who Rejected Jesus Christ?

"And he began to teach them, that the Son of man must suffer many things, <u>and be rejected of the elders, and of the chief priests, and scribes, and be killed, and after three days rise again."</u>
- **Mark 8:31**

"He was in the world, and the world was made by him, and the world knew him not. ¹¹ He came unto his own, <u>and his own received him not. ¹² But as many as received him, to them gave he power to become the sons of God, even to them that believe on his name."</u>

- **John 1:10-12**

Thank God for His Mercy and His Grace.

GRACE - Getting what we "**DON'T**" deserve.
MERCY - Not getting what we "**DO**" deserve.

How to Keep from Falling Into Sin

"Simon Peter, a servant and an apostle of Jesus Christ, to them that have obtained like precious faith with us through the righteousness of God and our Savior Jesus Christ. Grace and peace be multiplied unto you through the knowledge of God, and of Jesus our Lord, according as his divine power hath given unto us all things that pertain unto life and godliness, through the knowledge of him that hath called us to glory and virtue whereby are given unto us exceeding great and precious promises that by these ye might be partakers of the divine nature, having escaped the corruption that is in the world through lust. And beside this, giving all diligence, add to your faith virtue; and to virtue knowledge; and to knowledge temperance; and to temperance patience; and to patience godliness; and to godliness brotherly kindness; and to brotherly kindness charity. For if these things are in you, and abound, they make you that ye shall neither be barren nor unfruitful in the knowledge of our Lord Jesus Christ. But he that lacketh these things is blind, and cannot see afar off, and hath forgotten that he was purged from his old sins. Wherefore the rather, brethren, give the diligence to make your calling and election sure, <u>for if ye do these things, ye shall never fall."</u>

-   2 Peter 1-10

The key in the scripture is: *"According to <u>His divine power hath given unto us all things that pertain unto life and godliness, through the knowledge of him</u> that hath called us to glory and virtue through the knowledge of God, and of Jesus our Lord."*

      This verse is so powerful. The most powerful tool you can ever have is the true knowledge of God. Let's read this important verse that explains the importance of having knowledge of God:

"My people are destroyed for lack of knowledge because thou hast rejected knowledge, I will also reject thee, that thou shalt be no priest to me <u>seeing thou hast forgotten the law of thy God, I will also forget thy children</u>."

- Hosea 4:6

God is saying that we lack knowledge of His law and we reject His commands so we fall into the lust of the flesh and find ourselves in trouble. What keeps us from practicing sin is having knowledge of God and His laws, statutes, and commands and to obey them. This is what true knowledge of God is. This is why it is so important to know the word of God for yourself. Many pastors do not teach God's law, statues, and commands and God tells us that they should.

Let's read this important verse: *"For the lips of a priest should keep knowledge, and people should seek the law from his mouth; for he is the messenger of the LORD of hosts."*

- Malachi 2:7

When we have the knowledge of God, His laws, statutes, and commands and know that He has given unto us all things that pertain unto life and godliness, we become partakers of the divine nature, having escaped the corruption that is in the world through lust. When we hear the true Gospel we will know the good news of Jesus Christ and that He was crucified as a sacrifice that atones for our sins—and not only our sins but the sins of all the world. Now this is the true knowledge of God that sets us free.

Let's read this important scripture:

"My dear children, I am writing this to you so that you will not sin. But if anyone does sin, <u>we have an advocate who pleads our case before the Father, He is Jesus Christ, the one who is truly righteous. He himself is the sacrifice that atones for our sins—and not only our sins but the sins of all the world.</u>

And we can be sure that we know him <u>if we obey his commandments</u>. If someone claims, "I know God," but doesn't obey God's commandments, that person is a liar and is not living in the truth. <u>But those who obey God's word truly show how completely they love him.</u> That is how we know we are living in him. Those who say they live in God should live their lives as Jesus did."

-     **1 John 2:1-6**

When you have the true knowledge of God: the knowledge of God's law, statues, and His commands, God will add to your faith virtue, virtue knowledge, knowledge temperance, to temperance patience, to patience godliness, to godly brotherly kindness, and to brotherly kindness charity.

Through the Holy Spirit, God gives us everything we need to be fruitful but the key is to have the knowledge of God and not to forget His laws, statutes, and commands. If we do not have the knowledge of God, we can never live our lives as Jesus did and that's what God requires of us. We must be Christ-like and to live like Jesus did and He obeyed God because He loved God and Jesus also loved His neighbors as Himself.

The Native American Slave Trade

There were scattered church records, wills, and trade transactions and footnotes in regards to the Native American Slave Trade. This business was initiated by the Spanish a year after Columbus landed in the Caribbean in 1492. Even though their history was lost, it will never be forgotten by the descendants of thousands of men, women, and children who were forced into slavery and enslaved to work for unknown masters throughout Europe, the Caribbean, and North America.

This enslavement continued up until the 18th century when slavery was replaced with the Africans. Every colonial power that competed for the supremacy of North America used indigenous slaves in mines, fields, and construction work. Can you imagine being stolen from your land and brought to an unknown country with different customs, culture, language, and clothing and not having your husband, wife or children with you any longer? To be treated as if you are not human as you stand naked, frightened, and powerless while you watch your family be torn apart to never see them again?

Native American Indians were continually used for hard labor working in the fields, mines, and construction. They were in the hands of the French, English, and the Spanish who each had different strategies as well as economic ideas.

Native American slave trading was all based on the three European colonizing strategies in North America: the fur trade in the North East, the plantation system in the South, and the Spanish mission system in Florida

Local plantation owners hunted the slaves amongst the tribes and native groups. For example, the Apalachee tribe was a target for slave trading in Carolina and by 1704 the mission was devastated with bloodshed and non-stop enslavements. The Apalachee tribe was slaughtered and killed and left abandoned. The English even burned down their temples, and their beautiful council houses and their fields were abandoned.

Before the English slave traders came, the Apalachee tribe was flourishing 6,000 strong. But after the English they were down to a handful of survivors and the survivors were sent to Cuba.

Being enslaved was not the only problem that Native Americans had. They caught diseases. The most notable disease brought by Europeans was smallpox. Smallpox was lethal to many Native Americans, bringing sweeping epidemics and affecting the same tribes repeatedly.

In the summer of 1639, a Smallpox epidemic struck the Huron natives in the St. Lawrence and Great Lakes regions. Numerous other diseases were brought to North America including:

Measles, Scarlet fever, Typhoid, Typhus, Influenza, Pertussis, Whooping cough, Tuberculosis, Cholera, Diphtheria, Chickenpox, the common cold, and sexually transmitted diseases. Each of these brought destruction through sweeping epidemics, involving illness and extensive deaths. Many Native American tribes experienced great depopulation, averaging 25–50 percent of the tribe members.

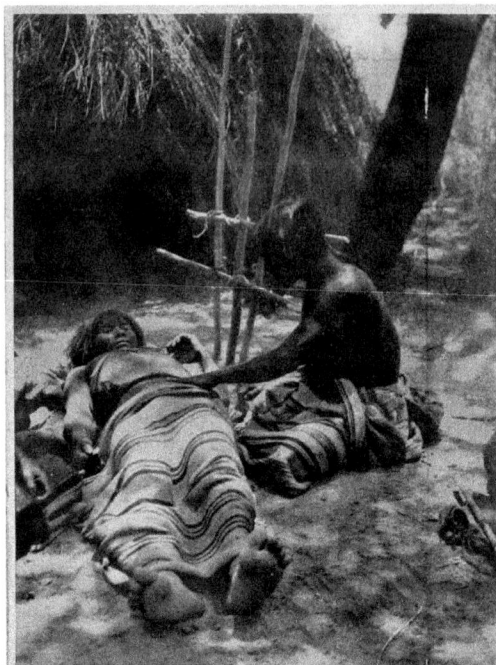

TREATMENT OF INVALIDS, ASHLUSLAY INDIANS.

The medicine-man rubs over the parts of the body which are ailing. In the background is to be seen the primitive invalid chair. It is made of three beams fixed in the ground and fastened together by cross-pieces. The invalid sits on the ground, leaning against these props, so as to rest himself.

Ashluslay Indian medicine man examining a sick patient, South America.
Photograph E. Nordenskjold. Library reference: ICV No 16280L
(Under Creative Commons Attribution S-A 4.0)

Slave trading was proven to be so profitable that Carolina English and Scottish slave traders and their Indian allies pushed themselves deep into Spanish and French territories looking for more captives.

The Native American Slave Trade was a vast enterprise that stretched as far west as Spanish New Mexico to as far North as the Great Lakes. Virtually every tribe living in these large areas like the Apalachee, Pawnee, Natchez, Choctaw, Osage, Nanzatico, Powhatan, Pequot, Wampanoag, Iroquois, Yamasee, Guale, Timucua, Cado, Wichita, Lipan, Natchez, Creek, and Westo were involved in this commerce either as a supplier of captives or middlemen.

178

Some of the first counts of slaves came through the lower parts of Louisiana like the Washa, Chawasha, Chitimacha tribes that went to Mobile. The primary source of slaves came out of the West. Many Indigenous Nations suffered due to enslavement. On the Atlantic seaboard, entire tribes were sold into slavery in the Caribbean. The Native Americans were another convenient source of free labor just like the Africans.

Indian slaves were shipped from ports like Mobile, Louisiana, and New Orleans. The English sent them to Barbados, French sent them to Martinique and Guadalupe, and the Dutch sent them to the Antilles. In 1636, about 300 men, women, and children were burned alive because of long-standing tensions between the Puritan English of Connecticut and Massachusetts Bay colonies and the Pequot. It escalated into open warfare. There was much confusion on both sides and when the tribe killed an Englishman thinking he was Dutch, the war was soon upon them.

The Mohegan and the Narragansett sided with the English. 1,500 Pequot were killed in battles or hunted down. Others were captured and distributed as slaves or household servants. A few escaped and were absorbed by the Mohawk or the Niantic on Long Island. Eventually, some returned to their traditional lands, where family groups of "friendly" Pequots had stayed. Of those enslaved, most were awarded to the allied tribes, but many were also sold as slaves in Bermuda. The Mohegan, in particular, treated their Pequot captives so severely that colonial officials of Connecticut Colony eventually removed them.

The Pequot tribe was sold out of the country to be enslaved in Bermuda. They also reached Europe, Bahamas, and New England. The first Indian slaves sent to Europe were the property of the King, Queen, and the church. They became wards of the state and property to people.

In April 1704, the Nanzatico complained to the House of Burgesses that English settlers were encroaching onto their remaining enclave, on both sides of the river. These complaints were never acted upon by the Virginia Colony. On August 30, a war party of ten Nanzatico men killed one of the encroaching settlers, John Rowley and his family. The tribe was told to tell the authorities who did it. The tribe told what men did the crime and then a colonial militia of Richmond County, Virginia hunted down and captured 49 Nanzaticos and tried them for murder.

Five men were hanged for the murder, and all the other Nanzaticos over age 12 were sold into slavery in the West Indies under a 1665 law that held communities responsible for any murders of English settlers. Children were forced to work as servants for officials of the Virginia Colony even though they cooperated and had nothing to do with the killings.

The English court system decided the whole Nanzatico tribe must pay. So the entire tribe was sold into slavery and sent to colonies in the Caribbean.

The Westo Indians and Native American slavery

Deuteronomy 28:32: *"Thy sons and thy daughters shall be given unto another people, and thine eyes shall look, and fail with longing for them all, the day long: and there shall be no might in thine hand."*

Native American Indians of the Columbia Plateau on horses in front of tipis, 1908. Author Benjamin A. Gifford

Sitting Bull - Teton Dakota Indian chief under whom the Sioux tribes united

Sitting Bull

The greatest records of Native American Slavery came from the Catholic Church. Many records show that the Native American Indians have been enslaved up into the 18th century. This is when they started to use the Africans instead.

The English found out that the Native Indians did not make good slaves because Indians caused a lot of trouble. In Barbados, they called a deportation of Indians. In 1676, Barbados issued an act prohibiting the use of Indian slaves. They felt the Native Americans were way too subtle, bloody, and dangerous to remain there.

This is when they started to look to Africans for slave labor due to wars and deportations with the Native Americans, but through this transition intermixing began with the Africans and Native American Indians. Mixed race offspring soon became people of color and the Indian identity soon disappeared.

They started calling this mix of people Mustic, Mulatto, Mestizo, and anything but Indian. They wanted to erase Indians from the record. They did not want a Native American presence. Even slave names were changed to European sounding names. Since the slave records changed people could not tell the true ethnicity of the slave being traded. The English found that what they could not accomplish with a torch and a gun they did accomplish with a stroke of a pen. This started in the 20th century when many records were altered in Virginia.

A man by the name of Walter Plecker began a racist crusade against Virginia's Native Americans and started to change records belonging to the Native Americans. Instead of saying they were 'Indian' he would put 'colored.' He did this on birth, death, marriage certificates, and on any record he could get his hands on. If you were recorded as Native Indian the record would be changed to 'colored.' This was how Indians were erased out of history and became invisible minorities.

So Native American and African American identity have been stolen. There are many African Americans today that are also of Native American descent and this is a recorded fact. There was a time when families were scared to say they were Native American because they wanted to protect themselves and their children. Even on many documents you were only able to check the box either for being 'white' or 'black.' There was no choice for Native American because they were pushed out completely.

When the senses came, they made the decision to put down what they thought you were rather than the truth. The Catholic records would also show that the Native Americans and African Americans would take on Catholic names like Maryann, Hector, John, Genevieve, Mary, Teresa and other names so they would not know the prior names or ethnicity of the person who were being enslaved.

The English alone sold over 50,000 slaves from 1650 to the 18th century. There were a lot more who were uncounted due to the heavy taxations.

A photo of enslaved Amazon Indians
From the 1912 book "The Putumayo, the Devil's Paradise"
Credit W Hardenberg

The earliest record of African and Native American contact occurred in April 1502, when Spanish explorers brought an African slave with them. In the early colonial days, Native Americans were enslaved along with Africans. They worked together, lived together in communal quarters, produced collective recipes for food, shared herbal remedies, myths and legends, and in the end they intermarried because both races were non-Christian. Europeans considered them to be inferior to Europeans. They worked to make enemies of the two groups.

In some areas, Native Americans began to slowly absorb the white culture and while Native Americans were fighting for their land from encroaching settlers, Africans were being captured and brought to America to be enslaved. Due to ignorance, prejudice, and racial hostility, the U.S. Government attempted to force American Indians with African heritage, as well as all American Indians, to reject their heritage.
(From Wikipedia Encyclopedia)

The family of Mixed African American and Native American heritage. The Oklahoma Historical Society has this image in their American Indian archives and lists the people as being from the Czarina Conlan Collection Photographs. Cheyenne Indians - (L. To R.): Mrs. Amos Chapman, her daughter Mrs. Lee Moore as an infant, Mrs. Chapman's sister, and an unidentified young black girl. Photo by "Soule View Artist". 1886. [2554].)

Black-Indian Diana Fletcher
(B. 1838) African-Seminole
Who joined the Kiowa tribe

Miskito Indians living along the Prinzapolka river in Nicaragua.
1957-1961

Seminole's were also known as black runaway slaves that escaped and lived amongst an Indian Tribe and intermixed.

We may not have all the answers, but one thing we do know is that the so-called African Americans and Native Americans, both fit the biblical prophecies of going into slavery by ships. These two great nations of people have also intermixed and shared the same curses in Deuteronomy 28. Many are a part of the twelve Tribes of Israel. Some people may say that they do not believe that the Native Americans are a part of the twelve Tribes of Israel.

Let's read what the Holy Bible says:

"And they assembled all the congregation together on the first day of the second month, <u>and they declared their pedigrees after their families, by the house of their fathers</u>, according to the number of the names, from twenty years old and upward, by their polls."
                          -    **Numbers 1:18 KJV**

Pedigree Definition:
 A line of ancestors; a lineage.
A list of ancestors; a family tree.
A chart of an individual's ancestors used in human genetics to analyze Mendelian inheritance.

        We know through historical fact that African Americans and Native Americans have intermixed and in God's written word it says in Numbers 1:18 that a person's lineage went also by the house of the father so if the father is an Israelite then so is his children.

"Take ye the sum of all the congregation of the children of Israel, after their families, <u>by the house of their fathers</u>, with the number of their names, every male by their polls."
                          -    **Numbers 1:2 KJV**

"And the LORD spake unto Moses, saying, Speak unto the children of Israel, and bid them that they make them fringes in the borders of their garments throughout their generations, and that they put upon the fringe of the borders a ribband of blue."
                          -    **Numbers 15:37-39**

Native Indians also wore fringes (Library Photo Info Unknown)

Source: The Untold Legacy of Native American Slavery Written out of History.

Written out of History blends historical facts with accounts of the forgotten legacy of Native American slavery and is written by Indigenous scholars and anthropologists. Check out the video by Max Carocci and Simona Piantieri:

(https://vimeo.com/11927488)

Black Indians of Wampanoag and African Heritage:
https://www.youtube.com/watch?v=qzrh5_ou-7c

African, Native Americans in Indian Country; "Black Indians:"
https://www.youtube.com/watch?v=qzrh5_ou-7c

Secret Ancient American History:
https://www.youtube.com/watch?v=g1c3L0qfNko

Some Symbols used by Indians in decorating Silverware, Pottery, Jewelry, Rugs, etc. 67144 G41

	Symbol	Meaning		Symbol	Meaning
	Sun Symbols	Life		Man, Woman	Human Life
	Clouds, Rain Clouds	Rain		Thunderbird	Plenty
	Moon "Nezheh"	Female		Horse	Journey
	Lightning	Speed		Dog	Fidelity
	Rain	Prosperity		Snake	Wisdom
	Running Water. Rivers, etc.	Same as Rain		Man on Horseback	Warrior
				Butterfly	Fertility
	Mountains	Majesty		Deer	Speed
	Rainbows	Happiness		Lizard	Rain
	4 Directions Paths Crossing			Bear	Strength
	Star	Night		Tree	Age
	Arrow	War		Cactus	Desert
	Crossed Arrows	Friendship		Cactus Flower	Beauty
	Broken Arrow	Peace		Corn	Food
	Teepee	Home		Corn Maiden	Divinity
	Head-dress	Dance		Squash	Food
	Feathers	Prayer		Squash Blossom	Courtship
	Hammer, Axe	Work		Seeds	Male
	Rope	Security		Leaves	Lightness
	All-Seeing Eye			Vine	Tenderness

An Indian Silversmith

67144

Some symbols used by Indians in decorating silverware, pottery, jewelry, rugs, etc. An Indian silversmith
By Southwest Arts & Crafts, Santa Fe, New Mexico; Tichnor Bros. Inc., Boston, Mass. 1930 - 1945

Kuna Indian sewing in Panama   Ouray - Chief of the Utes

Earth teach me freedom as the eagle, which soars in the sky Earth teach me regeneration as the seed which rises in the spring. Earth teach me to forget myself as melted snow forgets its life. Earth teach me to remember kindness as dry fields weep with rain. - Ute Prayer

188

Black Wall Street

"A Hidden Story"
(Date: May 31-June 1,1921)

One of the most violent race riots happened in Tulsa, Oklahoma. It happened in June of 1921 and history does not mention it. I find this information very important because African Americans are shown in movies as slaves, thugs, or prisoners. I can turn on the news tonight and I am bombarded with black on black crimes or another African American being killed unjustly as if that's all they can contribute. African Americans are one of the greatest nations on the planet. Many do not like to talk about the black holocaust that happened in Tulsa, Oklahoma in 1921.

In 1906, O.W. Gurley, a wealthy African American from Arkansas, moved to Tulsa and purchased over 40 acres of land. Gurley also used the area to give refuge to African Americans that were running from the harsh oppression of Mississippi.

I love knowing what my sisters and brothers had built and created in Tulsa, Oklahoma. They had built a Black Beverly Hills. They had all black-owned businesses and they owned commercial properties despite the odds against them, and the previous history of being enslaved.

Many Black Americans moved to Oklahoma in the years before and after 1907, which is the year Oklahoma became a state. In the early 1900s, Tulsa, Oklahoma experienced a major oil boom, attracting thousands. This was a place to get away from slavery and a chance for black Americans to get away from the harsh racism of their previous homes. Most of them traveled from other states, and Oklahoma offered hope and provided all people with a chance to start over. They traveled to Oklahoma by wagons, horses, trains, and even on foot. Many of the black Americans who traveled to Oklahoma had ancestors who could be traced back to Oklahoma. A lot of the settlers were relatives of black Americans who had traveled on foot with the five Civilized Tribes along the Trail of Tears. Others were the descendants of people who had fled to Indian Territory. Many Black residents were also from the various Muskogee-speaking peoples, such Creeks, Seminoles, and the Yuchi, while some had been adopted by the tribe after the Emancipation Proclamation.

They were able to live freely in the Oklahoma Territory. With the Jim Crow laws, the blacks were free but segregated from the Europeans. They were divided in one great city with Europeans on one side of the tracks and blacks on the other.

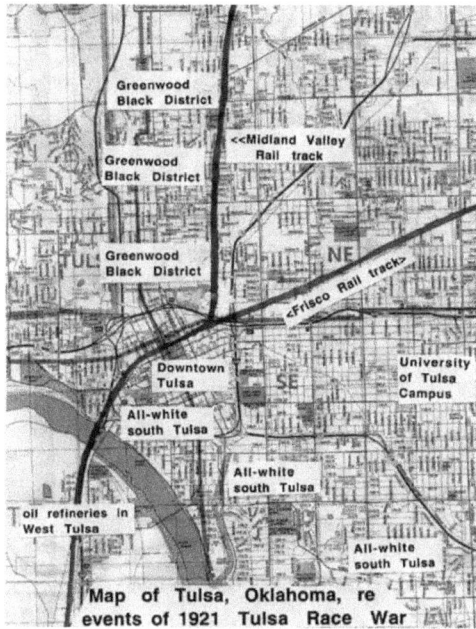
Map of Tulsa, Oklahoma, re
events of 1921 Tulsa Race War

The blacks had to pull up their bootstraps to make a life for themselves and they did. They started building in their own communities and so the money stayed in their community and started to quickly grow. This allowed them to continue building and venture out and establish 600 businesses. They had 21 restaurants, 30 grocery stores, 2 movie theaters, a hospital, a bank, a post office, libraries, schools, law offices, 6 private airplanes, a bus system, 21 churches and so much more.

Black Wall Street

Black Wall Street was no different than all the great upscale stores you see today. The only difference was they were all black-owned and ran by black people in their own community. When Tulsa became a booming and rather well-noted town in the United States, many people considered Tulsa to be two separate cities rather than one city united. The European residents of Tulsa referred to the area north of the Frisco railroad tracks as "Little Africa." This community later acquired the name Greenwood and by 1921 it was home to about 10,000 black residents.

People in Tulsa Were Leading in Luxury Possessions

In a time when the entire state of Oklahoma had only two airports, six Black families owned their own planes. The average income for a Black family was well over what minimum wage is today. Dr. Simon Berry, who owned the bus system in Tulsa, recalls that in 1910 his average income was around $500 a day, according to reports from sfbayview.com

They had strong black-owned businesses that prospered. The money in this black community did not turn over. It would take a year before the money went out of the community. This was good strong, honest black-owned businesses that were just thriving. Many people today, despite the evidence, will not believe that such atrocities happened in America not very long ago.

In 1921 Tulsa, Oklahoma was known as the Oil Capital of the World. It had a population of about 100,000, with a chamber of commerce, an Opera House, and a petroleum club. The Ku Klux Klan hated blacks let alone black communities that were doing very well for themselves and by themselves. The Ku Klux Klan hated to see beautiful communities ran by professional black people who lived in nice mansions and homes overlooking their great city.

Black Wall Street Business Owners
Creative Commons Attribution 4.0 License
http://creativecommons.org/licenses/by/4.0/

The theater was owned by Loula who had several theaters. Here the community enjoyed films and musicals. The theater seated over 700 people.

The damage to the Williams Dreamland Theatre in Greenwood,
Tulsa Historical Society

When thousands of European men came back from World War I and could not find jobs the Ku Klux Klan would enlist these men and blame their problems on the Jews, African Americans, and Catholics. So what happened to this beautiful black thriving community?

Tulsa was a segregated city where Jim Crow practices were in effect. Black people were not allowed to use toilet facilities used by Europeans and there was no separate facility for blacks at the shine parlor where Dick Rowland, an African-American teenage shoe shiner worked. The owner had arranged for black employees to use a segregated "Colored" restroom on the top floor of the nearby Drexel Building at 319 S. Main Street.

On May 30, 1921 Rowland attempted to enter the Drexel building elevator and as he entered he did not look down and because of the unevenness of both floors, he stumbled and, trying to save himself from falling, he touched the arm of a 17-year-old European woman, Sarah Page who was the elevator operator. Startled, the elevator operator screamed and Rowland freaked out and in fear ran out the elevator and the building.

The European clerk in a first-floor store called the police to report Rowland fleeing from the elevator and the building. The clerk on the first floor reported the incident as an attempted assault. They said Sarah had scratches on her hands and face. They tried to paint a picture of Sarah Page as this orphan girl working to pay her way through college as an elevator operator and was assaulted by a Negro when later they found out she was not an orphan girl. She had deserted her husband two months before and was going through a divorce and had not one scratch on her.

Rowland was arrested the following day. The Tulsa Tribune printed a front page story of this event, saying "Nab Negro for Attacking Girl In an Elevator".

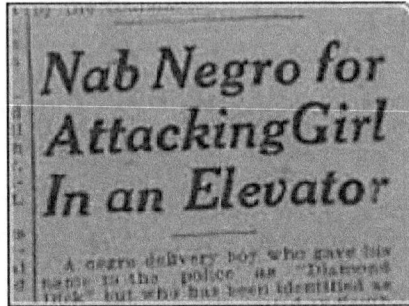

According to some witnesses, the same edition of the Tribune included an editorial warning of a potential lynching of Rowland and entitled "To Lynch Negro Tonight." All original copies of that issue of the paper have apparently been destroyed, and the relevant page is missing from the microfilm copy.

After news articles were released not an hour later lynch talk hit the streets and by evening European crowds gathered around the courthouse and the burning cross became viable by the Ku Klux Klan who was looking for any excuse to kill and destroy what they hated most: black people. During this time two black people a week were being lynched by Europeans. This was a Ku Klux Klan practice.

Many Tulsa blacks were veterans of World War I and armed. A group went to the courthouse and offered to help defend the jail and the prisoner. The sheriff told them to go home and everything would be alright. As the men began to walk away a European man walked up to the tall black vet and says to him, "where are you going with that gun, Nigger" and he replied, "I am going to use it if I have to" and the man says "like hell you give it to me." A struggle started and a shot went off and the worst riot started in American History.

Many of the residents left town and others stayed to fight. It was a block by block battle. It was horrible. People opened fire on each other as many died on the spot. The Europeans went into black homes and after looting the home they then set fire to them. The authorities came in and started arresting some blacks and others were taken to far out places so they could not defend their families or protect their businesses.

National Guard and wounded during 1921 Tulsa race riots.
This caption claims that the wounded are being taken to the Brady theater. Creative Commons Attribution 4.0 License http://creativecommons.org/licenses/by/4.0/

A black man said he remembers the day. He hid his wife and his five children in the attic right when the European authorities came to his door. He could hear them say, "Nigger, do you have a gun," and the man replied, "no, don't set my house on fire, please" and the authorities left and minutes after his home was set on fire and the man had to scramble out before he died.

This was a hate crime. The young man who fell into the elevator was innocent. The Europeans were looking for an excuse to destroy the blacks. They were very jealous because the black men also served in the military but they had jobs and built successful businesses waiting for them when they returned home. The blacks never had it easy. They worked extra hard because of segregation and since they were limited. It was unbelievable that they were able to build 600 businesses.

Black Wall Street 1921

The Europeans wanted them to fail by not investing in their businesses. But blacks were flourishing and prospering and raising up beautiful families. The Europeans hated that the black families were united, running successful businesses, and had children that were going to school to be well educated. The young black boys wore suits and ties to school and the young ladies wore dresses.

The Europeans were looking for a way to destroy them. During this riot their hate for blacks was very evident and they started dropping bombs from the air down onto this black community.

Black Wall Street in flames, June 1921 The "Little Africa" section of Tulsa, OK in flames during the 1921 race riot.
Creative Commons Attribution 4.0 License http://creativecommons.org/licenses/by/4.0/

Can you believe this? The riot fires were caused by Europeans dropping explosives from World War I planes. They purposely destroyed every home and business in Greenwood, 35 square blocks. In all, everything was burned and damaged. Can you believe that instead of being happy that blacks complemented and participated in growing Tulsa into being a great flourishing town they hated them for it? These poor, innocent families lost their homes and businesses all because of hate, jealousy, racism, and envy.

Later in that day, martial law was declared and National Guard troops patrolled the streets. The dead were everywhere, bodies were lying where they fell. Photographers turned these pictures into souvenir postcards.

Most were buried quickly in unmarked graves around town. There were no funerals because the European authorities outlawed them. There were no coffins, headstones, and no records of the burials but a ten-year-old boy saw it all. Clyde Eddy saw some men digging. He saw these big wooden crates. He walked over and opened the door to the crate and saw three black men laying in it. He then walked over to a larger crate and opened the lid on it. Four black bodies were thrown in it as well. He saw many other wooden crates. A man saw Clyde looking at the crates and ran him out.

The National Guard report said 88 were wounded and 35 died during the riot. Witnesses knew that the numbers of deaths were untrue. The American Red Cross estimated that over 300 persons were killed. The Red Cross also listed 8,624 persons in need of assistance, in excess of 1,200 homes and businesses destroyed, and the delivery of several stillborn infants. Not to forget that 10,000 blacks were left homeless by the riot, but zero Europeans were homeless.

Black Wall Street left desolate after the riot in 1921

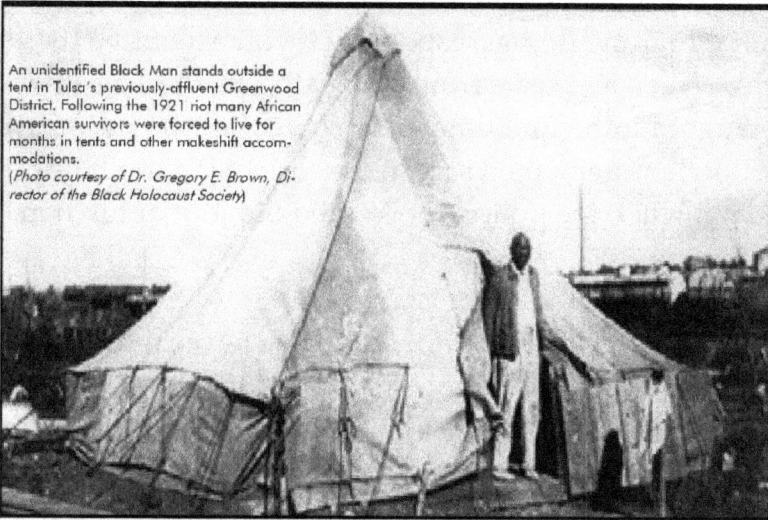

An unidentified Black Man stands outside a tent in Tulsa's previously-affluent Greenwood District. Following the 1921 riot many African American survivors were forced to live for months in tents and other makeshift accommodations.
(Photo courtesy of Dr. Gregory E. Brown, Director of the Black Holocaust Society)

Due to the loss of their homes, many were forced to endure winter living in tents.

The survivors lived in tents and shacks they built themselves and it was funded by the Red Cross. The city said they were going to rebuild Greenwood but they lied. Not a dime was given to rebuild a city they destroyed. Just to keep the blacks out there was a bill that was passed stating you cannot rebuild on a land that had been previously burned. All black insurance claims were rejected. No one wanted to admit that the riot in Tulsa really happened. Many tried to cover this history up like they did the history of the Native Americans.

A man by the name of Bill Graves, a state representative at that time, had opposed setting up a commission to pay back and to help the surviving families of the Tulsa riot. He made a chilling statement saying: "The sons do not pay for the sins of the fathers, only for their own sins." He smiled and then went on to say we need to put the past where it belongs. I only have one thing to say to all who feel as he does: "tell God that," because guess what? We will all go before God on judgment day and God will judge us by how we treated one another.

201

This is why we all must examine our hearts and repent for all our wrong doings, especially if you benefitted by the deaths, sweat, and tears from our brethren. The Tulsa Race Riot was taught for the first time in Tulsa public schools in 2012. Dick Rowland remained safe in the county jail until the next morning, when the police transported him out of town in secrecy.

All charges were dropped and he never returned to Tulsa. No reparations have been paid to those who lost their homes and businesses. An all-European jury found Black Tulsans responsible for the attack. They declared the land that belonged to the owners of Black Wall Street a fire zone and not long after the city put the land up for sale. The Mayor and city commissioner started a half million dollar building fund.

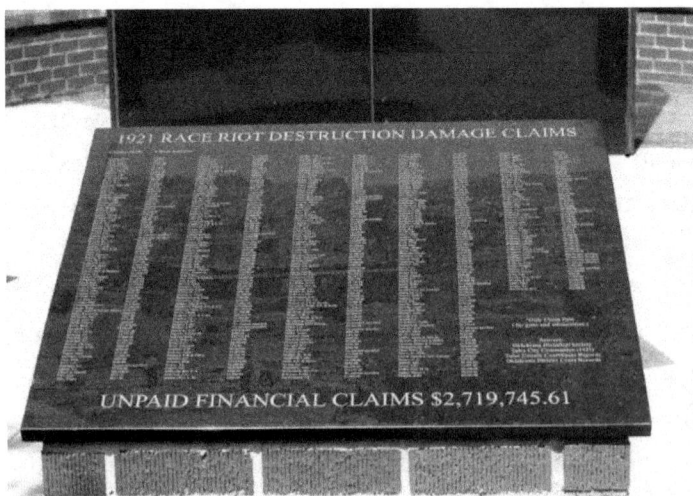

Source: Black Wall Street: Tulsa's Dirty Little Secret Riot

https://www.youtube.com/watch?v=ivCODTY7fmQ
https://en.wikipedia.org/wiki/Tulsa_race_riot
https://www.youtube.com/watch?v=YAhxUgYaalU

The Twelve Tribes of Israel

Over 4000 years ago, God told Abraham to get out of the country, and from his kindred, and from his father's house, and go into a land that God will show him **(Genesis 12:1-2).** And God said He would make Abraham a great nation so Abraham listened to God and went into the Promised Land of Canaan where he lived with his son Isaac and grandson Jacob. Jacob's name was later renamed Israel. The names of the twelve sons are Reuben, Gad, Benjamin, Joseph, Naphtali, Asher, Dan, Issachar, Zebulon, Judah, Levi, and Simeon.

Israel and his twelve sons went down to Egypt because they had a famine. They ended up staying in the land and they multiplied and became a great nation in Egypt, but then the Egyptians felt threatened that Israel was becoming a powerful nation so they decided to enslave them to gain control and to keep Egyptian rulership. They made it hard for the Israelites by putting them into hard bondage and heavy labor for over 400 years.

Moses led them out of bondage and then crossed the Red Sea, where they received the Moral Laws of God on Mount Sinai. The laws are also called the Ten Commandments. When the generation of Israelites would not obey God, they were not allowed to see the Promised Land along with Moses because of their on-going lack of faith in God. They ended up wandering in the wilderness for forty years until a new generation rose up that trusted the Lord and entered the Promised Land with Joshua.

For about 400 years the twelve Tribes of Israel were ruled by the judges according to the Law of Moses, but the Israelites desired to have a King to judge them like all the other nations **(1 Samuel 8:5).** So Saul became their King and reigned over them for about forty years, followed by King David who also reigned forty years. Then David's son Solomon reigned for forty years. Now during the reign of Solomon, Israel was at its most glorious and the first temple was built, but Solomon's heart turned away from the Lord. God told Solomon that ten tribes would not be ruled by his son. So after the death of Soloman, the Kingdom of Israel was divided. The Northern Kingdom, which were the ten tribes, were ruled by different wicked kings who were not descendants of David but they retained the name of Israel and Samaria was their capital city.

The smaller Southern Kingdom were two tribes. They were called Judah, Jerusalem was their capital, and they were ruled over by the descendants of David. The people of the Southern Kingdom became known as Jews after the name of the Kingdom of Judah. The Northern Kingdom began to become wicked and because of their wickedness they were overthrown and taken captive by the Assyrians. The Israelites intermingled with the other heathen nations that occupied the land. These people were known as the Samaritans.

The ten tribes of Northern Israel would never be a nation again. Now the Southern Kingdom of Judah would eventually be taken as captives into Babylon as a punishment for serving other gods and the temple would be destroyed. After seventy years, the Jews returned and rebuilt the temple in Jerusalem and continued to be ruled by King David's descendants. At the time of Christ, the Nation of Judah had become known as Judea and was under Roman rulership.

Jesus Christ and His disciples preached the Gospel throughout Judea and sought after the lost sheep of the house of Israel after 3 1/2 years of ministry. The Jews rejected Jesus as their Lord and Savior (Messiah) and convinced the Roman governor to crucify Him. Three days later, Jesus rose again and Jesus showed Himself alive to all His disciples before, ascending up to the right hand of the Father in heaven.

Before Jesus was crucified, He prophesied that as a punishment for rejecting Him they would be led away captive into all nations and Jerusalem would be burned down and the temple would be destroyed. This prophecy was fulfilled in 70 AD when Titus conquered Jerusalem. For over 1800 years, the Jews remained scattered among all nations.

"Those are the ten tribes, which were carried away prisoners out of their own land in the time of Osea the king, whom Salmanasar the king of Assyria led away captive, and he carried them over the waters, and so came they into another land. But they took this counsel among themselves, that they would leave the multitude of the heathen, and go forth into a further country, where never mankind dwelt, That they might there keep their statutes, which they never kept in their own land. And they entered into Euphrates by the narrow places of the river. For the most High then shewed signs for them, and held still the flood, till they were passed over. For through that country, there was a great way to go, namely, of a year and a half and the same region is called Arsareth (2 Esdras 13: 40- 47)*

ARZARETH: The name of the land beyond the great river, far away from the habitation of man, in which the Ten Tribes of Israel will dwell, observing the laws of Moses, until the time of the restoration, according to IV Esd. xiii. 45. Columbus identified America with this land. (Jewish Encyclopedia)
Source: - http://www.jewishencyclopedia.com/articles/1867-arzareth

The Great Deception

In 1948, the State of Israel was founded and the Jews once again possessed the Promised Land. Many Christians proclaimed this as a miracle and a blessing from God. But was it really or was something else going on as people celebrated with blinders on?

Once the Jews were dispersed to the four corners of the earth the nature of Judaism was changed and began to be a religion of the Rabbis and of their traditions. It stopped being the religion of the Old Testament and no longer based on the Holy Bible. Many people in the Jewish religion now use what they call the oral Torah. They use their own books that are referred to as the Talmud, which they say is the Holy Book of the Jews. These are the oral sayings of the Rabbis and not the Word of God.

It's known as the wisdom of the Rabbi which means the wisdom of men and not God's word. It's an Encyclopedia of Jewish knowledge. It's a Jewish Wikipedia of the ages. Several hundred authors have had their hands in it and they believe the Talmud is inspired by God, even though the Talmud has a book that says Jesus was a Sorcerer, Sanhedrin 43a. It calls Jesus "Yeshu" and in footnote #6, Yeshu "the Nazarene" and said He was executed because He practiced sorcery. The Talmud has nothing to do with scripture or the word of God because they do not believe in the Torah, the five books of Moses. They believe in the traditions of the elders.

"Howbeit in vain do they worship me, teaching for doctrines the commandments of men." **Mark 7:7**

The Talmud is the doctrine of men. They have over thirty volumes. If Christians knew what was in the Talmud it would make them angry to read all the unkind things that are said about the Gentiles and our Lord and Savior.

The Talmud was written hundreds of years after Jesus Christ lived on the earth. In the Talmud, they call Jesus a bastard and said He learned black magic in Egypt and this was how He performed miracles. We know this is a lie. They hide all of these writings in the Talmud by writing it in Hebrew so if you do not read Hebrew you would not be able to understand what is written.

It is really frustrating that some Christian organizations send money to Israel and fund these Jewish Rabbis that have hidden agendas thinking they love Jesus and not knowing they hate Our Lord and Savior Jesus Christ. Get the book "Jesus In The Talmud." They said Jesus was born to a whore. They call Mary, Jesus's mother, a whore and go on to call Jesus a fool. The Talmud gloats about Jesus being crucified, saying Jesus got what He deserved. These men are evil and hateful. They are unbelievers and to continue to support them It is nothing less than insane.

Messianic Jewish people want to make the Talmud Christian as if that would ever happen with all these recorded lies about our Lord and Savior Jesus Christ. The Talmud goes on to say that Jesus Christ is burning in hell today. Can you believe this nonsense? They also believe that the New Testament is a wonderful book of myths. They do not believe there is a hell either, so basically not all but many of the Jewish people do not believe in the Holy Bible period, not even the Torah.

Many Christians believe that they have to bless Israel to get a blessing. They use this scripture in **Genesis 12:1-3:**

"Now the LORD had said unto Abram, Get thee out of thy country, and from thy kindred, and from thy father's house, unto a land that I will shew thee: And I will make of thee a great nation, and I will bless thee, and make thy name great; and thou shalt be a blessing: And I will bless them that bless thee, and curse him that curseth thee: and in thee shall all families of the earth be blessed."

First of all, God is talking to Abraham. 'Thee' is singular and means Abraham, that He will bless Abraham.

Also in **Galatians 3:16** it says: *"Now to Abraham and his seed were the promises made. He saith not, And to seeds, as of many, but as of one, And to thy seed, which is Christ."*

The blessing is onto Abraham and Our Lord and Savior Jesus Christ. Now when we say we are heirs onto Christ let's read that scripture in Galatians 3:29. It says: *"And if ye be Christ's then ye Abraham's seed and heirs according to the promise."*

So this scripture makes it clear that we must be believers. We just read about these unbelievers in the Middle East and the Jewish people that are in the land of Israel that are not Christians. They put their faith in the Talmud. They are not in Christ and most of them do not believe in Jesus Christ. Christians need to wake up from sleep and follow scripture and not these false prophets. The promise is on to the Israelites who are scattered all over the world. Not just Israel.

"James, a servant of God and of the Lord Jesus Christ, to the twelve tribes which are scattered abroad, greeting."

- James 1:1

We see in scripture according to **James 1:1** that the twelve Tribes of Israel are all scattered outside of their previous home (Israel) and this is what abroad means, to be outside of your home, area and among the other nations. This means there is more than one nation of people, but yet the focus is always in Israel.

The twelve tribes will be united and brought back to the land when Christ comes back so the logic of sending money to converts and ignoring what the Bible is really saying makes no sense. I am not against Jewish people. I am against the trickery and money being sent under false pretenses. They are not all in Christ Jesus so they are not the seed of Abraham. If you want the blessing keep God's commandments and obey God.

In late 1800, persecution of the Jews in Russia and elsewhere intensified. They felt the only way to prosper would be to have a state of their own. This belief became known as Zionism. A man by the name of Theodore Hertzel founded Zionism. He came to the idea that the cause of Anti-Semitism was because the Jewish did not have a state of their own. He wrote a little book called the *State of the Jews*. He said the only way that the Jewish people can be protected was to leave Europe and settle in their own land, the land of Israel. Hertzel's book became like the Bible of Zionism.

Zionism was the hope for the rebirth. It started with World War I and "The Balfour Declaration." This was a major document and a letter in regards to British policies. In World War I, Turkey was an ally of Germany, who was on the losing side. So the Turkish Ottoman Empire was dismantled and the British Lord Balfour wrote a declaration saying it should be a homeland for the Jewish.

So tens of thousands of Jewish people came mainly from eastern Europe and they went to settle in Israel. The Balfour Declaration was a letter written to Lord Rothschild so in order to understand "The Balfour Declaration" you have to know who Rothschild was. Mayer Amschel Bauer was a money lender and a goldsmith. He later changed his name to Rothschild. Rothschild soon learned that loaning money to governments and kings was more profitable than loaning money to private individuals. Not only were the loans bigger but they were secured by the nation's taxes. Mayer Rothschild had five sons who he trained in the skills of money creation.

Mayer Rothschild told his five sons to open banks in different countries so they did. They opened banks in London, Paris, Frankfurt, Naples, and Vienna. He told his sons that there will be many wars in Europe and in other nations so money would need to be transported. Having banks in different locations would be wise and people would go through the Rothschild's for money loans because it would be safe. He told his sons to always work together and this would be their power.

When Mayer Rothschild died, he left a will instructing his sons on how to continue to operate his legacy. He said all key positions in the House of Rothschild were to be held by members of the family. The family was to intermarry with their own first and second cousins, thus preserving the vast fortune. Rothschild's heirs were strictly forbidden from ever disclosing the amount of their wealth. The whole family was driven by the lust for money and power. They financed European wars and dominated European banking. By the mid-1800 they were the richest family in the world.

In 1947, the United Nations declared that there would be two states: a Jewish State and a Palestine State. So Israel became a state, but did not allow Palestine to become a state. Then in 1948, they established Israel to become a Jewish State. A new Government came in and they now have a nation of their own.

The problem is that throughout the Bible all who had unbelief in God were always taken out of the land or not allowed to go in so knowing that many do not believe in Jesus Christ tells us that God did not bring these people in the land. It was the United Nations that brought these people into the Holy Land. They even designed a state flag with a six-point star on it, they call it a symbol of hope. Some call the symbol the Star of David. Some even wear this symbol around their neck. This is nowhere in the Bible. There is no passage about the Star of David. The strange thing is that when people would turn away from God and worship other gods the only star they talk about is the star of Remphan.

Let's read the Biblical text:

"You also took up the tabernacle of Moloch, And the star of your god Remphan, Images which you made to worship And I will carry you away beyond Babylon." **Acts 7:43**

In the Bible, it mentioned how they would turn away from God and worship these other gods. They would even sacrifice their children to these gods by burning them and God would become very angry.

Here is another text that talks about a star that refers to other gods:

"But ye have borne the tabernacle of your Moloch and Chiun your images, the star of your god, which ye made to yourselves. Therefore, will I cause you to go into captivity beyond Damascus, saith the Lord, whose name is The God of hosts."

- **Amos 5:26-27**

The Masons use the Star of David on the Masonic Temples because masonry is based on Judaism and the Kabala. They believe in the god of Moloch, the great architect known as the star god.

"Behold, I will make them of the synagogue of Satan, which say they are Jews, and are not, but do lie; behold, I will make them come and worship before thy feet, and to know that I have loved thee."
- **Revelations 3:9**

Not everyone who goes around and calls themselves a Jew is a follower of Christ. Do your homework and study the word of God for yourself and make sure that you're not worshipping other gods that God repeatedly warns us about.

"Study to shew thyself approved unto God, a workman that needeth not to be ashamed, rightly dividing the word of truth."
- **2 Timothy 2:15**

God examines our hearts and He knows if we are putting our faith in Him or idols.

"For he is not a Jew, which is one outwardly; neither is that circumcision, which is outward in the flesh But he is a Jew, which is one inwardly; and circumcision are that of the heart, in the spirit, and not in the letter; whose praise is not of men, but of God."

- **Romans 2:28-29**

Who is an Anti-Christ?

This following scripture makes it very clear how to tell who is an Anti-Christ, which means they do not believe that Jesus Christ is the Messiah. God loves all His children regardless of color, however you must be in Christ Jesus. Do not be fooled and let the deceiver lie and have you following a false God.

Christians believe in the second coming and most not all Jewish believe in the first coming and that Jesus never came the first time so they call Jesus a blasphemer and not the son of God.

"Who is a liar but he that denieth that Jesus is the Christ? He is the antichrist, that denieth the Father and the Son."
- **1 John 2:22**

"You are of your father the devil, and the desires of your father you want to do. He was a murderer from the beginning and does not stand in the truth because there is no truth in him. When he speaks a lie, he speaks from his own resources, for he is a liar and the father of it."
- **John 8:44**

"Whoever denies the Son does not have the Father either; he who acknowledges the Son has the Father also." **1 John 2:23**

"So all of Israel will not be saved only a person is a Jew, which is one inwardly not outward so we must learn to read all scripture, not just one line."
- **Romans 2:28-29**

The Anti-Christ wants mainstream Christianity to unite with all the non-believers and their false doctrines despite the rejection of Christ Jesus which is not even Biblical. The Anti-Christ, the devil, wants all believers in Jesus Christ to unite with the unbelievers so the Anti-Christ can transition into His seat and bring much more destruction. If anyone speaks negatively about the Jewish they call them an Anti-Semitic so they will back off and not bring truth to the people.

I will stand with the Jewish people in Israel who are in Christ Jesus and follow the clear teaching of the New Testament. I am not supporting anyone or any churches that are supporting an entrance for the Anti-Christ, period! They can call me whatever they want because at the end of the day only God can save me. The true Jew are God's chosen people, not these demons who bring their own teaching to pull God's children away from Him by discrediting God's word and His Doctrine of Truth.

Here is a really eye-opening scripture:

"Whosoever transgresseth and abideth not in the doctrine of Christ hath not God. He that abideth in the Doctrine of Christ he hath both the father and the son. If there come any unto you, and bring not this Doctrine receive him not into your house neither bid him God speed for he who bids him God speed is partaker of his evil deeds."
- **2 John 9-11**

This scripture clearly tells us that we are not to support the non-believers or we will have God's wrath come upon us. This scripture also tells us not to help finance these false teachers because you become a part of helping a false doctrine continue to go forth and deceive God's people.

216

Some believe we do not need to evangelize the non-believing Jewish person which is a lie. We must win the lost regardless.

"God says He that believeth on the son hath everlasting life, and he that believeth not the son shall not see life but the wrath of God abideth on him."

- John 3:36

There is hope to win the lost and there are many Jewish people who have turned away from man and are now following Jesus Christ. We do not need to support the non-believers and their actions of destruction and turning away from God. Again, I am talking about the ones who do not believe. I know that there are believers in Christ Jesus in Israel who are Jewish. I am only speaking of the non-believers that hate Jesus Christ.

If you want to convert to becoming Jewish the first thing you have to do is renounce from Christianity and Jesus Christ and go through unbiblical rituals to cleanse you from your previous religion. This is a rule. Now would a true or real ambassador of Jesus Christ renounce the Messiah? It is said you cannot be a Jewish and a Christian. It is one or the other.

I know people would much rather stay in a lie then to "Poke The Bear" they fear being attacked when the reason there is no peace is because of these lies and many false doctrines going forth. If you go to Israel, it is illegal to even pass out tracts in certain areas. You may even get arrested because they do not all believe in Jesus Christ. The ones who do not believe are the enemies of the gospel.

Tel Aviv is voted the number one gay city in the world amongst the gay community, not San Francisco or New York but Tel Aviv.

The Jerusalem gay pride parade is an annual pride parade taking place in Jerusalem. Since the first march for Pride and Tolerance in 2002, Jerusalem Pride—"Love Without Border"—has become an established event in Jerusalem, each year bringing in additional partners and supporters.

Tel Aviv was the first location in Israel were "gay" events were organized and also the first city in Israel to host a gay pride parade.

We must be careful with any new age teaching and images that have nothing to do with our Father of Abraham, Isaac, and Jacob.

Let's stay in prayer about God's will for our lives and trust in Him and His word that the Holy Spirit will always keep us discerning these false teachings. God loves all who are in Christ Jesus. However, if you are adding these false doctrines and teachings along with your spiritual walk you will soon fall back into being disobedient to God and following man's teachings, actually believing that you're doing what is right.

"For there is no difference between the Jew and the Greek for the same Lord over all is rich unto all that call upon him."
- **Romans 10:12**

"But avoid foolish questions, and genealogies, and contentions, and strivings about the law; for they are unprofitable and vain."
- **Titus 3:9**

"Neither gives heed to fables and endless genealogies, which minister questions, rather than godly edifying which is in faith: so do."
- **1 Timothy 1:4**

"Neither, because they are the seed of Abraham, are they all children but, In Isaac shall thy seed be called. That is, They which are the children of the flesh, these are not the children of God, but the children of the promise are counted for the seed."
- **Romans 9: 7-8**

God is saying that it is not our DNA that makes us children of God; it is our faith and our belief in Jesus Christ and not the people who are unbelievers but the people who know Jesus Christ as their Messiah. Amen to this!

"Know ye therefore that they which are of faith, the same are the children of Abraham." **Galatians 3:7**

"There is neither Jew nor Greek, there is neither bond nor free, there is neither male nor female: for ye are all one in Christ Jesus. And if ye be Christ's, then are ye Abraham's seed, and heirs according to the promise." - **Galatians 3: 28-29**

"Wherefore remember, that ye being in time past Gentiles in the flesh, who are called Uncircumcision by that which is called the Circumcision in the flesh made by hands That at that time ye were without Christ, being aliens from the commonwealth of Israel, and strangers from the covenants of promise, having no hope, and without God in the world But now in Christ Jesus ye who sometimes were far off are made nigh by the blood of Christ." - **Ephesians 2:11-13**

 "Now, therefore, ye are no more strangers and foreigners, but fellow-citizens with the saints, and of the household of God."
-Ephesians 2:19

When we believe in Jesus Christ, we are no more strangers and foreigners, but fellow-citizens with the saints, and of the household of God. So my point is we need to know our true doctrine and continue to witness to the non-believers because without Jesus there is no hope. As believers, we need to help our people. The real Israel are those who love God and put their faith in the finished works of Jesus Christ.

"Not as though the word of God hath taken none effect. For they are not all Israel, which are of Israel." - **Romans 9:6**

"Therefore say I unto you, the kingdom of God shall be taken from you, and given to a nation bringing forth the fruits thereof. "
- **Mathew 21:43**

When is Jesus's Birthday?

Nowhere in the Bible does it say Jesus was born in December. However, when we read this scripture in Luke it gives us a timeline for when Jesus was actually born. Let's Read:

"And the child grew, and waxed strong in spirit, filled with wisdom and the grace of God was upon him. ⁴¹ Now his parents went to Jerusalem every year at the feast of the Passover.⁴² And when he was twelve years old, they went up to Jerusalem after the custom of the feast."

- **Luke 2:40-42**

The scripture in Luke is the only biblical reference to any date around Jesus's age or birthday. It is written when Jesus turned 12 years old and it was on Passover. Passover is in the springtime not the Winter. Jesus's birthday was probably towards the end of March or in April, not December.

We know that in December the god Saturn was worshiped as he was a god in ancient Roman religion and its influence is still felt in the celebration of Christmas and the Western world's New Year. He was the first god of the Capitol known since the most ancient times as Saturnius Mons, and was seen as a god of generation, dissolution, plenty, wealth, agriculture, periodic renewal, liberation, and time.

They celebrated Saturnalia in a week-long celebration of lawlessness. It was an ancient Roman festival in honor of the deity Saturn, held on December 17 of the Julian calendar and later expanded with festivities through to December 25. The holiday was celebrated with a sacrifice at the Temple of Saturn, in the Roman Forum, and a public banquet, followed by private gift-giving, continual partying, and a carnival atmosphere that overturned Roman social norms. Masters provided table service for their slaves and a lot of gluttonous feasting, drunkenness, gambling, orgies, and public nudity happened on this day.

I am not saying don't celebrate the birth of Jesus Christ, what I am saying is it would be wise to examine your heart. If you are just running around worried about having money for Christmas, gift-giving, and parties this behavior would be the same way they celebrated and worshiped the god Saturn and has nothing to do with Jesus who came into the world to save sinners. God has rescued us through Christ. It was Jesus death on the cross and His resurrection that achieved our salvation so Jesus birth means everything. Our focus should be on Jesus, anything else would be idolatry.

Hear the word which the LORD speaks to you, O house of Israel. Thus says the LORD, "Do not learn the way of the Gentiles Do not be dismayed at the signs of heaven, For the Gentiles are dismayed at them. For the customs of the peoples are futile For one cuts a tree from the forest, The work of the hands of the workman, with the ax. They decorate it with silver and gold They fasten it with nails and hammers So that it will not topple. They are upright, like a palm tree, And they cannot speak; They must be carried, Because they cannot go by themselves. Do not be afraid of them, For they cannot do evil, Nor can they do any good." Inasmuch as there is none like You, O LORD you are great, and Your name is great in might
(Jeremiah 10:1-6)

This scripture in Jeremiah 10: 1-6 is from the Old testament so this type of worship celebration was before Jesus Christ, so the tree had nothing to do with Jesus's birth.

"Therefore, brethren, stand fast and hold to the traditions which ye have been taught, whether by word or our epistle."
- **2 Thessalonians 2:15**

The Lord's Prayer

When one of Jesus' disciples asks Him,
"Lord, teach us to pray," Jesus replied pray in this manner,
then He began to recite The Lord's Prayer.
There are two biblical accounts of The Lord's prayer.
(Matthew 6:9-13 and Luke 11:2-4)

My Personal Interpretation of the Lord's Prayer:

- **"Our Father who art in heaven"**

Jesus said to call no man your father upon the earth
for one is your Father, which is in heaven
(Matthew 23:9). God is the Father, the creator of the
universe, and the creator of the human race. There is
only one God and He is the same God and the Father of
Abraham, Issac, and Jacob.

- **"Hallowed be Thy name,"**

To render honor, respect and treat God as holy
and to hold Him sacred.

- **"Thy kingdom come,"**

God is Sovereign, God reigns, and God rules.

- **"Thy will be done on earth as it is in heaven,"**

God's government system, His laws, statutes, and
commands, will be followed on the Earth now
and when Jesus Christ returns.

- **"Give us this day our daily bread,"**

We pray that God will provide our spiritual and physical
needs like knowledge, food, clothing, and shelter.

- **"And forgive us our debts, as we forgive our debtors.** We ask God to forgive us knowing that we have to extend that same mercy to others in order for God to forgive us for our sins.

- **"And lead us not into temptation,"** We pray for grace through persecution, spiritual conflicts, and agonies of the body or of spirit. These may come to us as a test or as a discipline. We know Jesus was led into the wilderness so we may also be led and ask for His grace. (Matthew 4:1)

- **"But deliver us from evil,"** God protects us from both physical and spiritual harm. Only God can deliver us from our enemies.

- **"For thine is the kingdom, and the power, and the glory."** Everything belongs to God and comes from God and exists by the power of God and is intended for God's glory. All glory to God forever! Amen.

Are We Perfect?

"Be ye, therefore, perfect, even as your Father which is in heaven is perfect."

-   Matthew 5:48

Jesus said to be perfect like God in heaven is perfect. Most believe that it is impossible to be perfect. We also believe that only God is perfect, but God said He wants us to be perfect like Him but how? Let's find out by reading the Word of God.

"And God said, Let us make man in our image, after our likeness."

-   Genesis 1:26

Here we read that God made us after His image and likeness so from the beginning we were perfect. So we should strive for perfection?

"What then? Shall we sin, because we are not under the law but under grace? God forbid."

-   Romans 6:15

We are under grace and at the same time while we await Jesus's return, He forbids us from practicing sin. He wants us to grow spiritually and strive to be more like Christ but how? We must follow His commands and be obedient to His word. Doing so makes us perfect in God's eyes because when He sees us walking in the spirit, He sees Jesus in us which is perfection.

Let's read about what is perfect according to God:

"Let your heart, therefore, be perfect with the LORD our God, to walk in his statutes, and to keep his commandments, as at this day."

-   1 Kings 8:61

Here it says to let your heart, therefore, be perfect with the Lord our God. This means we need Jesus to be perfect, so yes, we can be perfect in our flesh. Let's read the proof in **Job 1**:

"There was a man in the land of Uz, whose name was Job; and <u>that man was perfect and upright, and one that feared God, and eschewed evil.</u>"

Now we read here that Job is perfect and Job was in the flesh like us so what made him perfect? First of all, he feared God and "the fear of the LORD is the beginning of wisdom" **(Proverbs 9:10).**

So Job was knowledgeable and he also stayed away from evil. The scripture also mentioned that he was an upright man which means he was honorable and honest. So it's not about being perfect by our definition; it is by God's definition of what is perfect to God and that is fearing Him and following His commands. That makes us perfect. So yes we are perfect in Christ Jesus. Amen to this!!!

"The fear of the LORD is the beginning of wisdom. A good understanding have all they that do His commandments. His praise endures forever." - **Psalms 111:10**

Let us hear the conclusion of the whole matter: *"Fear God, and keep His commandments: for this is the whole duty of man"* **(Ecclesiastes 12:13).**

"The law of the LORD is perfect, converting the soul: the testimony of the LORD is sure, making wise the simple."

- **Psalms 19:7**

Who Am I?

I am no longer a stranger, but a citizen. I am a part of the household of God with the rest of the body of Christ. (Ephesians 2:19)

I am righteous and holy in the likeness of God. (Ephesians 4:24)

I am a citizen of heaven. (Ephesians 2:6 and Philippians 3:20)

I have died and now my life is hidden with Christ in God. (Colossians 3:3)

I am chosen of God, holy, and beloved. (Colossians 3:12)

I am of the children of light and not of darkness. (1 Thessalonians 5:5)

I am a holy brother and partaker of a heavenly calling. (Hebrews 3:1)

I am a partner of Christ. (Hebrews 3:14)

I am one of God's living stones and am being built up as a spiritual house through Christ. (1 Peters 2:5)

I am a part of a chosen race, a royal priesthood, a holy nation, a people for God's own possession to proclaim the mighty acts of Him. (1 Peters 2:9, 10)

I am an enemy of the devil. (1 Peters 5:8)

I am born of God; the evil one (the devil) can't touch me. (1 John 5:18)

I am the salt of the earth. (Matthews 5:13)

I am the light of the world. (Matthews 5:14)

I am a child of God. (Romans 8:16 and John 1:12)

I am part of the true vine, a branch of His (Jesus). (John 15:1, 5)

I am Jesus's friend. (John 15:15)

I am chosen and appointed by Jesus to bear His fruit. (John 15:16)

I am a personal witness of Christ. (Acts 1:8)

I am a slave of righteousness. (Romans 6:18)

I am enslaved to God. (Romans 6:22)

I am a son of God. God is my "Father." (Galatians 3:26, 4:6 and Romans 8:14, 15)

I am a joint-heir with Christ, sharing His inheritance with Him. (Romans 8:17)

I am a temple (home) of God. His Spirit dwells in me. (1 Corinthians 3:16; 6:19)

I am joined to the Lord and one spirit with Him. (1 Corinthians 6:17)

I am a member of Christ's body.
(Ephesians 5:30 and 1 Corinthians 12:27)

I am a new creation and a new person. (2 Corinthians 5:17)

I am reconciled to God and am a minister of reconciliation.
(2 Corinthians 5:18, 19)

I am an heir of God since I am a son of God. (Galatians 4:6, 7)

I am a saint. (1 Corinthians 1:2; Philippians 1:1; Colossians 1:2; Ephesians 1:1)

I am God's workmanship, created in Christ to do the work He planned before hand to be our way of life. (Ephesians 2:10)

Now That I Am Saved

I have direct access to God through the Spirit. (Ephesians 2:18)

I may approach God with boldness, freedom, and confidence through faith in him. (Ephesians 3:12)

I have been delivered (rescued) from the domain of darkness (Satan's rule) and transferred to the kingdom of Christ. (Colossians 1:13)

I have been redeemed and forgiven of all my sins the records are erased and the demands of my sins are nailed to the cross. (Colossians 2:13, 14 and Colossians 1:14)

Christ Himself is in me. (Colossians 1:27)

I have been spiritually circumcised and my old nature has been cut away. (Colossians 2:11)

I have been made complete in Christ. (Colossians 2:10)

I have been buried, raised, and made alive with Christ. (Colossians 2:12, 13)

I have been raised up with Christ. I have died with Christ, so now my life is now hidden with Christ in God. Christ is now my life. (Colossians 3:1-4)

I have been given a spirit of power, love, and self-discipline. Not fear. (2 Timothy 1:7)

I have been saved and called and set apart.
(2 Timothy 1:9 and Titus 3:5)

Because I am sanctified and am one with the Sanctifier (Christ), He is not ashamed to call me brother. (Hebrews 2:11)

I have a right to come boldly before the throne of God to find mercy and find grace in time of need. (Hebrews 4:16)

I have been given exceedingly great and precious promises of God by which I am a partaker of God's divine nature.
(2 Peter 1:4)

I have been justified by faith, so I have peace with God through our Lord Jesus Christ. (Romans 5:1)

I died with Christ and died to the power of sin's rule in my life.
(Romans 6:1-6)

I am free forever from condemnation. (Romans 8:1)

I have received the Spirit of God into my life that I might know the gifts freely given to me by God. (1 Corinthians 2:12)

I have been bought with a price. I am not my own. I belong to God. Therefore, I Glorify God in my body.
(1 Corinthians 6:19, 20)

Since I have died, I no longer live for myself, but for Christ.
(2 Corinthians 5:14, 15)

I have been made righteous. (2 Corinthians 5:21)

I have been blessed with every spiritual blessing.
(Ephesians 1:3)

I have been chosen in Christ before the foundation of the world to be holy and without blame before Him. (Ephesians 1:4)

I was predestined (determined by God) to be adopted as a son. (Ephesians 1:5)

I have been redeemed, forgiven, and am a recipient of His grace. (Ephesians 1:7, 8)

I have been made alive together with Christ by grace I am saved. (Ephesians 2:5)

I have been raised up and seated with Christ in heavenly places. (Ephesians 2:6)

Who Am I in Christ Jesus?

I am faithful. (Ephesians 1:1)

I am God's child. (John 1:12)

I have been justified. (Romans 5:1)

I am Christ's friend. (John 15:15)

I belong to God. (1 Corinthians 6:20)

I am a member of Christ's body. (1 Corinthians 12:27)

I am assured all things work together for good. (Romans 8:28)

I have been established, anointed and sealed by God.
(2 Corinthians 1:21-22)

I am a citizen of heaven. (Philippians 3:20)

I am hidden with Christ in God. (Colossians 3:3)

I have not been given a spirit of fear, but of power, love and a
sound mind. (2 Timothy 1:7)

I am born of God, He protects me and the evil one cannot touch
me. (1 John 5:18)

I am blessed in the heavenly realms with every spiritual
blessing. (Ephesians 1:3)

I am chosen before the creation of the world. (Ephesians 1:4, 11)

I am holy and blameless. (Ephesians 1:4)

I am adopted as His child. (Ephesians 1:5)

I am sealed with the promised Holy Spirit. (Ephesians 1:13)

I am the salt and the light of the earth. (Matthew 5:13-14)

I am a personal witness of Jesus Christ. (Acts 1:8)

I am God's coworker. (2 Corinthians 6:1)

I am a minister of reconciliation. (2 Corinthians 5:17-20)

I am alive with Christ. (Ephesians 2:5)

I am seated with Christ in the heavenly realms. (Ephesians 2:6)

I have been brought near to God through Christ's blood. (Ephesians 2:13)

I have peace with God. (Ephesians 2:14)

I have access to the Father. (Ephesians 2:18)

I am a member of God's household. (Ephesians 2:19)

I am a holy temple. (Ephesians 2:21; 1 Corinthians 6:19)

I am a dwelling for the Holy Spirit. (Ephesians 2:22)

I share in the promise of Christ Jesus. (Ephesians 3:6)

I know God's power works through me. (Ephesians 3:7)

I can approach God with freedom and confidence. (Ephesians 3:12)

I can grasp how wide, long, high and deep Christ's love is with all the saints. (Ephesians 3:18)

I am completed by God. (Ephesians 3:19)

I can bring glory to God. (Ephesians 3:21)

I have been called. (Ephesians 4:1; 2 Timothy 1:9)

I can be humble, gentle, patient, tolerant and loving towards others. (Ephesians 4:2)

I can mature spiritually. (Ephesians 4:15)

I can have a new mindset and live a new lifestyle in true righteousness and holiness. (Ephesians 4:21-32)

I can be kind and compassionate to others. (Ephesians 4:32)

I can forgive others. (Ephesians 4:32)

I am a light to others, and can show goodness, righteousness and truth. (Ephesians 5:8-9)

I can understand what God's will is. (Ephesians 5:17-21)

I can give thanks for everything. (Ephesians 5:20)

I can honor God through marriage. (Ephesians 5:22-33)

I can be strong in Christ. (Ephesians 6:10)

I have God's power. (Ephesians 6:10)

I can stand firm in the day of evil. (Ephesians 6:13)

I am not alone. (Hebrews 13:5)

I am prayed for by Jesus Christ. (John 17:20-23)

I am united with other believers. (John 17:20-23)

I am provided for by God. (Philippians 4:19)

I am promised eternal life. (John 6:47)

I promise a full life. (John 10:10)

I am victorious. (1 John 5:4)

I am protected my heart and mind are guarded with God's peace. (Philippians 4:7)

I am chosen and dearly loved. (Colossians 3:12)

I am blameless. (1 Corinthians 1:8)

I am set free. (Romans 8:2; John 8:32)

I am crucified with Christ. (Galatians 2:20)

I am a light in the world. (Matthew 5:14)

I am more than a conqueror. (Romans 8:37)

I am the righteousness of God. (2 Corinthians 5:21)

I am safe. (1 John 5:18)

I am part of God's kingdom. (Revelation 1:6)

I am healed from sin. (1 Peter 2:24)

I am no longer condemned. (Romans 8:1, 2)

I am not helpless. (Philippians 4:13)

I am overcoming. (1 John 4:4)

I am protected. (John 10:28)

I am born again. (I Peter 1:23)

I am a new creation. (2 Corinthians 5:17)

I am delivered. (Colossians 1:13)

I am redeemed from the curse of the Law. (Galatians 3:13)

I am victorious. (1 Corinthians 15:57)

Key Scriptures

What is the love of God? That we keep His Commands.

"For this is the love of God, that we keep his commandments. And his commandments are not burdensome. **(1 John 5:3)** *And this is love, that we follow his commandments; this is the commandment, as you have heard from the beginning, that you follow love."* **(2 John 1:6)**

What is truth? God's law, statues, and commands.

"Thy righteousness is an everlasting righteousness, and thy law is the truth." **(Psalms 119:142)**

True repentance means you no longer live a sinful life.

"Now repent of your sins and turn to God, so that your sins may be wiped away." **(Acts 3:19)**

Not fearing God keeps you from wisdom and understanding.

"The fear of the LORD is the beginning of wisdom a good understanding have all they that do his commandments his praise endures forever." **(Psalms 111:10)**

The truth is God's Law so following His law will make you free.

"And ye shall know the truth, and the truth shall make you free." **(John 8:32)**

Read the Bible yourself, then you will know what is true.

"Seeing to it that no one makes a prey of you by philosophy and empty deceit, according to human tradition, according to the elemental spirits of the universe, and not according to Christ." **(Colossians 2:8)**

"For the time is coming when people will not endure sound teaching, but having itching ears they will accumulate for themselves teachers to suit their own likings, [4] *and will turn away from listening to the truth and wander into myths."* **(2 Timothy 4:3-4)**

240

The believers of God are doers, they follow His laws.

"Wherefore the Lord said, Forasmuch as this person draw near me with their mouth, and with their lips do honor me, but have removed their heart far from me, and their fear toward me is taught by the precept of men." **(Isaiah 29:13)**

Listen to God's instructions doing what is good and not evil.

"Guard your steps when you go to the house of God; to draw near to listen is better than to offer the sacrifice of fools; for they do not know that they are doing evil." **(Ecclesiastes 5:1)**

Many look to alter God bringing false beliefs and death.

"Lift up thine eyes unto the high places, and see where thou hast not been lien with. In the ways hast thou sat for them, as the Arabian in the wilderness; and thou hast polluted the land with thy whoredoms and with thy wickedness." **(Jeremiah 3:2)**

There is only one God, which will bring peace and unity.

"Endeavoring to keep the unity of the Spirit in the bond of peace.
⁴ There is one body, and one Spirit, even as ye are called in one hope of your calling; ⁵ One Lord, one faith, one baptism, ⁶ One God and Father of all, who is above all, and through all, and in you all."
(Ephesians 4:3-6)

Paul's message was Jesus Christ and His crucifixion.

We preach Christ crucified, unto the Jews a stumblingblock, and unto the Greeks foolishness **(1 Corinthians 1:23)**

God has given His word to the chosen to share the Gospel.

"He sheweth his word unto Jacob, his statutes and his judgments unto Israel.²⁰ He hath not dealt so with any nation and as for his judgments, they have not known them. Praise ye the LORD."
(Psalms 147:19-20)

Now faith is the substance of things hoped for, the evidence of things not seen.

"For we walk by faith, not by sight." **(2 Corinthians 5:7)**

He who says they know God will keep His commandments.

"And by this we may be sure that we know him, if we keep his commandments. ⁴ He who says "I know him" but disobeys His commandments is a liar, and the truth is not in him."
(1 John 2:3-4)

We are destroyed when we reject God and His laws.

"My people are destroyed for lack of knowledge; because you have rejected knowledge, I reject you from being a priest to me. And since you have forgotten the law of your God, I also will forget your children." **(Hosea 4:6)**

The Holy spirit comes to those who believe.

"He that believeth on me, as the scripture hath said, out of his belly shall flow rivers of living water." **(John 7:38)**

Sin is breaking God's law, statute, and commands.

"Whosoever committeth sin transgresseth also the law: for sin is the transgression ("rebellion") of the law." **(1 John 3:4)**

The evil knows what is coming. They run from believer's who trust in God.

"The wicked flee when no man pursueth: but the righteous are bold as a lion." **(Proverbs 28:1)**

God requires the following:

"And now, Israel, what doth the LORD thy God require of thee, but to fear the LORD thy God, to walk in all his ways, and to love him, and to serve the LORD thy God with all thy heart and with all thy soul, To keep the commandments of the LORD, and his statutes, which I command thee this day for thy good? ¹⁴ Behold, the heaven and the heaven of heavens is the LORD's thy God, the earth also, with all that therein is." **(Deuteronomy 10:12-14)**

Whom shall He teach knowledge? And whom shall He make to understand doctrine?

"Them that are weaned from the milk and drawn from the breasts. For precept must be upon precept, precept upon precept; line upon line, line upon line; here a little, and there a little." **(Isaiah 28:9-10)**

What is righteousness?

"And it shall be our righteousness if we observe to do all these commandments before the LORD our God, as he hath commanded us." **(Deuteronomy 6:25)**

You can only love in action:

"Dear children, let's not merely say that we love each other; let us show the truth by our actions." **(1 John 3:18)**

A fool is an unbeliever.

"The fool says in his heart, "There is no God." They are corrupt, they do abominable deeds. There is none that does good." **(Psalms 14:1)**

What is the Grace of God for?

"For the grace of God that bringeth salvation hath appeared to all men teaching us that, denying ungodliness and worldly lusts, we should live soberly, righteously, and godly, in this present world; looking for that blessed hope, and the glorious appearing of the great God and our Saviour Jesus Christ." **(Titus 2:11-13)**

We are followers of Jesus Christ

"For to this you have been called, because Christ also suffered for you, leaving you an example, that you should follow in his steps. He committed no sin; no guile was found on his lips." **(1 Peter 2:21-22)**

The Truth about Tithes and Offerings

Let's get some understanding about tithing. Let's find out why people in the Old Testament gave a tenth of their earnings and what it was for. I believe that the true Christians should follow Christ and be a generous giver to share with others, whether they are in need or not just as God shares with us.

I remember when I wrote my first book, *A Turn in My Belly*. I gave out hundreds of copies for free to people who were incarcerated. Even though I was able to give the book to them free of charge does not mean the book did not cost anything to print. I still had to receive donations and offerings to help with the printing cost and postage so this is a perfect example of Christians giving back so we can share the Gospel to advance God's Kingdom.

This also teaches us that giving an offering is not only to the church building. We are the church as believers so you can give to any ministry that is expanding God's Kingdom Amen to this!!

It is also important that when you give you should never be under pressure or guilt. Let's read the scriptures that give us knowledge about who gave tithes and what the tithe was for.

"And behold, I have given the children of the Levites, all the tenth in Israel for an inheritance, for their service which they serve, even the service of the tabernacle of the congregation."
- **Numbers 18:21**

"But the tithes of the children of Israel, which they offer as a heave-offering unto the LORD, I have given to the Levites to inherit, therefore I have said unto them, Among the children of Israel they shall have no inheritance."

- **Numbers 18:24**

The tithes were for the Levites. They are the priests and God had given the children of Levi a tenth as an inheritance for their service to the tabernacle and of the congregation. The Levites would then take the tithes back to the temple of God in Jerusalem.

The Levite's job was to take the Israelite's money and care for the poor while having money to support themselves as well. It is so sad that many pastors have robbed widows and their communities by taking the scriptures out of context such as this one in Malachi. Let's read it:

"Will a man rob God? Yet ye have robbed me. But ye say, wherein have we robbed thee? In tithes and offerings."

- **Malachi 3:8**

They use this scripture to put guilt and fear into people. Many senior citizens and widows are targeted even though they are on fixed incomes and in need themselves. Not all churches, but many churches will go after them to get money. How? When the first of the month comes around the pastors know their social security checks arrive at this time, so some churches will send their envelopes out to these homes trying to get their hands on some of their social security. Some may even use this scripture in **Malachi 3:8** and the poor widow or senior citizen feels that if they do not give their money they are robbing God.

Now here is the key verse that will explain how people in Biblical days used tithes and who benefitted from the tithe and offerings:

"Bring ye all the tithes into the storehouse, that there may be meat in mine house, and prove me now herewith, saith the LORD of hosts, if I will not open you the windows of heaven, and pour you out a blessing, that there shall not be room enough to receive it. And I will rebuke the devourer for your sakes, and he shall not destroy the fruits of your ground; neither shall your vine cast her fruit before the time in the field, saith the LORD of hosts."

- **Malachi 3:10-11**

So tithing was dealing with your crops. Let's read the Biblical text in Deuteronomy that explains it even better:

"You shall tithe all the yield of your seed, which comes forth from the field year by year. [23] *And before the LORD your God, in the place which he will choose, to make his name dwell there, you shall eat the tithe of your grain, of your wine, and of your oil, and the firstlings of your herd and flock; that you may learn to fear the LORD YOUR God always.* [24] *And if the way is too long for you, so that you are not able to bring the tithe, when the LORD your God blesses you, because the place is too far from you, which the LORD your God chooses, to set his name there,* [25] *then you shall turn it into money, and bind up the money in your hand, and go to the place which the LORD your God chooses,* [26] *and spend the money for whatever you desire, oxen, or sheep, or wine or strong drink, whatever your appetite craves; and you shall eat there before the LORD your God and rejoice, you and your household.* [27] *And you shall not forsake the Levite who is within your towns, for he has no portion or inheritance with you.* [28] *"At the end of every three years you shall bring forth all the tithe of your produce in the same year, and lay it up within your towns;* [29] *and the*

Levite, because he has no portion or inheritance with you, and the sojourner, the fatherless, and the widow, who are within your towns, shall come and eat and be filled; that the LORD your God may bless you in all the work of your hands that you do."

- **Deuteronomy 14:22-29**

So tithing was dealing with your crops. You would give a tenth of your corn, wine, oil, and the firstlings of your herds and your flocks. If the way was too long for you, so that you are not able to carry the crops, then you turned it into money, and bound up the money in your hand, and went to the place which the Lord your God chose. You would then spend the money for whatever you desire: oxen, sheep, wine or strong drink, whatever your appetite craves; and you and your household shall eat there before the LORD your God and rejoice.

But here is the important part: <u>God said you shall not forsake the Levites.</u> The tithe was for the Levites and the Israelites were to give a tenth to the Levites and then the Levites were to give God His dues out of their tithes and give back to the temple to help the needy. The tithe was for the Levites who didn't share in the inheritance of the Land of Israel, as did all the other Tribes. It was the way God provided for His full-time servants who devoted their lives to serving Him. The tithe that went back to God was for God's care for the poor, orphans, and widows; not to buy planes, Bentleys, and mansions. The Levites helped the less fortunate.

By giving tithes the Israelites also recognized that they were giving back a portion to the Lord, who had helped them prosper. They also respected the role of the priest and the Levites as God's representatives and acknowledged their right to receive support for the spiritual service they performed on the people's behalf. That's why God said, "Bring ye all the tithes into the storehouse, that there may be meat in mine house."

It was the Israelites' job to take care of the Levites because the Levites served God full-time and did not own any land of their own to have crops and oil. What was given to the Levites was dispersed amongst the sojourner, the fatherless, and the widows, and not only them but others who also were in need. The tithe was for the Levites' spiritual service and to give back to the temple of God for the people who had a need. It is important to understand why they gave a tenth and what it was for.

Today it is much different. We have a lot of false prophets, teachers, and leaders that prey on people by making them feel guilty and pressuring them to give more than what they can actually afford. Squeezing God's people for money is not Biblical. This scripture will help you and guide you on how you can give to God's house today.

Let's read: *"He who sows sparingly will also reap sparingly, and he who sows bountifully will also reap bountifully. Each one must do as he has made up his mind, not reluctantly or under compulsion, for God loves a cheerful giver. And God is able to provide you with every blessing in abundance, so that you may always have enough of everything and may provide in abundance for every good work. As it is written, "He scatters abroad, he gives to the poor; his righteousness endures forever." He who supplies seed to the sower and bread for food will supply and multiply your resources and increase the harvest of your righteousness. 11 You will be enriched in every way for great generosity, which through us will produce thanksgiving to God; 12 for the rendering of this service not only supplies the wants of the saints but also overflows in many thanksgivings to God. Under the test of this service, you will glorify God by your obedience in acknowledging the gospel of Christ, and by the generosity of your contribution for them and for all others; while they long for you and pray for you, because of the surpassing grace of God in you. Thanks be to God for his inexpressible gift!"*

- **2 Corinthians 9:6-15**

Yes, we should always support God's Kingdom and if all you have is a few dollars to give that is okay. God is not thinking you are robbing Him, He actually speaks highly of the ones who are struggling and gives out of their poverty. Do not let anyone make you feel like God is not going to bless you because you're on a fixed income and not able to give more. God knows our heart.

"He looked up and saw the rich putting their gifts into the treasury; ² and he saw a poor widow put in two copper coins. ³ And he said, "Truly I tell you, this poor widow has put in more than all of them; ⁴ for they all contributed out of their abundance, but she out of her poverty put in all the living that she had."

- **Luke 21:1-4**

Heaven And Hell

Many of us often wonder is there really a Heaven or a Hell? The answer is yes. The bible actually describes both.

Let's read the Biblical text referring to Heaven and Hell:

The Son of Man will send out his angels, and they will weed out of his kingdom everything that causes sin and all who do evil. [42] *They will throw them into the blazing furnace, where there will be weeping and gnashing of teeth.* [43] *Then the righteous will shine like the sun in the kingdom of their Father. Whoever has ears, let them hear.*
-**Matt 13:41-43**

The scripture tells us that the angels will weed out the evil doers and everything that causes sin. They will throw them into the blazing furnace. Then the righteous will shine like the sun in the kingdom of their Father. So now we know that there is a Heaven and a Hell.

Who did God originally prepared this everlasting fire for?

Lord, when did we ever see you hungry and feed you? Or thirsty and give you something to drink? Or a stranger and show you hospitality? Or naked and give you clothing? When did we ever see you sick or in prison and visit you?' "And the King will say, 'I tell you the truth when you did it to one of the least of these my brothers and sisters, you were doing it to me! Then the King will turn to those on the left and say Away with you, you cursed ones, into the eternal fire prepared for the devil and his demons. For I was hungry, and you didn't feed me. I was thirsty, and you didn't give me a drink. I was a stranger, and you didn't invite me into your home. I was naked, and you didn't give me clothing. I was sick and in prison, and you didn't visit me.' - **Mathew 25:37-46**

Jesus teaches us that all of us has a free will to live a life of sin or to live a life of righteousness. So if a person chooses to reject Jesus and not follow his commands and stay in sin by doing evil that person will be thrown into the blazing furnace, where there will be weeping and gnashing of teeth. Weeping means people in Hell are wailing out a loud cry full of grief and pain. Their teeth grind because they are in complete anguish.

The scripture makes it clear that the people that end up in Hell will be the ones who cause sin and all who do evil.

Let's read the Biblical text of a man cast into Hell:

There was a certain rich man, which was clothed in purple and fine linen, and fared sumptuously every day. And there was a certain beggar named Lazarus, which was laid at his gate, full of sores, And desiring to be fed with the crumbs which fell from the rich man's table moreover the dogs came and licked his sores. And it came to pass, that the beggar died, and was carried by the angels into Abraham's bosom the rich man also died, and was buried; And in hell he lift up his eyes, being in torments, and seeth Abraham afar off, and Lazarus in his bosom.

And he cried and said, Father Abraham, have mercy on me, and send Lazarus, that he may dip the tip of his finger in water, and cool my tongue; for I am tormented in this flame. But Abraham said, Son, remember that thou in thy lifetime receivedst thy good things, and likewise Lazarus evil things: but now he is comforted, and thou art tormented.

And beside all this, between us and you, there is a great gulf fixed so that they which would pass from hence to you cannot; neither can they pass to us, that would come from thence. Then he said, I pray thee, therefore, father, that thou wouldest send him to my father's house for I have five brethren; that he may testify unto them, lest they also come into this place of torment.

Abraham saith unto him, They have Moses and the prophets; let them hear them. And he said, Nay, father Abraham but if one went unto them from the dead, they will repent. And he said unto him, If they hear not Moses and the prophets, neither will they be persuaded, though one rose from the dead.

- Luke 16:19-31

When Jesus is telling the story we learn that the rich man died, and was buried and now in hell being tormented. This is a very sad story because once he had gone to Hell, it was now too late for repentance and no one could help him because he was now in a place of separation. No one could get over to the side where the rich man remained in torments even if they wanted to, it's like having a wide gap between you so you can't walk over to them and they can not walk over to you.

We also find out that the rich man in Hell had a request he said he had five brothers and wanted to send a message to them about Hell so they would not end up there and this request was denied. Once this man ended up in Hell, he was denied all privileges, including a drop of water to cool his tongue.

The rich man had many chances to help his neighbor Lazarus, who had no money or food and needed medical assistance. Now the rich man is in Hell begging for help But Abraham said, Son, remember that thou in thy lifetime received thy good things, and likewise Lazarus evil things but now he is comforted, and thou art tormented.

Remember, God told us to love the Lord thy God with all thy heart, and with all thy soul, and with all thy mind, and with all thy strength this is the first commandment. And the second is Thou shall love thy neighbor as thyself. There is none other commandment greater than these.

- Mark 12:30-31

Did the Rich man follow the great commandments?
The answer is NO. We have to follow God's commands and help our neighbors.

Let's read the Biblical text of being cast into Hell, when we reject Jesus:

The kingdom of heaven is like a certain king who arranged a marriage for his son, and sent out his servants to call those who were invited to the wedding, and they were not willing to come. Again, he sent out other servants, saying, Tell those who are invited, "See, I have prepared my dinner; my oxen and fatted cattle are killed, and all things are ready. Come to the wedding. But they made light of it and went their ways, one to his own farm, another to his business.

And the rest seized his servants, treated them spitefully, and killed them. But when the king heard about it, he was furious. And he sent out his armies, destroyed those murderers, and burned up their city. Then he said to his servants, 'The wedding is ready, but those who were invited were not worthy. Therefore go into the highways, and as many, as you find, invite to the wedding. So those servants went out into the highways and gathered together all whom they found, both bad and good. And the wedding hall was filled with guests.

But when the king came in to see the guests, he saw a man there who did not have on a wedding garment. So he said to him, Friend how did you come in here without a wedding garment?' And he was speechless. Then the king said to the servants, 'Bind him hand and foot, take him away, and cast him into outer darkness; there will be weeping and gnashing of teeth. For many are called, but few are chosen."

- Mathew 22:1-14

When the king came in to see the guests, he saw there a man which had not on a wedding garment and was cast into outer darkness (Hell) When we read the text we have learned that when God calls us we must come in our wedding garments. What are wedding Garments?

When we read the verse in Revelations it gives us the answer to the meaning of wearing our wedding garments let's read:

Let us be glad and rejoice, and give honor to him for the marriage of the Lamb is come, and <u>his wife hath made herself ready</u>. And to her was granted that <u>she should be arrayed in fine linen, clean and white for the fine linen is the righteousness of saints.</u> And he saith unto me, Write, Blessed are they which are called unto the marriage supper of the Lamb. And he saith unto me, These are the true sayings of God.

Rev 19:7 -10

The proper attire would correspond to all that Jesus said was required for entrance into the Kingdom of Heaven, true repentance for sin and faith in Christ, and to love the Lord thy God with all thy heart, and with all thy soul, and with all thy mind, and with all thy strength. Jesus also said if you loved me, you would keep my commandments

- John 14:15

So this man through his lifetime did not follow what God had commanded. He rejected Jesus and came to the wedding feast with self-righteousness with no faith in Jesus, he was unconverted (No change)

And the LORD commanded us to do all these statutes, to fear the LORD our God, for our good always, that he might preserve us alive, as it is on this day. And it shall be our righteousness if we observe to do all these commandments before the LORD our God, as he hath commanded us." (Deuteronomy 6:24-25)

Jesus said, "For many are called, but few are chosen."
The ones who continue to reject Jesus by not following his commands will be cast away.

Heaven

"Don't let your hearts be troubled. Trust in God, and trust also in me. ²*There is more than enough room in my Father's home. If this were not so, would I have told you that I am going to prepare a place for you?* ³*When everything is ready, I will come and get you, so that you will always be with me where I am.* **John 14:1-3**

A Picture Of Heaven

And now, dear brothers and sisters, we want you to know what will happen to the believers who have died so you will not grieve like people who have no hope. ¹⁴*For since we believe that Jesus died and was raised to life again, we also believe that when Jesus returns, God will bring back with him the believers who have died.*

We tell you this directly from the Lord We who are still living when the Lord returns will not meet him ahead of those who have died. ¹⁶*For the Lord himself will come down from heaven with a commanding shout, with the voice of the archangel, and with the trumpet call of God. First, the believers who have died will rise from their graves.*

Then, together with them, we who are still alive and remain on the earth will be caught up in the clouds to meet the Lord in the air. Then we will be with the Lord forever. So encourage each other with these words.

-1 Thessalonians 4:13-18

Will we know one another in Heaven?

Notice in Mathew 17:1-5 Peter knew Moses and Elijah, though they had been dead for hundreds of years

Six days later Jesus took Peter and the two brothers, James and John, and led them up a high mountain to be alone. ² As the men watched, Jesus' appearance was transformed so that his face shone like the sun, and his clothes became as white as light. ³ Suddenly, Moses and Elijah appeared and began talking with Jesus.

⁴ Peter exclaimed, "Lord, it's wonderful for us to be here! If you want, I'll make three shelters as memorials one for you, one for Moses, and one for Elijah."

Mathew 17:1-5

We will be with Jesus in Heaven

And one of the elders answered, saying unto me, What are these which are arrayed in white robes? and whence came they?

¹⁴ And I said unto him, Sir, thou knowest. And he said to me, These are they which came out of great tribulation, and have washed their robes, and made them white in the blood of the Lamb.

¹⁵ Therefore are they before the throne of God, and serve him day and night in his temple and he that sitteth on the throne shall dwell among them.¹⁶ They shall hunger no more, neither thirst any more; neither shall the sun light on them nor any heat.

¹⁷ For the Lamb which is in the midst of the throne shall feed them, and shall lead them unto living fountains of waters: and God shall wipe away all tears from their eyes. **Revelation 7:13-17**

The Final Day Of Judgement

And the devil that deceived them was cast into the lake of fire and brimstone, where the beast and the false prophet are, and shall be tormented day and night forever and ever. Rev 20:10

The Great White Throne Judgment

And I saw a great white throne, and him that sat on it, from whose face the earth and the heaven fled away; and there was found no place for them.[12] And I saw the dead, small and great, stand before God; and the books were opened: and another book was opened, which is the book of life: and the dead were judged out of those things which were written in the books, according to their works.

[13] And the sea gave up the dead which were in it; and death and hell delivered up the dead which were in them: and they were judged every man according to their works.[14] And death and hell were cast into the lake of fire. This is the second death.

*And whosoever was not found written in the book of life was cast into the lake of fire. **Revelation 20:11-15***

Read more about Hell in the Apocrypha in the book of
2 Esdras 7:36-105. Here is a PDF version you can read online:

(http://www.polohco.com/get/70verses.pdf)

Black Jews in the Catacombs of Rome

The Catacombs of Rome are ancient catacombs, underground burial places. Though most famous for Christian burials, either in separate catacombs or mixed together, people of all the Roman religions are buried in them, beginning in the 2nd century AD. The Christian Catacombs are extremely important for the history of Early Christian art, as they contain the great majority of examples from before about 400 AD, in fresco and sculpture, as well as gold-glass medallions.

Pictures from the 3rd century, Catacomb of Priscilla, Rome.
For more information, visit (https://www.youtube.com/watch?v=sfuav0DNVVc)

Samson and the lion. Wall-painting c. 350-400.
Via Latina Catacomb, Rome

Dura-Europos synagogue painting: Moses and the burning bush: 303 B.C. - 256 A.D.

Saint Clement is said to have known St. Peter, St. Luke, Barnabas and even St. Paul personally, and he even traveled with them on several occasions. After St. Peter and his first two successors, Linus and Cletus were martyred, he was appointed Bishop of Rome and the 3rd successor of Saint Peter (The 4th Pope).

Saint Benedict

Pope Gregory the Great c.1363
Chapel of the Holy Cross

Christ and His Angels and the Prophets.

Early Christian painting of a Baptism
Saint-Calixte Catacomb - 3rd century

Jesus in the middle Russian CA 1500

Notre Dame du Puy, Cathedrale Notre Dame du Puy, Le Puy-en-Velay (Haute-Loire)
James I of Aragon in 1254 passing through Le Puy on his return from the
Holy Land, gave to the cathedral an ebony image of the Blessed Virgin clothed in
gold brocade, one of the many dozens of venerable "Black Virgins" of France:
It was destroyed in the Revolution, but replaced at the Restoration with a copy

262

Apostle Paul, 2nd century

Noah is praying in the Ark,

The Good Shepherd painted c. 250-300 CE,
Catacomb of Priscilla.

Drawing of Cleopatra made by Michelangelo
Between 1533 and 1534. From the Wikimedia Commons.

Christ Between Peter and Paul, 4th century

Saint Moses (Coptic: (330–405)

The Prophet Nahum. The Holy Prophet Nahum, whose name means "God consoles," was from Galilee. He lived during the seventh century B.C. The Prophet Naum prophesies the ruin of the Assyrian city of Nineveh because of its iniquity, the destruction of the Israelite kingdom, and the blasphemy of King Sennacherib against God.

Michael Archangel.
(London) Early 6th century

Eastern icon of Thomas, 1st century AD

The Prophet Nahum

264

The earliest known icons of the Apostles Peter and Paul
Date from the second half of the 4th century. (Rome)

Madonna and Child 170 AD, the Catacombs, St Pricilla
The world's Oldest known picture of an image of Mary

Beheading of St. John the Baptist

The Four Men in the Fiery Furnace 15th century

The prophet Jonah being thrown into the sea. The story: Ordered by God to go to the city of Nineveh to prophesy against it "for their great wickedness is come up before me," Jonah seeks instead to flee from "the presence of the Lord" by going to Jaffa and sailing to Tarshish, which, geographically, is in the opposite direction. A huge storm arises and the sailors, realizing this is no ordinary storm, cast lots and learn that Jonah is to blame. Jonah admits this and states that if he is thrown overboard the storm will cease. The sailors try to dump as much cargo as possible before giving up, but feel forced to throw him overboard, at which point the sea calms. The inspired sailors then offer sacrifices to God. Jonah is miraculously saved by being swallowed by a large fish specially prepared by God where he spends three days and three nights. Catacomb of Saints Marcellino & Pietro, circa 300 A.D. Rome

More very old paintings

The Archangels   **King David**   **Moses**

More very old paintings

Adam and Eve 3rd Century Catacombs in Rome

**Photograph supplied courtesy of Real History
(http://www.realhistoryww.com)**

Dura-Europos synagogue painting: Jeremiah or
Ezra holding/reading a scroll: 303 B.C.-256 A.D.
(The Original picture).

(Peter and Paul Russian, Circa 1800)

Dura-Europos synagogue painting: Moses and the Hebrews crossing the Red Sea, pursued by Pharoah: 303 B.C. - 256 A.D.

268

This wall painting, depicting the Healing of the Paralytic, is the earliest known representation of Jesus, dating from about 235 AD. The painting was found in 1921 on the left-hand wall of the baptismal chamber of the house-church at Dura-Europos on the Euphrates River in modern Syria. It is now part of the Dura Europos collection at the Yale University Gallery of Fine Arts.

Earliest surviving paintings of Jesus, from the church in the ruined city of Dura-Europos on the Euphrates (Dating from the first half of the 3rd Century AD)

This fresco of the Good Shepherd was found on the ceiling of the Vault of Lucina in the Catacomb of Callixtus in Rome. The construction of the vault itself has been dated to the second half of the 2nd century, but the use of the red and green lines to divide the space (similar to the chambers under San Sebastiano) has suggested the first half or middle of the 3rd century for this fresco. The image of Jesus as the Good Shepherd was an especially popular motif in the early Christian centuries. It was based on several biblical passages, including the 23rd Psalm and sayings of Jesus, and is also an adaptation of a popular pagan image.

Christ Among the Apostles 4th-century

Agape feast or Last Supper (3rd cent)

Archaeologists in Spain have found one of the world's earliest known images of Jesus: The figure is engraved on a glass plate dating back to the 4th Century A.D, according to Spanish reports. He is flanked by two figures, believed to be apostles Peter and Paul. Unlike later depictions, Jesus has no beard, with short, curly haired Afro. Story in the DailyMail - 5 October 2014.

This fresco of Christ Among the Apostles is in an arcosolium of the Crypt of Ampliatus in the Catacombs of St. Domitilla in Rome. The Catacombs of Domitilla date from the 2nd through 4th centuries. According to W.F. Volbach, The extent to which the type of the apostolic group has been developed suggests a 4th-century origin for this particular fresco.

An Original Depiction of Jesus, ca 400 A.D., Roman catacombs.

Medieval Monastery of the Virgin Mary of Mavriótissa, Greece.
Close-up of Tree of Jesse figure.

Edith of England and Otto I, Holy Roman Emperor - Married in 929 A.D.

Portrait of a Moor Chieftain
Philadelphia Art Museum

Portrait of a Black Youth Richly dressed in Silk and holding a Bow.
Rigaud Hyacinthe (French) 1659-1743. Musée des Beaux-Arts de Dunkerque

The term Moors refers to the Muslim inhabitants of the Maghreb, North Africa, the Iberian Peninsula, Sicily, and Malta during the Middle Ages, who initially were Berber and Arab peoples from North Africa. When we talk about the Moors, these were also Africans who came In 711 AD, a tribe of newly converted Muslims from North Africa crossed the straits of Gibraltar and invaded Spain. They were called Moors.

Moors is another word that describes the color black (Negro) Moor is not a person, it is a word that is used to describe the color skin. So when you talk about the Moors you are talking about black people. Some people would associate the name Moors with being Muslims, however, all Moors were not Muslim some were Christian others practiced and celebrated African faith traditions.

Holy Roman Emperor Charles V - (1500~1558)

Unknown

Unknown

Portrait of a Moor Soldier

When the Moors came into Europe, they changed the appearance of the population that's why you see some Italians and Spaniards being darker they inner mixed with the other races in Europe just like we do today. The Moors (Black Africans) Brought knowledge into Europe, they were advanced in literacy, Science, Medicine, technology, mathematics, astronomy, arts, agriculture and so much more. The Moors ruled Spain for over 700 years.

A photo of the 1928 Moorish Science Temple Conclave in Chicago.
Noble Ali Drew can be seen in white in the front row center.

To learn more about the Moors, please watch: A Brief History of The Moors
https://www.youtube.com/watch?v=WWggxyk1L5Q
http://realhistoryww.com/world_history/ancient/Misc/True_Negros/The_True_Negro_2a.htm)

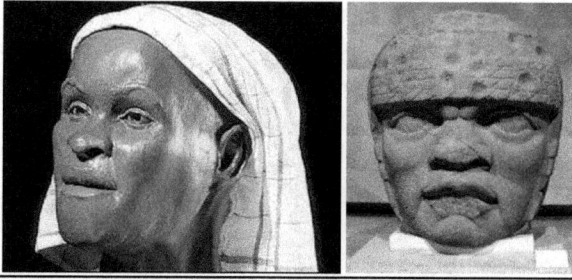

| Luzia | Olmec |

When we talk about the Indigenous people these were people who were already here in America before Christopher Columbus came and they were black people. Luzia is proof her skeleton was found in a cave in Brazil, South America. Some archaeologists believe the young woman may have been part of the first immigrants to come to South America.

They nicknamed her Luzia her name pays homage to the famous African fossil "Lucy", who lived 3.2 million years ago, the 11,500-year-old skeleton was found in Lapa Vermelha, Brazil, in 1975 by archaeologist Annette Laming-Emperaire. Others believe that Luzia was a member of the Olmec civilization because Her skull matches the African facial features of the Olmec heads.

 Luzia is considered to be Brazil's oldest woman, based on remains found that have been dated from 11,500 to 12,000 years old. After Luzia skull was analyzed scientist agreed that her bone structure was of Negroid and Australian Aborigines. She is one of the oldest humans remains found so far in the Americas. Luzia may have perished in an accident or was killed by an animal attack. She was in her 20's when she died and stood just under five feet tall.

Image: Truganini: full-face portrait, 1866,   Truganini in 1870
(Photographer: C. A. Woolley, Collection: Tasmanian Museum and Art Gallery (Q177.2)

Truganini is known for being the last surviving full-blooded Tasmanian Aborigine she was born in 1812 on Bruny Island, located south of the Tasmanian capital Hobart. She took part in her people's traditional culture, but Aboriginal life was disrupted by the European invasion. When Lieutenant Governor George Arthur arrived in Van Diemen's Land in 1824, he implemented two policies to deal with the growing conflict between settlers and the Aborigines.

First, bounties were awarded for the capture of Aboriginal adults and children, and secondly an effort was made to establish friendly relations with Aborigines in order to lure them into camps. When Truganini met George Augustus Robinson, the Protector of Aborigines, in 1829, her mother had been killed by sailors, her uncle shot by a soldier, her sister abducted by sealers, and her fiancé brutally murdered by timber-cutters, who then repeatedly sexually abused her. In 1830, Robinson moved Truganini and her husband, Woorrady, to Flinders Island with the last surviving Tasmanian Aborigines, numbering approximately 100.
Truganini was born in 1812 and Died May 8, 1876 aged 63–64

First Americans were Black:
Aborigines: https://www.youtube.com/watch?v=r6IrMjfbh6E&t=822s
Resource: https://en.wikipedia.org/wiki/Truganini

Our Lady of Anjony - In the chapel of the 15th century
fort Château d'Anjony, France.

The Black Virgin of Montserrat: A copy at Barcelona Cathedral
The original is said to have been made by St. Luke in 54 A.D

Fresco from the Via Latina Catacomb, Rome (cubiculum C), painted about 320 A.D.
Abraham raises his sword to slay his son Isaac.

The Black Madonna of Einsiedeln Switzerland - 1400s

Medieval Monastery of the Virgin Mary of Mavriótissa, Greece - The Tree of Jesse.
The Tree of Jesse refers to a passage in the Biblical Book of Isaiah which describes metaphorically
the descent of the Messiah (Jesus) from Jesse of Bethlehem, through his son King David.

Pope Francis and Pope Emeritus Benedict XVI pray together
In front of the Black Madonna & baby Jesus

Panama - gold pendant - 500 A.D.

Panama-Gold Pendant -500 A.D

Resources

Photograph supplied courtesy of Real History
(http://www.realhistoryww.com)

&

The catacombs of Rome clearly shows paintings of the Jews
who lived in Rome during 1st through the 6th century CE
(https://www.youtube.com/watch?v=sfuav0DNVVc)

Jerusalem which is above is free, which is the mother of us all
- Galatians 4:26

THE 50 FRUITS OF PRIDE

Pride Is the Root of All Evil
(Genesis 3:5; 1 Timothy 3:6; 1 John 2:15-17)

Rate yourself from 1 to 5

1. SELF SUFFICIENT

I tend to be self-sufficient in the way I live my life. I don't live with a constant awareness that my every breath is dependent upon the will of God. I tend to think I have enough strength, ability and wisdom to live and manage my life. My practice of the spiritual disciplines is inconsistent and superficial. I don't like to ask others for help.

I ------------------------ I
1   2   3   4   5

2. ANXIOUS

I am often anxious about my life and the future. I tend not to trust God and rarely experience His abiding and transcendent peace in my soul. I have a hard time sleeping at night because of fearful thoughts and burdens I carry.

I ------------------------ I
1   2   3   4   5

3. OVERLY SELF-CONSCIOUS

I am overly self-conscious. I tend to replay in my mind how I did, what said, how I am coming across to others, etc. I am very concerned about what people think of me. I think about these things constantly.

I ------------------------ I
1   2   3   4   5

284

4. FEAR OF MAN

I fear man more than God. I am afraid of others and make decisions about what I will say or do based upon this fear. I am afraid to take a stand for things that are right. I am concerned with how people will react to me or perceive my actions or words. I don't often think about God's opinion on a matter and rarely think there could be consequences for disobeying him. I primarily seek the approval of man and not of God.

```
I ------------------------ I
1    2    3    4    5
```

5. INSECURE

I often feel insecure. I don't want to try new things or step out into uncomfortable situations because I'm afraid I'll fail or look foolish. I am easily embarrassed.

```
I ------------------------ I
1    2    3    4    5
```

6. COMPARE MYSELF

I regularly compare myself to others. I am performance oriented. I feel that I have greater worth if I do well.

```
I ------------------------ I
1    2    3    4    5
```

7. SELF-CRITICAL

I am self-critical. I tend to be a perfectionist. I can't stand for little things to be wrong because they reflect poorly on me. I have a hard time putting my mistakes behind me.

```
I ------------------------ I
  1    2    3    4    5
```

8. DESIRE CREDIT AND RECOGNITION

I desire to receive credit and recognition for what I do. I like people to see what I do and let me know that they noticed. I feel hurt or offended when they don't. I am overly concerned about my reputation and hate being misunderstood.

```
I ------------------------ I
  1    2    3    4    5
```

9. DESIRE TO MAKE GOOD IMPRESSION

I want people to be impressed with me. I like to make my accomplishments known.

```
I ------------------------ I
  1    2    3    4    5
```

10. DECEPTIVE

I tend to be deceptive about myself. I find myself lying to preserve my reputation. I find myself hiding the truth about myself, especially about sins, weaknesses, etc. I don't want people to know who I really am.

```
I ------------------------ I
  1    2    3    4    5
```

11. SELFISHLY AMBITIOUS

I am selfishly ambitious. I really want to get ahead. I like having a position or title. I far prefer leading to following.

```
I ------------------------ I
  1    2    3    4    5
```

12. OVERLY COMPETITIVE

I am overly competitive. I always want to win or come out on top and it bothers me when I don't.

```
I ------------------------ I
  1    2    3    4    5
```

13. CENTER OF ATTENTION

I like to be the center of attention and will say or do things to draw attention to myself.

```
I ------------------------- I
  1    2    3    4    5
```

14. TALK ABOUT MYSELF

I like to talk, especially about myself or persons or things I am involved with. I want people to know what I am doing or thinking. I would rather speak than listen. I have a hard time being succinct.

```
I ------------------------- I
  1    2    3    4    5
```

15. SELF-SERVING
I am self-serving. When asked to do something, I find myself asking, "How will doing this help me, or will I be inconvenienced?"

```
I ------------------------- I
  1    2    3    4    5
```

16. NOT EXCITED ABOUT OTHERS' SUCCESS

I am not very excited about seeing or making others successful. I tend to feel envious, jealous or critical towards those who are doing well or being honored.

```
I ------------------------- I
  1    2    3    4    5
```

17. FEELINGS OF SUPERIORITY

I feel special or superior because of what I have or do. For example:

» my house
» my neighborhood
» my physical gifting
» my spiritual gifting
» my intellect or education

» being a Christian
» my position or job
» my car
» my salary
» my looks

I ------------------------ I
1   2   3   4   5

18. THINK HIGHLY OF SELF

I think highly of myself. In relation to others I typically see myself as more mature and more gifted. In most situations, I have more to offer than others even though I may not say so. I don't consider myself average or ordinary.

I ------------------------ I
1   2   3   4   5

19. GIVE MYSELF CREDIT

I tend to give myself credit for who I am and what I accomplish. I only occasionally think about or recognize that all that I am or have comes from God.

I ------------------------ I
1   2   3   4   5

20. SELF- RIGHTEOUS

I tend to be self-righteous. I can think that I really have something to offer *God*. I would never say so, but I think God did well to save me. I seldom think about or recognize my complete depravity and helplessness apart from God. I regularly focus on the sins of others. I don't credit God for any degree of holiness in my life.

```
I ------------------------- I
   1   2   3   4   5
```

21. FEEL DESERVING

I feel deserving. I think I deserve what I have. In fact, I think I ought to have more considering how well I have lived or in light of all I have done.

```
I ------------------------ I
   1   2   3   4   5
```

22. UNGRATEFUL
I often feel ungrateful. I tend to grumble about what I have or my lot in life.

```
I ------------------------ I
   1   2   3   4   5
```

23. SELF-PITY

I find myself wallowing in self-pity. I am consumed with how I am treated by God and others. I tend to feel mistreated or misunderstood. I seldom recognize or sympathize with what's going on with others around me because I feel that I have it worse than they do.

```
I ------------------------ I
   1   2   3   4   5
```

24. JEALOUS OR ENVIOUS

I can be jealous or envious of others abilities, possessions, positions, accomplishments. I want to be what others are or want to have what others have. I am envious of what others have thinking that I should have it or deserve it. I find it hard to rejoice with others when they are blessed by God.

I ------------------------ I
1   2   3   4   5

25. INSENSITIVE

I am pretty insensitive to others. I feel that some people just aren't worth caring about. I have a hard time showing compassion.

I ------------------------ I
1   2   3   4   5

26. KNOW-IT-ALL ATTITUDE

I have a know-it-all attitude. I am impressed by my own knowledge. I feel like there isn't much I can learn from other people, especially those less mature than me.

I ------------------------ I
1   2   3   4   5

27. HARD TIME LISTENING

I have a hard time listening to ordinary people. I listen better to those I respect or people I want to leave with a good impression. I don't honestly listen when someone else is speaking because I am usually planning what I am going to say next.

I ------------------------ I
1   2   3   4   5

28. LIKE TO REVEAL OWN MIND

I like to reveal my own mind. I have an answer for practically every situation. I feel compelled to balance everyone else out.

I ------------------------ I
1   2   3   4   5

29. INTERRUPT PEOPLE
I interrupt people regularly. I don't let people finish what they are saying.

I ------------------------ I
1   2   3   4   5

30. COMPELLED TO STOP PEOPLE

I feel compelled to stop people when they start to share something with me I already know.

I ------------------------ I
1   2   3   4   5

31. HARD TO ADMIT WHEN I DON'T KNOW SOMETHING

I find it hard to admit it when I don't know something. When someone asks me something I don't know, I will make up an answer rather than admit I don't know.

I ------------------------ I
1   2   3   4   5

32. DON'T GET MUCH OUT OF TEACHING

I don't get much out of teaching. I tend to evaluate a speaker rather than my own life. I grumble in my heart about hearing something a second time.

I ------------------------ I
1   2   3   4   5

33. LISTEN TO TEACHING WITH OTHER PEOPLE IN MIND
I listen to teaching with other people in mind. I constantly think of those folks who need to hear the teaching and wish they were here.

I ------------------------ I
1   2   3   4   5

34. NOT OPEN TO INPUT

I'm not very open to input. I don't pursue correction for my life. I tend to be unteachable and slow to repent when corrected. I don't really see a correction as a positive thing. I am offended when people probe the motivations of my heart or seek to adjust me.

I ------------------------ I
1   2   3   4   5

35. HARD TIME ADMITTING TO BEING WRONG

I have a hard time admitting that I am wrong. I find myself covering up or excusing my sins. It is hard for me to confess my sins to others or to ask for forgiveness.

I ------------------------ I
1   2   3   4   5

36. RESENT CORRECTION

I view correction as an intrusion into my privacy rather than an instrument of God for my welfare. I can't identify anyone who would feel welcome to correct me.

I ------------------------ I
1   2   3   4   5

37. I RESENT PEOPLE

I resent people who attempt to correct me. I don't respond with gratefulness and sincere appreciation for their input. Instead I am tempted to accuse them and dwell on their faults. I get bitter and withdraw.

I ------------------------ I
1   2   3   4   5

38. CONTENTIOUS, AND ARGUMENTATIVE

When corrected, I become contentious and argumentative. I don't take people's observations seriously. I minimize and make excuses or give explanations.

```
I ----------------------- I
1    2    3    4    5
```

39. EASILY ANGERED AND OFFENDED

I am easily angered and offended. I don't like being crossed or disagreed with. I find myself thinking, "I can't believe they did that to me." I often feel wronged.

```
I ----------------------- I
1    2    3    4    5
```

40. PERSONALITY CONFLICTS

I have "personality conflicts" with others. I have a hard time getting along with certain kinds of people. People regularly tell me that they struggle with me.

```
I ----------------------- I
1    2    3    4    5
```

41. SELF-WILLED AND STUBBORN

I am self-willed and stubborn. I have a hard time cooperating with others. I really prefer my own way and often insist on getting it.

```
I ------------------------ I
  1    2    3    4    5
```

42. INDEPENDENT AND UNCOMMITTED

I am independent and uncommitted. I don't really see why I need other people. I can easily separate myself from others. I don't get much out of our small group meetings.

```
I ------------------------ I
  1    2    3    4    5
```

43. UNACCOUNTABLE

I am unaccountable. I don't ask others to hold me responsible for following through on my commitments. I don't really need accountability for my words and actions. I think I can take care of myself.

```
I ------------------------ I
  1    2    3    4    5
```

44. UNSUBMISSIVE

I am unsubmissive. I don't like being under the authority of another person. I don't see submission as a good and necessary provision from *God* for my life. I have a hard time supporting and serving those over me. I don't "look up" to people and I like to be in charge. Other people may need leaders but I don't. It is important that my voice is heard.

```
I ------------------------ I
  1    2    3    4    5
```

45. LACK RESPECT

I lack respect for other people. I don't think very highly of most people. I have a hard time encouraging and honoring others unless they really do something great.

```
I ------------------------ I
  1    2    3    4    5
```

46. SLANDERER

I am a slanderer. I find myself either giving or receiving evil reports about others. Often times the things I say or hear are true about other people. I am not concerned about the effect of slander on me because of my maturity level. I think I can handle it. I only share with others the things I really think they need to know. I don't tell all.

```
I ------------------------ I
  1    2    3    4    5
```

47. DIVISIVE

I am divisive. I tend to resist or resent authority. I don't like other people to give me orders or directions.

```
I ------------------------- I
  1    2    3    4    5
```

48. DEMEAN

I like to demean or put others down. I often think people need to be adjusted and put in their place. This includes leaders. Other people need to be more humble and have a "sober" assessment of themselves.

```
I ------------------------- I
  1    2    3    4    5
```

49. CRITICAL

I tend to be critical of others. I find myself feeling or talking negatively about people. I subtlety feel better about myself when I see how bad someone else is. I find it far easier to evaluate than to encourage someone else.

```
I ------------------------- I
  1    2    3    4    5
```

50. I THINK I'M HUMBLE

I really appreciate somebody taking the time to put this paper together. It will really be a big help to my friends and family. However, I don't really need this because I think I'm pretty humble already.

```
I ------------------------- I
  1    2    3    4    5
```

Briceida Ryan Aka (Bre)

I am so proud of my mother Briceida Ryan since I was a child my mother would tell me over and over how she felt almost as if she was used as an experiment. She found it very hard to believe that what she had seen and experienced spiritually and physically others have not.

I decided to scan a copy of her book entitled "Opened Eyes" so I can share her knowledge, testimonies and encounters she has experienced.

One thing I have noticed about people who are in the faith not all but many have this belief that if they did not experience what another sister or brother in the Lord has experienced then it must not be true. It's time to awaken out of sleep and Open Your Eyes.

Opened Eyes

by Briceida Ryan

Dedication

This book is dedicated with love to my children: Audrena, Andrew and Angelina Dominguez; to my grandchildren: Andrew, Anthony and Alexander Dominguez, Sophia Barraza, and Taylor Vernali; and to each member of my family and especially to my son, Kirk P. Ryan Jr., who is no longer with us. I wish abundance in wealth, prosperity and happiness in your lives. I love you all very much.

Preface

In *Opened Eyes* I have compiled some of my true-life experiences. I'm excited to share them with you.

When I was young child, spirits would visit and communicate with me like friends coming over to visit. Spirit, saints and angels have come at will and I've never needed to perform special tasks for this to occur.

My desire with this book, *Opened Eyes,* is to share this experience in a comfortable reading environment that may clarify ideas about the spiritual world from my own perspective, outlook and point of view.

I'm very grateful that Jesus Christ rescued me from death from an inoperable brain tumor and gave me the needed time to get my last days in order and get my book, *Opened Eyes,* in your hands.

I hope you enjoy reading this book.

Thank you,

Briceida Ryan

My Expression of Gratitude

My loving Jesus Christ, I will always be eternally grateful for your love and generosity. My life has been overfilled with joy because of your care and guidance in my life.

When I was hit by a car at the tender age of five and my body was bounced off of three cars, the only injury was a scar left on my skull when I should have been dead.

At the hospital when I was giving birth, I was left unattended for many hours and was close to death. It was Jesus who visited and stroked my right hand and instantly restored my life.

On December 14, 2009, when a tumor took over and I died, Jesus Christ gave me life, partial vision and certainty when I needed it the most.

I consider myself very lucky and blessed to call Jesus Christ a life-long friend. Thank you Jesus for being in my life.

Briceida Ryan

My Purpose

I believe I was placed here on Earth for a reason. I have never met anyone who has the same heightened senses and awareness that I have. I am able to see spirits as if they were a living person in front of me. I do feel as if this life was a test and I am very grateful for all the goodwill that has been sent my way. This book is a testament to some of my experiences. My memory has been blocked due to a brain tumor. Nonetheless, I'm excited to share these true stories with you.

My Beginnings

I was born in Panama. My Panamanian mother's name was Siliva Elena Suncin. My Salvadorian father, Fernando Enrique Suncin, was the one who raised me since my biological father passed away before I was born. I am the oldest of ten children.

My parents decided to move to the United States early in their marriage. My aunt already lived in San Francisco and secured a place in North Beach on Filbert and Columbus for our family.

Your Spirit/Soul

Let's be clear; the spirit and soul are the same concept. Your spirit/soul is a part of you. It's just like a heartbeat and it attempts to look out for you by relaying different messages or hunches that you can relate to and work from.

The personality is who you are, it is how you act and it learns to react to the spirit/soul.

A spirit/soul communicates through instant messages your body receives: the goose bumps, the hair that rises from your skin, the butterflies that flutter in your stomach and many other feelings. Intuition is your spirit/soul talking to you. Vibes are never taught; they are understood, and your personality learns how to listen.

As a person grows older, the personality and spirit can both blend with each other and keep separate identities. Even when you pass, these two elements are so important that they will be a part of you and cannot be taken away. This is a personal compass you learn to respond to and use for your best interest.

A dream is a tool that the spirit uses to communicate to the personality. To clarify, the personality is who you are.

A dream is a clear message of important events you must not ignore. It is an immediate channel used by spirits/souls to inform you of good or bad events. Should an event be negative, you have the authority to change it.

As a young child, I recognized my own ability for foretelling future events through dreams. By listening to the dreamer, I was able to interpret present and future events for them. From the reactions that I witnessed, I became aware that what I translated was accurate.

Spiritual Encounters

A person may have different encounters with the spiritual world. Some spirits, angels and even passed people visit many of us at random. With these experiences, your spirit immediately knows who appears before you.

My assumption is that these messengers receive permission to visit to deliver an important message with a limited time span.

Personally, I am able to see and communicate with those who have passed away. This skill is as natural to me as breathing. When spirits contact me, they introduce themselves, the time they walked on earth and the message of positive future events or events that need to be prevented.

Crystal Clear Dreams

When I was very young, I was visited by Jesus Christ and it was understood that I'd write a dictionary for dreams. When Jesus appeared in my living room decades later inquiring the whereabouts of the promised book, *The Ultimate Dictionary of Dream Language,* it was the motivation to bring this project to completion. Your dreams bring concrete information that you can reflect from to form greater decisions. *The Ultimate Dictionary of Dream Language* is an instrument that can help you define those images and meanings of all your dreams for the best outcome in life.

Throughout this five-year process, I was visited by 800 souls who created imaginary dream segments. The meanings I received became definitions for any reader who wants to understand their dreams.

One evening, I was greeted with a surprise reception by those 800 souls celebrating the completion of the book. These souls were the key to unlock the mystery of dreams. Without their contribution of creating thousands of dreams, this work would have never been completed. They were instrumental to this work and enabled me to connect the dreams and the interpretations to help you, the reader, understand your present and future events.

Dreams are maps to incoming treasures and they help you figure out your needs and wants. Dreams also display future positive and negative events you can reflect on to make smart decisions.

Guides

Everybody has their own guides, and I say guides because most people have more than one. In my opinion, guides are with you twenty-four hours a day to make an account of any incidents: what you were doing, where you were, who was with you, and who did what to you. My belief is that they are witnesses for the Lord Jesus Christ.

Rescued by an Angel

My first encounter was around 1945. My mother was having difficulties delivering while in the hospital. That particular night, while I was home, my mother appeared on the wall. I remember her telling me that she was dying and that I must come with her. I felt a pull toward the wall and started screaming. When my father ran in to console me, I explained what had just happened. His eyes widened and left me with my aunt to rush to the hospital.

Mother had an experience all her own. My screams and fears must have alerted someone in the heavens that she was in danger and experiencing death, because simultaneously an angel appeared in front of her.

A tall beautiful angel quickly flew into the room and stated, "I can assist you further, if you have a pair of scissors." My mother interpreted this as a signal to accept help from this angel and she responded, "If I had scissors, I'd give them to you." By the time my father ran into the room my mother had already given birth without complications.

Guidance by Jesus Christ

My friend Jesus Christ visited me. His emanating light filled the room and motioned me to follow him.

He turned my normal living room into a real life tropical paradise. I was in awe of what I saw; my fireplace became a cascading waterfall, colorful tropical birds flew in many directions, and flowers swayed from side to side, I couldn't believe it.

Jesus politely stepped in front of the beautiful scene, smile graciously with arms extended out and asked, "Where's the book you promised to write?" I quickly responded, it would be ready in a year.

And then he, along with the beautiful paradise, vanished. Throughout my life, it was known I'd write a book. The appearance by Jesus Christ made me realize I had the maturity to start on the book and I had to start soon.

Jesus on Jackson Street

After I wrote my dream book, *The Ultimate Dictionary of Dream Language,* I knew I wanted to thank Jesus Christ. I was walking with my grandkids on Jackson Street and Jesus Christ appeared a block away. I quickly ran toward him, kissed him on the cheek to thank him for his encouragement, inspiration and drive to finish the book. I then woke up from this dream.

St. Veronica's Appearance

The following paragraphs are proof for me that the heavens are always watching us and that our words are being accounted for.

At the time I was writing *The Ultimate Dictionary of Dream Language* I explained to a family member I didn't have any drive to leave the house and I couldn't understand this feeling.

That night after I went to bed, an illuminating glowing light filled the room, revealing a mysterious woman I didn't know. She came close to examine my face and asked me if there was anything wrong with me. And I responded, from my understanding there wasn't. She left indicating that she would return.

A few nights later she appeared glowing and said, "In life, you will not be uncomfortable and there isn't anything wrong with you." As she walked away, she held up a veil with the face of Jesus Christ. Instantly, I knew it was St. Veronica.

I was honored that St. Veronica visited. Her appearance was a blessing that inspired my own curiosity as to why I didn't leave the house.

St. Veronica, I can truthfully answer yes, there was something wrong with me then. After many years, a tumor grew and mimicked the form of my brain. Only when I was in the hospital and Jesus restored my life, were the doctors finally able to identify this problem.

The Doctor's Visit

It must have been around 2 o'clock in the morning when my bedroom lit up as three people appeared in my room. A gentleman arrived in a doctor's outfit and two women beside him wore nurses' uniforms. They introduced themselves as legitimate doctors and nurses and mentioned what years they practiced as professionals on this Earth.

From my bed, the doctor raised my body into levitation, and examined my stomach. This was an out-of-the-ordinary experience so naturally I was frightened. He then pointed to the air as a scrolling list of diseases appeared and said, "You will never suffer from any of these diseases." As he lowered my body back to the position I was in, he said, "We're here to verify there is nothing wrong with you," and they disappeared immediately. This event left me uneasy and I thought to myself, if I will not suffer from those ailments, what will I suffer from? Thirty five years later x-rays would reveal that I had an inoperable brain tumor.

The Unwelcomed Visitors

This particular day I came home early from school and for some odd reason, no one was home. While in my room I heard a commanding voice say, "Hide," then I heard the front door open, footsteps walking up the stairs and a whispered conversation between two men.

While they were searching the house and making their way toward my room, I heard a loud noise. Spooked, they decided to run out. I'm thankful for that warning noise and voice that commanded me to hide.

Anacleto

My mother had come over to visit and had fallen asleep in my room. Keep in mind this was a two-story house and both myself and my mother were on the second floor. I was standing at the top of the stairs when I saw a white man with blond hair running up. I asked him, "Who are you? What are you doing here?" He had a shocked, numb look on his face, apparently surprised that I could see

see him. He responded, "I am Anacleto and I'm here to see Silvia." I moved out of his way and motioned him to my room. When my mother woke up that day, I asked her "Who is Anacleto?" My mother's eyes grew wide and she said, "He's my father, your grandfather." In awe, her eyes filled with tears. She was surprised I knew his name because he had died when she was a baby and no one had ever mentioned my grandfather's name to me, not even my mother.

An Unexpected Appearance

When I was born in Panama in 1943, my grandmother witnessed my birth and held me in her arms. My parents and I left the country a couple of months after later. Because I was so young, I didn't remember what she looked like. In 1970, my grandmother appeared before me and said, "Get in touch with your mom, and talk to her about sending your jewelry back to you immediately." I called my mother in San Diego to request these items. She agreed to send both her and my valuable items together.

I was thankful that my grandmother appeared and reminded me to gather my belongings because soon after when my mother was admitted to the hospital, her house was broken into.

My Father's Visit

I never met my father since he passed before I was born. Just like anyone who has never met their passed parents, I was curious to know who he was and what he looked like. One night I had a dream where a handsome Chinese gentleman with a white streak that ran through his hair stood in front of me. I spoke to my mother about the gentleman with the streak in his hair, and with that detail, she verified it was my father.

Contrary Events

Here are two separate events that happened at the same time, but have no connection. Be careful with significant events in your life since those occurrences may or may not coincide.

I was picking up groceries and a friendly woman approached me. We had a conversation in which she mentioned that she was out of work, looking for a job and she had children to feed. We parted ways after we left the check out counter and went on with our lives.

When I walked out of the grocery store, across the street I saw The Virgin Mary and Jesus Christ happily waving to me. I was left contemplating both situations; the woman's ordeal and this visit by The Holy Family. I chose to clutch my children's' hands and hurry home.

When I arrived home, an ambulance and crowd were surrounding the house across the street. The same woman I had spoken to in the store had hung herself. I had no idea she lived so close.

That same day Andy Turner, my real estate broker, approached me about buying a new property in Pacifica. During this time in my life, my family was growing and my husband and I spoke of moving to a bigger home that would be put in my name so I could establish some credit. Andy informed me of a young pilot about 25 years old who was selling his home to move closer to his fiancée. With four bedrooms and two bathrooms and a spectacular view of the ocean, I fell in love with this property and bought it. Interestingly enough, the gentleman I bought the property from never once doubted my ability to buy my own property.

Buying a house was a part of my life plan, and the visit from Jesus and The Virgin Mary was to congratulate and encourage me for the move. It had nothing to do with the incident that occurred with the woman across the street.

For your information, when The Virgin Mary appears, she is responding to a request or giving a reward. She wears garments that you are familiar with and can reflect from.

Bell Shaped Flowers

In 2005, The Virgin Mary appeared to me. She had a happy look on her face. She stood between two large trees and she said to me " It's a good time for you to move into a new house of your own." To be clear, these were mature trees with large bell-shaped flowers that swung back and forth and they repeated The Virgin Mary's message to me.

That same day I asked a friend who was joining me for lunch if she'd like to go to an open house. She looked surprised, but agreed. Once I saw the house, I knew right then I'd be the owner of that property.

Later on, a young tenant called me to introduce herself. She welcomed me as the new owner, and said she had a small gift, two plants for the back yard that she intended to take care of. I was really happy and appreciated her kindness. My only request was that she plant them in two separate places since it would look more aesthetically pleasing. Little did I know that her plants would grow to become the same trees as in the dream premonition with The Virgin Mary. I was elated.

Six years later, this story repeated itself. I had picked up two tiny trees that I wanted to plant in the yard of the home that I owned for most of my life. To my surprise, of all the places around my house the gardener chose to plant them on each side of the Virgin Mary statue. Guess what? These trees will soon bloom bell-shaped flowers.

The Virgin Mary and Kirk Ryan Jr.

It was 3 o'clock in the morning when my room lit up. I saw my youngest son surrounded in a huge light, stating, "Mom, I'm leaving now and I want you to see who I'm leaving with." He extended his arm, and there stood The Virgin Mary, glowing. Then, they left together.

I knew in my heart that his saying goodbye meant he was no longer alive. Instantly I began looking for my son and called every number that I could reach him on. Eventually, my family and I found out he had passed away in a drowning accident.

The Miracle

I was in the hospital waiting to give birth. In those days, women were tied to the gurney while being transferred to the delivery room. This was what happened to me. The doctors left me unattended with plans of returning. My guess was there was some miscommunication between the doctors and I was left in the room for many hours.

Feeling that my baby was near birth, I yelled for help. I was suffering, my mouth was dry and I felt death was near. Then a miracle took place: Jesus appeared at the last moment and stroked the top of my right hand, then disappeared. Instantly, I felt life was returned to my body. The baby had come out by the time shocked and panicked-looking doctors arrived at the scene.

While my baby was healthy, my body wasn't. For the next three months, my right leg had no sensation. I decided to pray about it, and it slowly recuperated. The next six years after this experience, I would constantly feel the sensation of Jesus Christ's touch on my right hand.

Chicken Over Rice

This early morning I had just woken up when all of a sudden a large glowing baby with piercing blue eyes appeared. It spoke to me and said, "Please tell my mother that I need to be born immediately. And tell her for lunch she will be served chicken over rice."

I found out what hospital the mother of the baby was admitted to and rushed to the hospital. The mother was surprised by my visit and I said, "Your baby appeared to see me and had asked me to tell you that you will deliver today. You can stop your agony and disconnect yourself from these tubes because you'll have a healthy delivery." I added," If you need any verification, the baby told me to tell you that you will be eating "chicken over rice" for lunch.

Two nurses walked in and the mother asked them to disconnect her from all those apparatuses. She then asked what was on the hospital's menu for lunch. One nurse left the room she came back and responded, "Chicken over rice." At that moment, the mother started to go into labor.

My Honeymoon Morning

It was the morning of my honeymoon, my fiancé and I woke up as husband and wife. My husband had a sweet mysterious look on his face reflecting over a recent event. I asked what happened and laughing with a smile he responded, "I went for a walk with Jesus and all he spoke about was you, but don't ask what he said because I'm not telling." Being in our teens, he 17 and I 16, I chased and taunted him for the answer but to this day, I still don't know what was said.

A Sudden Scare

The kids and I were napping in bed. In my dream stage, I started screaming out, "Angelina!" my 2-year-old daughter's name. I woke up with a sense of extreme urgency and a need to act fast.

I hurried out of bed, screaming her name, but she was nowhere to be found in the house. I quickly opened the window, saw her walking outside, and yelled her name again. That made her come to an abrupt halt, seconds away from being run over by a car. The urgency that I felt in the dream helped to save my daughter's life.

A Beautiful Man

I was in San Francisco when I came across a man with a beautiful profile. I was delighted because when he turned around to look at me, it was my friend Jesus Christ. His purpose was to let me know that I was being rewarded for my kind acts. Whether you realize or not, you will always be rewarded for helping those in need.

Open Your Eyes

One night, I heard Jesus Christ say , "Open your eyes." I had the impression I had to be more watchful of significant future events.

That same night, I was visited by my aunt, her husband, and two couples. She reminded me of her past as a property owner and encouraged me to do the same. Jesus repeated in my ear, "Open your eyes." I woke up that morning excited and filled with ambition to start my new venture.

Numbers to Victory

Audrena, my daughter, and I were deciding on our next financial move. It had gotten late and we called it a night, going to sleep without making real plans. All of a sudden, in the middle of the night, both of us jumped up and looked at each other. Wide awake, Audrena said, "Someone just yelled over and over in my ear, '825.'" I had the same experience with a different number, 930. I questioned if she heard the right numbers.

What was interesting was that both of us were awakened by someone who yelled in our ears. Puzzled, we took the different numbers and compared them. What we received was a formula for the best selling dates for our properties. This proved to be correct and we reaped the financial benefits thanks to that message in our dreams.

Mystery Call from the Junkyard

It was 2 o'clock in the morning and my guest was leaving for his house after a two-week stay. I received a call from this guest, in a panic, stating that he had veered off the freeway 500 miles from his destination because his engine had died and on top of that, he had forgotten to recharge his cellphone.

Hours went by and although I didn't know what to do, I had faith that there would be an answer from the heavens. After some thought, I called auto-wrecking yards, because of their car expertise. Mechanics would have been an option to contact, but since it was Sunday, wrecking yards seemed like the best bet.

The next option was to leave messages to numerous junkyards that a person was in desperate need and I left a number where they could reach my guest.

Later on that morning, my guest happily called back and couldn't thank me enough because out of the blue, someone from the junkyard gave them specific directions to start up their car and it worked.

I don't know any junkyards that are open and receptive to phone calls on a Sunday morning between 5 and 7 a.m. Even today, we still are in awe and thankful to who ever responded so quickly.

St. Michael's Visit

I was visited by St. Michael Archangel and this was my experience. I was in despair because I was presented a problem that I was working through. My prayers were directed to St. Michael to aid this process and I received an immediate response. We all have the ability to request aid and connect with the heavens, all you have to do is ask.

When St. Michael appeared to see me, my back was turned, but my spirit was aware he was there and said, "Thank you St. Michael for coming to my aid." I turned around and saw a huge light emanating from St. Michael.

He is a tall, handsome, muscular man with long loose wavy black hair. He is known as a protector. When he appeared he was wearing a helmet, vest, outer garments and boots that looked to be made of platinum.

As I acknowledged him, a calming sensation ran through my body. Instantly I knew that whatever crisis I was dealing with would soon be over. I'm very grateful for the assistance and resolution I received.

I have seen St. Michael Archangel several times. One evening a thought came across my mind that I had not seen his wings. The next time I saw him, he was in flight, and I got to see them. With the presence of St. Michael, I become thankful that he's watching me and all of us and working toward a positive outcome. From what I sense, St. Michael along with other angels were created to defend us in crisis situations. Angels are constantly aware of what happens on earth.

Miracles come to people unexpectedly. Trials and

tribulations on Earth are being watched and are accounted for. Should you need to be rescued, you will be.

The Glow

Out of the blue I had a woman call me. She had heard about my reputation as a reader and wanted to meet me. She, too, had certain abilities, and we decided to meet up and exchange services.

When I arrived, she stood at the top of the stairs. As I walked up, her eyes grew wide and she appeared to be overjoyed. She greeted me with a hug, and tears filled her eyes explaining what she had just witnessed, an enormous illuminating light that accompanied me. I was happy to meet someone with this ability. While everyone has a light which no one can remove, it's unusual to meet someone who can see it.

The reading that she received from me was that she would be reuniting with her husband in Texas. I was lucky enough to meet her days before she left. I never saw her again.

These next three incidents happened years apart.

The Distressed Old Man

Most of the time, you don't know who you'll come across. An older man whom I didn't know was clearly in distress, and I felt the need to help him. No one was there to witness what occurred between us. We parted ways and went on with our lives.

That evening a woman whispered in my ear, "For helping that older man you received 1,000 points." What was around to witness this event. It left me a clear impression that everyone is being constantly viewed in their lives. Constantly.

The Flower Lady

A woman with a little girl approached me pushing a cart of flowers in San Francisco. The woman with a bouquet of flowers said to me, "Excuse me, Miss, these are for you." She refused payment and swiftly walked away.

The Man with the Statue

An older man approached me when I was walking to work in San Francisco. He was cradling A Virgin Mary statue and said, "This is for you." I was overjoyed and humbled to receive such a beautiful gift. I thanked him, and we both walked away.

I suppose these visits were gifts for good deed I have done in the past.

Visitations

The multiple times when I've been visited by people who have passed, it's usually around the eighth day after their death. Loved ones, friends, acquaintances and even co-workers are communicating their final significant words or apologies.

These are some of my experiences with visitations.

A Visit in the Garden

I was in my garden tending to my flowers one day. I stopped for some reason and turned around. All of a sudden, the spirit of a co-worker appeared to me. She had a surprised look on her face, and didn't say a word. I knew instantly she had passed away. It was as if her accidental passing took her and all of us, her coworkers, by surprise.

The Forgotten Response

During the time that my regular job was looking for grants, I worked with a travel agency. The agency enjoyed my job performance and every three years they would respond positively to my request for extra work. The last time I asked for hours, there was no response.

I had no alternative but to except another job. The new job was painful and overwhelming but I never thought about holding a grudge against the person who failed to call me. I moved on.

Years later when the travel agency's hiring manager passed, his spirit appeared with an apology for not returning my call. I never did forget this experience.

Floating Papers

I was working with an executive director on an important project. The work was completed and the information was left on my desk so that it could be reviewed for a meeting. Later, the paperwork was nowhere to be found.

Looking for a solution, I focused on my options for retrieval before I went to bed.

I felt I was transported to the heavens where I was able to speak to two women about my dilemma. My assumption was that they were waiting for me, as if this episode in my life was preplanned. I immediately asked where I could find the documents I was looking for

Telepathically they informed me I would have the needed paperwork the same day, time and place next week.

This experience reinforced my belief that the heavens are watching all of us.

Mischievous Little Girl

This next incident happened when I was admitted into the hospital.

I've been able to see spirits since I was born, but most spirits I've come across don't know this.

I was in and out of consciousness at the hospital when I saw a spirit approach me and jump into my body. I had the impression he didn't fit because of his gender and large frame, so he jumped out.

Later in the same week, I noticed a little girl sitting in front of me, pondering. I don't think she knew I could see her. The next moment I saw her jump into my body, moving my arms and legs into different and interesting poses.

I passed out due to my condition, but I knew this wasn't right, so I was ready for her next attempt.

I saw her approach me again. She jumped and moved my body into positions I wouldn't ever think to make while the doctor checked up on me. My doctor grew aware of this strange behavior and quickly left. I was embarrassed. When he had walked away, and when I felt safe enough, I yelled at the top of my lungs, "Get out!"

She must have freaked out, because she left my body so quickly. Luckily, I haven't experienced that again.

The Revealing Visit

Before I was diagnosed with a brain tumor, the spirit of an old friend appeared at my front door. This soul revealed the name of a person who would help me if I ever needed assistance. Once a year for three years, I was visited and was given the same message. I didn't understand the soul because the tumor hadn't affected my body at that time and I was very healthy.

Once it was revealed I had a brain tumor, I was released from the hospital with the condition that I would need a 24-hour caretaker. When I was conducting interviews, I instantly remembered the given name as the best candidate for the job. To this day, she remains my caretaker and friend. I'd like to thank that caring soul who gave me the helpful information.

My Life after Death Experience

I had a strong desire to open an antique gift shop when I reached a certain age. That night when I went to sleep, I had a clear vision of what the store would look like on the opening night. This rehearsal vision included many of my friends celebrating this accomplishment.

All of a sudden, it felt like a curtain was pulled down. I was in a different dimension. Right then, I knew I had passed away.

It was a dimly lit place, where I saw a strange man walking closer and closer to me pretending to be preoccupied with something else. A strong feeling of danger overcame me.

I knew I was in trouble and needed to escape. A clear

whisper said, "Do not run, you will not make it." It stopped me in my tracks. Deciding to fight, I ran and jumped on the man's shoulders, and called for Jesus. The strange man looked caught off guard, opened his toothless mouth and transformed himself into a shadow drifting away.

I had died. My soul floated horizontally and my guides were with me crying and looking upset. My guides are four blonde, blue-eyed, tall, good-looking white women. At this time, they were pacing back and forth as if they were waiting for someone. Jesus Christ hurried in making a concerned face.

My four guides started speaking simultaneously and told Jesus that at the moment I died, I was asleep and they couldn't stop my journey. Somehow, their dialogue was projected in the air and visible for all and anyone to read.

I was drifting horizontally in the air then Jesus directed me into an upright standing position. He looked directly in my right eye, then in my left eye and quietly spoke, "You need to go back."

I wasn't expecting to come back to life. My spirit was traveling mid-air in a pitch black arena, where I'd see large explosions and small bright lights passing me by. All of a sudden, my soul floated slowly back into my body.

Coming back was a horrendous task. I didn't come back with the memory of what my life was about. I didn't remember who I was, where I was or who was around me. My surroundings felt unpredictable. I was lucky to have my family's support. They took me to the hospital, where we all found out weeks later that I had an inoperable brain tumor.

My family took the news hard, but to be truthful, it didn't affect me emotionally. My vision and my abilities had been severely diminished, but I strongly believe that Jesus removed the emotional pain that is connected with this hardship. I was glad the doctors sent me home to tie up loose ends.

A Wake-Up Call

I was released from the hospital with the information that I would have a short life span with limited abilities caused by an inoperable brain tumor. I was sent home to put my life plans in order. It was as if the tumor turned off my personality and my memory had vanished into thin air.

One morning, I decided I needed something from the top kitchen cabinet. By using a fold-up chair, I was able to gain the height I required. On the way down, the chair folded, positioning me where my head would have hit the kitchen floor first. I felt someone from the heavens catch me and break the impact of the fall, otherwise I wouldn't be here to tell this story.

My feeling is that whoever broke my fall must have notified Jesus Christ of this incident because two or three days later he appeared. I was in the kitchen and my spirit recognized Jesus was behind me. He extended his arms and his hands hovering over my head, directing a miracle to the brain. I say miracle because my thinking improved immensely. I cannot be grateful enough.

The Unborn Child

A friend of mine didn't think she would have children due to some past trauma. One night a large glowing unborn child came to see me. Playfully, the baby made different poses as it spoke, "Soon I will be born."

When I told this friend that she was pregnant she couldn't believe me. Once she delivered her child, it was the exact same one who visited me.

Vision of the End

There's a lot of talk about the end of this world. I'll never forget my vision and what I saw. It was as if something hot hit and altered the Earth. With each step that was taken, glittery shiny ashes were kicked into the air. The glittery substances were like ground petrified glass raining down on everyone.

As I finished walking this path, I was met with a huge line of people. Those of us who had survived had somber and sad looking faces. At the beginning of the line was a woman who was taking down names of people as they were escalated up into a two-street, block-sized, white-grayish saucer-type vehicle.

Book Contributors

Thank you Stephanie Fernández for your effort and help each morning to bring this special project into completion. Your curiosity, enthusiasm and passion to finish this book helped immensely. I'm happy I was able to work with you and I appreciate your efforts.

Thank you Renee Batti for your assistance in proof reading this work.

Editor's Note

After my time working on this project, I have a feeling that we are all visited and have miracles occur to us just like Briceida but we may not have the capacity to see or recognize it as such. Whether you see them or not, The Holy Family, angels, guides and spirits have and will continue to visit you, too.

My time with Briceida writing this book has been a blessing. Her positivity, charisma and energy is infectious. She has the ability to light up a room and I'm sure, this is one of many characteristics that people enjoy about her.

I am very happy I was chosen to be a part of this project. I enjoyed every minute of it. My life has changed since meeting this interesting, smart, kind woman, Briceida Ryan.

Stephanie Fernández

About the Author

Opened Eyes is a collection of memories of the life of Briceida Ryan. She is confident that her life was spared to share these events with you. Her hope is that her one-of-a-kind experiences with The Holy Family, saints, angels and spirits unborn and passed will open a comfortable dialogue for you and others to enjoy.

Briceida Ryan has been involved in dream interpretation for over fifty years, beginning at the age of nineteen. According to her family members, she had demonstrated psychic abilities and experienced dream premonitions from an early age. Briceida's ability to precisely predict future events based on the dreams of others was self taught. She has interpreted dreams for people all over the world and from all walks of life.

Briceida Ryan is bilingual in English and Spanish and this has enabled her to work with a broad spectrum of ethnic groups during her time as a health educator with The Department of Obstetrics and Gynecology with the University of California in San Francisco. Her work extended to St. Luke's Hospital and San Francisco General. Briceida Ryan contributed and promoted the starting phases of the midwifery program at UCSF and the WIC program (a subsidized food program).

She presently lives in Pacifica raising her orchids.

Opened Eyes

by Briceida Ryan

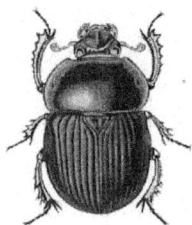

Other Published Books

Brieceida's first book, *The Ultimate Dictionary of Dream Language,* continues to sell and receive excellent reviews.

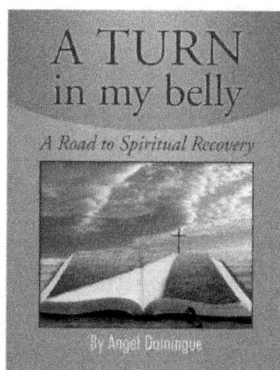

A Turn In My Belly By Angel Domingue

Read the Bible in One Year

This is an awesome way to stay on track. Check off each day's reading as you complete it. You can also highlight your favorite scriptures.

- o **Day 1** - Genesis 1-2; Matthew 1
- o **Day 2** - Genesis 3-5; Matthew 2
- o **Day 3** - Genesis 6-8; Matthew 3
- o **Day 4** - Genesis 9-11; Matthew 4
- o **Day 5** - Genesis 12-14; Matthew 5:1-26
- o **Day 6** - Genesis 15-17; Matthew 5:27-48
- o **Day 7** - Genesis 18-19; Matthew 6
- o **Day 8** - Genesis 20-22; Matthew 7
- o **Day 9** - Genesis 23-24; Matthew 8
- o **Day 10** - Genesis 25-26; Matthew 9:1-17
- o **Day 11** - Genesis 27-28; Matthew 9:18-38
- o **Day 12** - Genesis 29-30; Matthew 10:1-23
- o **Day 13** - Genesis 31-32; Matthew 10:24-42
- o **Day 14** - Genesis 33-35; Matthew 11
- o **Day 15** - Genesis 36-37; Matthew 12:1-21
- o **Day 16** - Genesis 38-40; Matthew 12:22-50
- o **Day 17** - Genesis 41; Matthew 13:1-32
- o **Day 18** - Genesis 42-43; Matthew 13:33-58
- o **Day 19** - Genesis 44-45; Matthew 14:1-21
- o **Day 20** - Genesis 46-48; Matthew 14:22-36
- o **Day 21** - Genesis 49-50; Matthew 15:1-20
- o **Day 22** - Exodus 1-3; Matthew 15:21-39
- o **Day 23** - Exodus 4-6; Matthew 16
- o **Day 24** - Exodus 7-8; Matthew 17
- o **Day 25** - Exodus 9-10; Matthew 18:1-20
- o **Day 26** - Exodus 11-12; Matthew 18:21-35
- o **Day 27** - Exodus 13-15; Matthew 19:1-15
- o **Day 28** - Exodus 16-18; Matthew 19:16-30

- Day 29 - Exodus 19-21; Matthew 20:1-16
- Day 30 - Exodus 22-24; Matthew 20:17-34
- Day 31 - Exodus 25-26; Matthew 21:1-22
- Day 32 - Exodus 27-28; Matthew 21:23-46
- Day 33 - Exodus 29-30; Matthew 22:1-22
- Day 34 - Exodus 31-33; Matthew 22:23-46
- Day 35 - Exodus 34-36; Matthew 23:1-22
- Day 36 - Exodus 37-38; Matthew 23:23-39
- Day 37 - Exodus 39-40; Matthew 24:1-22
- Day 38 - Leviticus 1-3; Matthew 24:23-51
- Day 39 - Leviticus 4-6; Matthew 25:1-30
- Day 40 - Leviticus 7-9; Matthew 25:31-46
- Day 41 - Leviticus 10-12; Matthew 26:1-19
- Day 42 - Leviticus 13; Matthew 26:20-54
- Day 43 - Leviticus 14; Matthew 26:55-75
- Day 44 - Leviticus 15-17; Matthew 27:1-31
- Day 45 - Leviticus 18-19; Matthew 27:32-66
- Day 46 - Leviticus 20-21; Matthew 28
- Day 47 - Leviticus 22-23; Mark 1:1-22
- Day 48 - Leviticus 24-25; Mark 1:23-45
- Day 49 - Leviticus 26-27; Mark 2
- Day 50 - Numbers 1-2; Mark 3:1-21
- Day 51 - Numbers 3-4; Mark 3:22-35
- Day 52 - Numbers 5-6; Mark 4:1-20
- Day 53 - Numbers 7; Mark 4:21-41
- Day 54 - Numbers 8-10; Mark 5:1-20
- Day 55 - Numbers 11-13; Mark 5:21-43
- Day 56 - Numbers 14-15; Mark 6:1-32
- Day 57 - Numbers 16-17; Mark 6:33-56
- Day 58 - Numbers 18-20; Mark 7:1-13
- Day 59 - Numbers 21-25; Mark 7:14-37; Mark 8:1-21
- Day 60 - Numbers 26-27; Mark 8:22-38
- Day 61 - Numbers 28-29; Mark 9:1-29

- Day 62 - Numbers 30-31; Mark 9:30-50
- Day 63 - Numbers 32-33; Mark 10:1-31
- Day 64 - Numbers 34-36; Mark 10:32-52
- Day 65 - Deuteronomy 1-2; Mark 11:1-19
- Day 66 - Deuteronomy 3-4; Mark 11:20-33
- Day 67 - Deuteronomy 5-7; Mark 12:1-27
- Day 68 - Deuteronomy 8-10; Mark 12:28-44
- Day 69 - Deuteronomy 11-13; Mark 13:1-13
- Day 70 - Deuteronomy 14-16; Mark 13:14-37
- Day 71 - Deuteronomy 17-19; Mark 14:1-25
- Day 72 - Deuteronomy 20-22; Mark 14:26-50
- Day 73 - Deuteronomy 23-25; Mark 14:51-72
- Day 74 - Deuteronomy 26-27; Mark 15:1-26
- Day 75 - Deuteronomy 28; Mark 15:27-47
- Day 76 - Deuteronomy 29-30; Mark 16
- Day 77 - Deuteronomy 31-32; Luke 1:1-23
- Day 78 - Deuteronomy 33-34; Luke 1:24-56
- Day 79 - Joshua 1-3; Luke 1:57-80
- Day 80 - Joshua 4-6; Luke 2:1-24
- Day 81 - Joshua 7-8; Luke 2:25-52
- Day 82 - Joshua 9-10; Luke 3
- Day 83 - Joshua 11-13; Luke 4:1-32
- Day 84 - Joshua 14-15; Luke 4:33-44
- Day 85 - Joshua 16-18; Luke 5:1-16
- Day 86 - Joshua 19-20; Luke 5:17-39
- Day 87 - Joshua 21-22; Luke 6:1-26
- Day 88 - Joshua 23-24; Luke 6:27-49
- Day 89 - Judges 1-2; Luke 7:1-30
- Day 90 - Judges 3-5; Luke 7:31-50
- Day 91 - Judges 6-7; Luke 8:1-21
- Day 92 - Judges 8-9; Luke 8:22-56
- Day 93 - Judges 10-11; Luke 9:1-36
- Day 94 - Judges 12-14; Luke 9:37-62

- Day 95 - Judges 15-17; Luke 10:1-24
- Day 96 - Judges 18-19; Luke 10:25-42
- Day 97 - Judges 20-21; Luke 11:1-28
- Day 98 - Ruth 1-4; Luke 11:29-54
- Day 99 - 1 Samuel 1-3; Luke 12:1-34
- Day 100 - 1 Samuel 4-6; Luke 12:35-59
- Day 101 - 1 Samuel 7-9; Luke 13:1-21
- Day 102 - 1 Samuel 10-12; Luke 13:22-35
- Day 103 - 1 Samuel 13-14; Luke 14:1-24
- Day 104 - 1 Samuel 15-16; Luke 14:25-35
- Day 105 - 1 Samuel 17-18; Luke 15:1-10
- Day 106 - 1 Samuel 19-21; Luke 15:11-32
- Day 107 - 1 Samuel 22-24; Luke 16:1-18
- Day 108 - 1 Samuel 25-26; Luke 16:19-31
- Day 109 - 1 Samuel 27-29; Luke 17:1-19
- Day 110 - 1 Samuel 30-31; Luke 17:20-37
- Day 111 - 2 Samuel 1-3; Luke 18:1-17
- Day 112 - 2 Samuel 4-6; Luke 18:18-43
- Day 113 - 2 Samuel 7-9; Luke 19:1-28
- Day 114 - 2 Samuel 10-12; Luke 19:29-48
- Day 115 - 2 Samuel 13-14; Luke 20:1-26
- Day 116 - 2 Samuel 15-16; Luke 20:27-47
- Day 117 - 2 Samuel 17-18; Luke 21:1-19
- Day 118 - 2 Samuel 19-20; Luke 21:20-38
- Day 119 - 2 Samuel 21-22; Luke 22:1-30
- Day 120 - 2 Samuel 23-24; Luke 22:31-53
- Day 121 - 1 Kings 1-2; Luke 22:54-71
- Day 122 - 1 Kings 3-5; Luke 23:1-26
- Day 123 - 1 Kings 6-7; Luke 23:27-38
- Day 124 - 1 Kings 8-9; Luke 23:39-56
- Day 125 - 1 Kings 10-11; Luke 24:1-35
- Day 126 - 1 Kings 12-13; Luke 24:36-53
- Day 127 - 1 Kings 14-15; John 1:1-28

- o **Day 128** - 1 Kings 16-18; John 1:29-51
- o **Day 129** - 1 Kings 19-20; John 2
- o **Day 130** - 1 Kings 21-22; John 3:1-21
- o **Day 131** - 2 Kings 1-3; John 3:22-36
- o **Day 132** - 2 Kings 4-5; John 4:1-30
- o **Day 133** - 2 Kings 6-8; John 4:31-54
- o **Day 134** - 2 Kings 9-11; John 5:1-24
- o **Day 135** - 2 Kings 12-14; John 5:25-47
- o **Day 136** - 2 Kings 15-17; John 6:1-21
- o **Day 137** - 2 Kings 18-19; John 6:22-44
- o **Day 138** - 2 Kings 20-22; John 6:45-71
- o **Day 139** - 2 Kings 23-25; John 7:1-31
- o **Day 140** - 1 Chronicles 1-2; John 7:32-53
- o **Day 141** - 1 Chronicles 3-5; John 8:1-20
- o **Day 142** - 1 Chronicles 6-7; John 8:21-36
- o **Day 143** - 1 Chronicles 8-10; John 8:37-59
- o **Day 144** - 1 Chronicles 11-13; John 9:1-23
- o **Day 145** - 1 Chronicles 14-16; John 9:24-41
- o **Day 146** - 1 Chronicles 17-19; John 10:1-21
- o **Day 147** - 1 Chronicles 20-22; John 10:22-42
- o **Day 148** - 1 Chronicles 23-25; John 11:1-17
- o **Day 149** - 1 Chronicles 26-27; John 11:18-46
- o **Day 150** - 1 Chronicles 28-29; John 11:47-57
- o **Day 151** - 2 Chronicles 1-3; John 12:1-19
- o **Day 152** - 2 Chronicles 4-6; John 12:20-50
- o **Day 153** - 2 Chronicles 7-9; John 13:1-17
- o **Day 154** - 2 Chronicles 10-12; John 13:18-38
- o **Day 155** - 2 Chronicles 13-16; John 14
- o **Day 156** - 2 Chronicles 17-19; John 15
- o **Day 157** - 2 Chronicles 20-22; John 16:1-15
- o **Day 158** - 2 Chronicles 23-25; John 16:16-33
- o **Day 159** - 2 Chronicles 26-28; John 17
- o **Day 160** - 2 Chronicles 29-31; John 18:1-23

- Day 161 - 2 Chronicles 32-33; John 18:24-40
- Day 162 - 2 Chronicles 34-36; John 19:1-22
- Day 163 - Ezra 1-2; John 19:23-42
- Day 164 - Ezra 3-5; John 20
- Day 165 - Ezra 6-8; John 21
- Day 166 - Ezra 9-10; Acts 1
- Day 167 - Nehemiah 1-3; Acts 2:1-13
- Day 168 - Nehemiah 4-6; Acts 2:14-47
- Day 169 - Nehemiah 7-8; Acts 3
- Day 170 - Nehemiah 9-11; Acts 4:1-22
- Day 171 - Nehemiah 12-13; Acts 4:23-37
- Day 172 - Esther 1-3; Acts 5:1-16
- Day 173 - Esther 4-6; Acts 5:17-42
- Day 174 - Esther 7-10; Acts 6
- Day 175 - Job 1-3; Acts 7:1-19
- Day 176 - Job 4-6; Acts 7:20-43
- Day 177 - Job 7-9; Acts 7:44-60
- Day 178 - Job 10-12; Acts 8:1-25
- Day 179 - Job 13-15; Acts 8:26-40
- Day 180 - Job 16-18; Acts 9:1-22
- Day 181 - Job 19-20; Acts 9:23-43
- Day 182 - Job 21-22; Acts 10:1-23
- Day 183 - Job 23-25; Acts 10:24-48
- Day 184 - Job 26-28; Acts 11
- Day 185 - Job 29-30; Acts 12
- Day 186 - Job 31-32; Acts 13:1-23
- Day 187 - Job 33-34; Acts 13:24-52
- Day 188 - Job 35-37; Acts 14
- Day 189 - Job 38-39; Acts 15:1-21
- Day 190 - Job 40-42; Acts 15:22-41
- Day 191 - Psalm 1-3; Acts 16:1-15
- Day 192 - Psalm 4-6; Acts 16:16-40
- Day 193 - Psalm 7-9; Acts 17:1-15

- Day 194 - Psalm 10-12; Acts 17:16-34
- Day 195 - Psalm 13-16; Acts 18
- Day 196 - Psalm 17-18; Acts 19:1-20
- Day 197 - Psalm 19-21; Acts 19:21-41
- Day 198 - Psalm 22-24; Acts 20:1-16
- Day 199 - Psalm 25-27; Acts 20:17-38
- Day 200 - Psalm 28-30; Acts 21:1-14
- Day 201 - Psalm 31-33; Acts 21:15-40
- Day 202 - Psalm 34-35; Acts 22
- Day 203 - Psalm 36-37; Acts 23:1-11
- Day 204 - Psalm 38-40; Acts 23:12-35
- Day 205 - Psalm 41-43; Acts 24
- Day 206 - Psalm 44-46; Acts 25
- Day 207 - Psalm 47-49; Acts 26
- Day 208 - Psalm 50-52; Acts 27:1-25
- Day 209 - Psalm 53-55; Acts 27:26-44
- Day 210 - Psalm 56-58; Acts 28:1-15
- Day 211 - Psalm 59-61; Acts 28:16-31
- Day 212 - Psalm 62-64; Romans 1
- Day 213 - Psalm 65-67; Romans 2
- Day 214 - Psalm 68-69; Romans 3
- Day 215 - Psalm 70-72; Romans 4
- Day 216 - Psalm 73-74; Romans 5
- Day 217 - Psalm 75-77; Romans 6
- Day 218 - Psalm 78; Romans 7
- Day 219 - Psalm 79-81; Romans 8:1-18
- Day 220 - Psalm 82-84; Romans 8:19-39
- Day 221 - Psalm 85-87; Romans 9
- Day 222 - Psalm 88-89; Romans 10
- Day 223 - Psalm 90-92; Romans 11:1-21
- Day 224 - Psalm 93-95; Romans 11:22-36
- Day 225 - Psalm 96-98; Romans 12
- Day 226 - Psalm 99-102; Romans 13

- Day 227 - Psalm 103-104; Romans 14
- Day 228 - Psalm 105-106; Romans 15:1-21
- Day 229 - Psalm 107-108; Romans 15:22-33
- Day 230 - Psalm 109-111; Romans 16
- Day 231 - Psalm 112-115; 1 Corinthians 1
- Day 232 - Psalm 116-118; 1 Corinthians 2
- Day 233 - Psalm 119:1-48; 1 Corinthians 3
- Day 234 - Psalm 119:49-104; 1 Corinthians 4
- Day 235 - Psalm 119:105-176; 1 Corinthians 5
- Day 236 - Psalm 120-123; 1 Corinthians 6
- Day 237 - Psalm 124-127; 1 Corinthians 7:1-24
- Day 238 - Psalm 128-131; 1 Corinthians 7:25-40
- Day 239 - Psalm 132-135; 1 Corinthians 8
- Day 240 - Psalm 136-138; 1 Corinthians 9
- Day 241 - Psalm 139-141; 1 Corinthians 10:1-13
- Day 242 - Psalm 142-144; 1 Corinthians 10:14-33
- Day 243 - Psalm 145-147; 1 Corinthians 11:1-15
- Day 244 - Psalm 148-150; 1 Corinthians 11:16-34
- Day 245 - Proverbs 1-2; 1 Corinthians 12
- Day 246 - Proverbs 3-4; 1 Corinthians 13
- Day 247 - Proverbs 5-6; 1 Corinthians 14:1-20
- Day 248 - Proverbs 7-8; 1 Corinthians 14:21-40
- Day 249 - Proverbs 9-10; 1 Corinthians 15:1-32
- Day 250 - Proverbs 11-12; 1 Corinthians 15:33-58
- Day 251 - Proverbs 13-14; 1 Corinthians 16
- Day 252 - Proverbs 15-16; 2 Corinthians 1
- Day 253 - Proverbs 17-18; 2 Corinthians 2
- Day 254 - Proverbs 19-20; 2 Corinthians 3
- Day 255 - Proverbs 21-22; 2 Corinthians 4
- Day 256 - Proverbs 23-24; 2 Corinthians 5
- Day 257 - Proverbs 25-27; 2 Corinthians 6
- Day 258 - Proverbs 28-29; 2 Corinthians 7
- Day 259 - Proverbs 30-31; 2 Corinthians 8

- **Day 260** - Ecclesiastes 1-3; 2 Corinthians 9
- **Day 261** - Ecclesiastes 4-6; 2 Corinthians 10
- **Day 262** - Ecclesiastes 7-9; 2 Corinthians 11:1-15
- **Day 263** - Ecclesiastes 10-12; 2 Corinthians 11:16-33
- **Day 264** - Song of Solomon 1-3; 2 Corinthians 12
- **Day 265** - Song of Solomon 4-5; 2 Corinthians 13
- **Day 266** - Song of Solomon 6-8; Galatians 1
- **Day 267** - Isaiah 1-3; Galatians 2
- **Day 268** - Isaiah 4-6; Galatians 3
- **Day 269** - Isaiah 7-9; Galatians 4
- **Day 270** - Isaiah 10-12; Galatians 5
- **Day 271** - Isaiah 13-15; Galatians 6
- **Day 272** - Isaiah 16-18; Ephesians 1
- **Day 273** - Isaiah 19-21; Ephesians 2
- **Day 274** - Isaiah 22-23; Ephesians 3
- **Day 275** - Isaiah 24-26; Ephesians 4
- **Day 276** - Isaiah 27-28; Ephesians 5
- **Day 277** - Isaiah 29-30; Ephesians 6
- **Day 278** - Isaiah 31-33; Philippians 1
- **Day 279** - Isaiah 34-36; Philippians 2
- **Day 280** - Isaiah 37-38; Philippians 3
- **Day 281** - Isaiah 39-40; Philippians 4
- **Day 282** - Isaiah 41-42; Colossians 1
- **Day 283** - Isaiah 43-44; Colossians 2
- **Day 284** - Isaiah 45-47; Colossians 3
- **Day 285** - Isaiah 48-49; Colossians 4
- **Day 286** - Isaiah 50-52; 1 Thessalonians 1
- **Day 287** - Isaiah 53-55; 1 Thessalonians 2
- **Day 288** - Isaiah 56-58; 1 Thessalonians 3
- **Day 289** - Isaiah 59-61; 1 Thessalonians 4
- **Day 290** - Isaiah 62-64; 1 Thessalonians 5
- **Day 291** - Isaiah 65-66; 2 Thessalonians 1
- **Day 292** - Jeremiah 1-2; 2 Thessalonians 2

- o **Day 293** - Jeremiah 3-4; 2 Thessalonians 3
- o **Day 294** - Jeremiah 5-6; 1 Timothy 1
- o **Day 295** - Jeremiah 7-8; 1 Timothy 2
- o **Day 296** - Jeremiah 9-10; 1 Timothy 3
- o **Day 297** - Jeremiah 11-13; 1 Timothy 4
- o **Day 298** - Jeremiah 14-16; 1 Timothy 5
- o **Day 299** - Jeremiah 17-19; 1 Timothy 6
- o **Day 300** - Jeremiah 20-22; 2 Timothy 1
- o **Day 301** - Jeremiah 23-24; 2 Timothy 2
- o **Day 302** - Jeremiah 25-26; 2 Timothy 3
- o **Day 303** - Jeremiah 27-28; 2 Timothy 4
- o **Day 304** - Jeremiah 29-30; Titus 1
- o **Day 305** - Jeremiah 31-32; Titus 2
- o **Day 306** - Jeremiah 33-35; Titus 3
- o **Day 307** - Jeremiah 36-37; Philemon
- o **Day 308** - Jeremiah 38-39; Hebrews 1
- o **Day 309** - Jeremiah 40-42; Hebrews 2
- o **Day 310** - Jeremiah 43-45; Hebrews 3
- o **Day 311** - Jeremiah 46-48; Hebrews 4
- o **Day 312** - Jeremiah 49-50; Hebrews 5
- o **Day 313** - Jeremiah 51-52; Hebrews 6
- o **Day 314** - Lamentations 1-2; Hebrews 7
- o **Day 315** - Lamentations 3-5; Hebrews 8
- o **Day 316** - Ezekiel 1-3; Hebrews 9
- o **Day 317** - Ezekiel 4-6; Hebrews 10:1-23
- o **Day 318** - Ezekiel 7-9; Hebrews 10:24-39
- o **Day 319** - Ezekiel 10-12; Hebrews 11:1-19
- o **Day 320** - Ezekiel 13-15; Hebrews 11:20-40
- o **Day 321** - Ezekiel 16; Hebrews 12
- o **Day 322** - Ezekiel 17-19; Hebrews 13
- o **Day 323** - Ezekiel 20-21; James 1
- o **Day 324** - Ezekiel 22-23; James 2
- o **Day 325** - Ezekiel 24-26; James 3

- **Day 326** - <u>Ezekiel 27-28; James 4</u>
- **Day 327** - <u>Ezekiel 29-31; James 5</u>
- **Day 328** - <u>Ezekiel 32-33; 1 Peter 1</u>
- **Day 329** - <u>Ezekiel 34-35; 1 Peter 2</u>
- **Day 330** - <u>Ezekiel 36-37; 1 Peter 3</u>
- **Day 331** - <u>Ezekiel 38-39; 1 Peter 4</u>
- **Day 332** - <u>Ezekiel 40; 1 Peter 5</u>
- **Day 333** - <u>Ezekiel 41-42; 2 Peter 1</u>
- **Day 334** - <u>Ezekiel 43-44; 2 Peter 2</u>
- **Day 335** - <u>Ezekiel 45-46; 2 Peter 3</u>
- **Day 336** - <u>Ezekiel 47-48; 1 John 1</u>
- **Day 337** - <u>Daniel 1-2; 1 John 2</u>
- **Day 338** - <u>Daniel 3-4; 1 John 3</u>
- **Day 339** - <u>Daniel 5-6; 1 John 4</u>
- **Day 340** - <u>Daniel 7-8; 1 John 5</u>
- **Day 341** - <u>Daniel 9-10; 2 John</u>
- **Day 342** - <u>Daniel 11-12; 3 John</u>
- **Day 343** - <u>Hosea 1-4; Jude</u>
- **Day 344** - <u>Hosea 5-8; Revelation 1</u>
- **Day 345** - <u>Hosea 9-11; Revelation 2</u>
- **Day 346** - <u>Hosea 12-14; Revelation 3</u>
- **Day 347** - <u>Joel; Revelation 4</u>
- **Day 348** - <u>Amos 1-3; Revelation 5</u>
- **Day 349** - <u>Amos 4-6; Revelation 6</u>
- **Day 350** - <u>Amos 7-9; Revelation 7</u>
- **Day 351** - <u>Obadiah; Revelation 8</u>
- **Day 352** - <u>Jonah; Revelation 9</u>
- **Day 353** - <u>Micah 1-3; Revelation 10</u>
- **Day 354** - <u>Micah 4-5; Revelation 11</u>
- **Day 355** - <u>Micah 6-7; Revelation 12</u>
- **Day 356** - <u>Nahum; Revelation 13</u>
- **Day 357** - <u>Habakkuk; Revelation 14</u>
- **Day 358** - <u>Zephaniah; Revelation 15</u>

- ○ **Day 359** - Haggai; Revelation 16
- ○ **Day 360** - Zechariah 1-3; Revelation 17
- ○ **Day 361** - Zechariah 4-6; Revelation 18
- ○ **Day 362** - Zechariah 7-9; Revelation 19
- ○ **Day 363** - Zechariah 10-12; Revelation 20
- ○ **Day 364** - Zechariah 13-14; Revelation 21
- ○ **Day 365-** Malachi; Revelation 22

NOTEPAD

Date: _____

_____

_____

_____

_____

_____

_____

_____

_____

_____

_____

_____

_____

_____

_____

_____

_____

_____

NOTEPAD

Date: _____

_____

_____

_____

_____

_____

_____

_____

_____

_____

_____

_____

_____

_____

_____

_____

_____

NOTEPAD

Date: _____

_____

_____

_____

_____

_____

_____

_____

_____

_____

_____

_____

_____

_____

_____

_____

_____

_____

_____

_____

NOTEPAD

Date: _____

_____
_____
_____
_____
_____
_____
_____
_____
_____
_____
_____
_____
_____
_____
_____
_____
_____
_____
_____

NOTEPAD

Date: _____

_____

_____

_____

_____

_____

_____

_____

_____

_____

_____

_____

_____

_____

_____

_____

_____

_____

_____

_____

NOTEPAD

Date: _____

_____

_____

_____

_____

_____

_____

_____

_____

_____

_____

_____

_____

_____

_____

_____

_____

_____

_____

NOTEPAD

Date: _____

_____

_____

_____

_____

_____

_____

_____

_____

_____

_____

_____

_____

_____

_____

_____

_____

_____

NOTEPAD

Date: _____

_____

_____

_____

_____

_____

_____

_____

_____

_____

_____

_____

_____

_____

_____

_____

_____

_____

_____

NOTEPAD

Date: _____

_____

_____

_____

_____

_____

_____

_____

_____

_____

_____

_____

_____

_____

_____

_____

_____

_____

_____

_____